P9-CDC-141

One of *The New York Times Book Review*'s Notable Books of 2017
One of NPR's Great Reads of 2017
One of *The New York Times* Critics' Top Ten Books of 2017 (Janet Maslin)
One of *The Telegraph*'s Fifty Best Books of 2017
One of *Foreign Affairs*' Best Books of 2017

"The first deeply insightful political narrative of the Trump era."
—David Leonhardt, *The New York Times*

"Indispensable."   —Jeffrey Toobin, *The New Yorker*

"Mr. Green is a talented reporter and a gifted storyteller. The anecdotes he records from the chaotic 2016 Trump campaign are both well chosen (they're there for thematic reasons, not as gratuitous gossip) and brilliantly told."
—*The Wall Street Journal*

"You won't be able to put it down. I certainly couldn't, surrendering a weekend I should have rightly spent with the kids. I spent it instead with a sixty-three-year-old nationalist whom *Time* magazine all but called the shadow President of the United States. . . . Addictive."   —*Newsweek*

"Deeply reported and compulsively readable . . . Green is consistently interesting on the subject of Trump. But the real value of *Devil's Bargain* is the story it tells about Bannon, some of which has been previously reported (not least by Green himself) but never so well synthesized or explained as it is here."
—Bret Stephens, *The New York Times*

"Tremendous."   —*GQ*

"Vividly pulls back the curtain on the symbiotic relationship between two of America's most polarizing figures . . . Green is nothing but prescient."
—*The Guardian* (London)

"Green saw Bannon as an important figure early on and began to track his career long before other journalists. As a result, Green had the material and access to produce a deeply researched and sharply observed account of a political figure and a movement that took most of the country by surprise. . . . Readers will find no better guide to Bannon's vision than this gripping and sometimes appalling account."   —*Foreign Affairs*

"One of the best, more thoroughly researched, and arguably most influential 2016 books to come out so far, *Devil's Bargain* is the product of years of interviews and tight reporting from journalist Joshua Green. He thrillingly tracks the influence of Steve Bannon and the alt-right on Trump's candidacy, persuasively arguing they were intrinsic to his rise and eventual victory. It's disturbing, fascinating stuff for anyone interested in this newly powerful fringe."

—*Entertainment Weekly*

"In this important and vivid book, the veteran journalist Joshua Green . . . examines the role of Bannon, the man who, on convincing evidence laid out here, was instrumental in securing the most improbable election victory in modern political history." —*The Times* (London)

"Intelligent, insightful, and fast-moving." —*The Washington Times*

"Delicious from page one." —*Pittsburgh Post-Gazette*

"Fast-paced, crisp, and cogent, this is a first look into a dark corner of history whose ramifications are only beginning to be understood." —*PopMatters*

"Joshua Green is an incredible storyteller, and Bannon is an incredible subject."

—*Paste*

"Splendid." —*Esquire*

"Fascinating . . . required reading for anyone interested in the future."

—Janet Maslin, *The New York Times*

"Absorbing . . . the first thing I've read in the last year and a half that manages to make some sense of the human catastrophic weather event that is Steve Bannon." —*The Millions*

"Behind the scenes and ripped from the headlines, Green's saga exuberantly traces Trump's wild ride to the presidency." —*Kirkus Reviews*

Donald J. Trump ✔
@realDonaldTrump

I love reading about all of the "geniuses" who were so instrumental in my election success. Problem is, most don't exist. #Fake News! MAGA

7:15 PM - 29 Jul 2017

💬 28K   ↻ 18K   ♡ 63K

PENGUIN BOOKS

DEVIL'S BARGAIN

Joshua Green is a national correspondent for *Bloomberg Business-week* and a CNN political analyst. Previously, Green was a senior editor of *The Atlantic*, a weekly political columnist for *The Boston Globe*, and an editor at *Washington Monthly*. He has also written for *The New Yorker*, *Esquire*, *Vanity Fair*, and other publications. Green regularly appears on CNN's shows, HBO's *Real Time with Bill Maher*, and PBS's *Washington Week* and *Frontline*.

DEVIL'S BARGAIN

STEVE BANNON, DONALD TRUMP, AND THE NATIONALIST UPRISING

JOSHUA GREEN

PENGUIN BOOKS

PENGUIN BOOKS
An imprint of Penguin Random House LLC
375 Hudson Street
New York, New York 10014
penguin.com

ISBN 9780735225022 (hardcover)
ISBN 9780735225046 (paperback)
ISBN 9780735225039 (ebook)

Printed in the United States of America
1   3   5   7   9   10   8   6   4   2

DESIGNED BY AMANDA DEWEY

Portions of this book have appeared in different form in *Bloomberg Businessweek*.

For Alicia

CONTENTS

PREFACE TO THE PAPERBACK EDITION

The voice on my phone was excited, as if the caller had downed a few too many cups of coffee. "I'm ready to go on the record," Steve Bannon told me. I hadn't expected to hear this.

It was August 18, 2017, nearly one year to the day after Bannon took over Donald Trump's floundering presidential campaign, and his tenure as White House chief strategist had just come to an abrupt end a few hours earlier.

Bannon's role in the White House had always struck me as a tenuous affair. He was a bomb thrower and an outsider with no experience operating the levers of government, a man with a gift for making enemies, and someone whose habit it was to feud bitterly with those with whom he disagreed. Trump's White House was full of them. Furthermore, Bannon was a radical who aimed to aggressively transform politics, not just in the United States but across the globe. Something had to give.

Accustomed to the unchallenged authority he had enjoyed during the final, tumultuous months of the Trump campaign—and besotted with the global celebrity he gained for masterminding Trump's stunning victory over Hillary Clinton—Bannon chafed at the strictures of life in the White House. He clashed repeatedly with everyone from Trump's daughter Ivanka and her husband, Jared Kushner (his close ally during the campaign), to the people he derisively referred to as "the globalists" or "the West Wing Democrats," a group of Goldman Sachs executives whom Trump appointed to senior positions in his administration: Treasury Secretary Steven Mnuchin, National Economic Council director Gary Cohn, and Deputy National Security Adviser Dina Powell.

But what finally did in Bannon was his public profile and the anger it aroused in his boss. As Bannon told me back in February 2017, after *Time* dubbed him "The Great Manipulator" and splashed his glowering face on the cover, "Trump doesn't want any costars." Knowing that this book would likely cause him further problems, Bannon had twice pushed (unsuccessfully) to delay its publication and then gone to ground as soon as the book arrived, in an effort to lower his profile.

It didn't work. The same morning he called me, August 18, *The Washington Post* reported that Trump was "upset about Bannon's participation in a book by *Bloomberg News* reporter Joshua Green, *Devil's Bargain*—particularly a cover photo giving equal billing to Trump and his chief strategist. Every time Green was on CNN, where he is now a contributor, Trump grew unhappy with his references to Bannon as a thinker and strategist—and upset that the conversation was not instead about Trump."

In the end, the notion that someone other than Trump alone was responsible for his victory—and that is precisely the thesis of this book—was something that the president couldn't abide. So Bannon's fate was sealed. He must have known this.

Still, Bannon didn't hold a grudge. Nor did he share Trump's belief that his historic victory was a one-man affair. To the contrary, Bannon often seemed to have a better understanding of that victory—of its meaning, its symbolism, and its potential to shape global affairs—than the man in the Oval Office for whom he now no longer worked. This is why he'd taken my call and decided to grant me his first interview upon leaving the White House: He knew that everyone, including the president, would sit up and listen.

And he had a message to deliver. Bannon wanted the world to know that while his time in the White House had run its course, his populist crusade would continue on the outside. "If there's any confusion out there, let me clear it up," he told me. "I'm leaving the White House and going to war for Trump against his opponents—on Capitol Hill, in the media, and in corporate America."

At a glance, Bannon's loyalty to Trump might seem puzzling. After all, he'd just been publicly cast out of a powerful White House position with walk-in privileges to the Oval Office. But Bannon was smart enough to know that publicly breaking with Trump would incite a swift backlash and undermine what now became his primary ambition: to advance the political movement that had captured the White House beyond Donald Trump. "*I'm* the leader of the nationalist movement in America," he insisted to a friend.

Privately, Bannon seethed over his departure from the White House. On the Friday he left, even as he told me that he was "going to war for Trump," he was so angry that he didn't take Trump's call when the president, anxious to maintain relations with his base, reached out to check on him. "I'm sick of playing wet nurse to a seventy-one-year-old man," he vented to associates. But at the same time, he understood that his own political power, at least for the time being, depended on the public perception that his relationship with Trump was intact. The irony was amusing: Bannon knew he would have free rein to build out a nationalist movement that didn't have to rely on Trump—so long as he claimed that the purpose of his endeavors was to glorify Trump and vanquish his detractors. With typical grandiosity, Bannon told friends that he was the American version of Charles de Gaulle, the French resistance leader who refused to accept his government's armistice with Nazi Germany and then, after the Allied victory, became president of France.

Bannon's self-appointed role as resistance leader battling the GOP establishment struck many of his old colleagues in the West Wing and on Capitol Hill as rich. Although he was accurately portrayed as the scourge of country club Republicans during the campaign and in his early days in the White House, the truth was that Bannon quickly acclimated to, and even came to like, many of the establishment figures he'd viciously attacked at *Breitbart News*. He struck an alliance with Reince Priebus, the White House chief of staff and former head of the Republican National Committee. He made regular visits to Capitol Hill to lobby members of Congress.

But his most surprising alliance was with a politician he had openly despised and once sought to destroy: House Speaker Paul Ryan. Early in 2017, as Bannon and the White House grappled with the difficulties inherent in writing major tax reform legislation, he recognized, to his own amused chagrin, that Ryan, a tax-policy wonk, was pushing a plan that lined up better with Trump's "America First" ethos than anything else under discussion. At the heart of Ryan's vision was a $1 trillion "border-adjusted tax" that would place a 20 percent levy on U.S. companies' domestic sales and imports, while exempting exports. Ryan liked the border-adjusted tax because the revenue it raised would offset the deep cuts to corporate rates he ardently desired. Bannon liked that it would reduce incentives for U.S. companies to ship jobs overseas and might even bring jobs back home. "It's the most nationalist plan that's feasible," he reasoned. Ryan, knowing he needed allies in the White House, embraced the Oscar-and-Felix partnership with his former tormenter. "I see a person that I have a common cause and purpose with," he explained to PBS. Bannon was even more colorfully effusive. "Ryan and I are asshole buddies," he joked to me, summoning an old term from his Navy days.

In the end, these inroads with mainstream Republicans proved futile. Objections from border-state congressmen and "West Wing Democrats" like Cohn and Mnuchin scotched the border-adjusted tax. Then White House chaos and mismanagement led to the dramatic collapse of Trump's first major legislative effort, an attempt to repeal Obamacare. Episodes like the white-nationalist rally in Charlottesville, Virginia, that descended into violence and left one woman dead showed that while Bannon could moderate his approach on some issues, deep fissures that couldn't be bridged ran through the party—and the White House—on issues of race, immigration, and cultural identity.

The investigation into Russian interference in the 2016 election, the firing of FBI director James Comey, and the indictments of senior Trump officials as a result of Robert Mueller's special counsel investigation put further pressure on a White House staff increasingly consumed by angry recriminations. Bannon's aggressive shivving of his West Wing rivals ensured that when retired Marine Corps general John Kelly replaced Priebus as chief of staff over the summer, his White House days were numbered.

xvi   PREFACE TO THE PAPERBACK EDITION

Almost as soon as he left the White House, Bannon launched into what he declared would be "a season of war" against the Republican establishment. Sprung free from the constraints of the West Wing, Bannon—who had cultivated an Oz-like image by always lurking off camera, even while leaking profusely to reporters—immediately recast himself as a colorful public figure, a kind of Che Guevara of American right-wing nationalism, all the way down to his grimy military field jacket.

He moved back into the Breitbart Embassy on Capitol Hill, only now with an exalted, folk-hero status among the Trump base. He was avidly courted by political and media figures, awarding *CBS News*'s Charlie Rose his first prime-time interview, on *60 Minutes*. Although the Trump administration was flailing and his tenure had been cut short, Bannon was still regarded by prominent political figures, both in the United States and abroad, as a kind of soothsayer who could understand and explain the populist forces roiling countries all over the world.

Members of Congress paid quiet visits to the Embassy to consult with him. Henry Kissinger twice had Bannon up to his weekend home in Connecticut for long discussions about global affairs, particularly Bannon's great preoccupation, China. Foreign officials concerned about growing nationalist sentiments in their own countries extended Bannon invitations to visit and share his views, invitations he gladly accepted. More often than not, he'd bring along a reporter from a national magazine or a film crew to document the role he was carving out for himself, the one he felt he'd deserved all along: that of the globe-trotting geostrategic thinker able to make sense of the world and divine where it was heading. He hopscotched from Japan to China to Abu Dhabi giving speeches. He went falcon hunting in Morocco.

In accordance with this elevated status, Bannon traveled exclusively by private jet. The Embassy's basement became headquarters to a bustling hive of functionaries who managed his jam-packed schedule and were constantly calling around to rich donors, financial titans, and state party leaders to line up the next jet and pilot crew. And of course, anyone important enough to consult with foreign eminences couldn't risk leaving himself unprotected. So Bannon, with funding from the Mercer family, hired a private security force to protect him at all hours. Whenever Bannon was whisked away on a trip, he was usually accompanied by two stocky, tattooed, gun-toting ex–Navy SEALs—who went by "Mo" and "X"—whom Bannon, a paranoiac, would bark at if unwanted reporters or hostile protesters got too close to him.

All the while, he was zigzagging across the country, giving speeches and collecting awards from conservative groups who still viewed him as the torchbearer and authentic protector of the Trump movement. His instinct for propaganda still razor-sharp, Bannon confided to me on the day he left the White House that he planned to "put the whole *Breitbart* apparatus to work" behind Roy Moore, a far-right social conservative twice removed from the Alabama Supreme Court, who was running in a special election to fill Jeff Sessions's Senate seat. "We're going in big for Judge Moore," Bannon said. "Just watch what happens." Bannon calculated that Moore, who had a strong following in Alabama, was poised to knock off the unpopular, establishment-friendly—and Trump-endorsed—placeholder, Luther Strange, who'd been appointed to fill the seat when Sessions became attorney general. Because Trump had been persuaded to endorse Strange at the behest of Jared Kushner and Mitch McConnell, his defeat would be a twin humiliation for Bannon's two great enemies, and a demonstration, for all the world to see, that "Trumpism" could succeed apart from Donald Trump—could, in fact, succeed *in opposition to* Trump.

And it did, briefly. When Moore handily defeated Strange in the GOP primary, Bannon looked like a kingmaker, while Trump, who was humiliated, looked like someone who'd lost touch with his own following.

For Bannon, however, Moore's primary victory marked the beginning of the end.

Throughout the fall, Bannon had traveled the country delivering what amounted to a political stump speech, one that genuinely connected with his audiences. He could feel this. Ostensibly, he was spreading the Gospel of Trump. But it was apparent to anyone who attended a speech or a rally that he was really spreading the Gospel of Bannon.

Bannon believed, or willed himself to believe, that the 2016 election was not really a referendum on Trump, but rather a ratification of a set of ideas Trump had championed—Bannon's ideas. Yet as soon as Trump made it to the White House, he showed how little fealty he had to this agenda. As the early failures mounted, the increasingly angry and erratic president looked like someone who wasn't going to last. Bannon told friends that Trump had only a 30 percent chance of finishing his term, according to *Vanity Fair*.

If Trump quit or was impeached, Bannon told friends, it would eliminate the first great champion of Trumpism—but it wouldn't be a negative judgment on the politics that had swept him into office. In such a scenario, who better to succeed Trump than the man who got him elected?

Bannon shared his interest in running for president with only a few close friends, and even they were never quite sure how seriously to take these flights of fancy. But Bannon had thought hard enough about a path to the White House that he'd even toyed with starting a new political party and settled on a name: the National Union Party. That was the temporary name that Abraham Lincoln and the Republican Party had adopted in 1864 to attract War Democrats and Unionists. In Bannon's vision, it would now unite disaffected populists on both ends of the political spectrum. With support from financial benefactors like the Mercer family, he seemed to imagine such a path might be viable, and that a true devotee of right-wing nationalism—rather than a charlatan like Trump—could succeed where his predecessor had failed.

But in truth, Bannon himself seemed only intermittently interested in the policies that were supposed to undergird this movement. While he did push forcefully for immigration crackdowns and refugee bans, Bannon did little to advance the economic populism that lay at the heart of Trump's campaign message. His efforts to refashion the GOP as a "workers' party" were mostly rhetorical. Toward the end of his White House tenure, Bannon briefly floated the idea of raising taxes on those making more than $5 million or more a year, understanding how powerful the symbolism of such a move would be. But he was quickly shut down. Once he'd left, he considered pushing Janet Yellen's reappointment as Federal Reserve chair, recognizing that her dovish monetary policy was helping boost wages and that a fiscal hawk of the sort most Republicans preferred might kill economic growth. "Yellen's my girl," he told me in September. "The *Breitbart* posse is in love with Janet Yellen. If we get behind her, that is the signal of signals—the realignment of American politics."

But Bannon never quite had the courage of his convictions. He did not endorse Yellen or speak out when Republicans passed a massive tax bill in December sharply slanted toward the interests of corporate America and the rich—the very antithesis of a worker-friendly bill. The candidates he recruited to wage his war on GOP incumbents weren't populists in any meaningful sense, but rather a motley assemblage of retreads and grifters.

Instead, Bannon's crusade against the GOP establishment, and McConnell in particular, was built primarily on personal animosity toward the Senate majority leader. It wasn't a grand clash of ideas; it was Hatfields versus McCoys. So committed was Bannon to destroying McConnell that he wouldn't abandon Roy Moore, even after news reports revealed that the judge had cruised the local mall preying on teenage girls well into his thirties. As Republicans rushed to sever ties with Moore, Bannon galloped in the other direction, elevating the Alabama race into a national referendum on his insurgent politics and on the president himself.

With encouragement from Bannon, whom he still consulted regularly, Trump, to the horror of his staff, began inching toward Moore, convinced, as Bannon was telling him, that the race was shaping up as a referendum on Trump—and that by forcefully weighing in for Moore, Trump could tilt it in his favor. Polls seemed to show Moore headed for a narrow victory. In the end, however, he lost to his Democratic opponent, Doug Jones, saddling Trump with another Bannon-orchestrated humiliation.

Flashing his stiletto, McConnell swiftly cut Bannon down to size. "He specializes in nominating people who lose," the majority leader declared afterward. Trump refrained from publicly burying his ex-strategist, but billboarded his own embarrassment by taking to Twitter to claim he'd thought Moore was going to lose all along.

The end came suddenly, on January 3. *The Guardian* obtained an early copy of an explosive new book, *Fire and Fury*, by the writer Michael Wolff, and published its major revelation: that Bannon had described a June 2016 meeting between Russian operatives and senior

Trump officials, including Donald Trump, Jr., as "unpatriotic" and "treasonous." He'd gone on to say, "They're going to crack Don Junior like an egg on national TV." At once, the article shattered the emerging Republican response to Robert Mueller's fast-encroaching Russia investigation, that it was all a partisan witch hunt. Here was Bannon, Trump's brain and alter ego, declaring with withering disgust that in fact it was not. "Even if you thought that this [meeting] was not treasonous, or unpatriotic, or bad shit, and I happen to think it's all of that, you should have called the FBI immediately," he'd told Wolff.

Trump finally snapped, dictating a furious statement that would excommunicate Bannon once and for all. "Steve Bannon has nothing to do with me or my Presidency. When he was fired, he not only lost his job, he lost his mind," Trump said. "Now that he is on his own, Steve is learning that winning isn't as easy as I make it look. Steve had very little to do with our historic victory, which was delivered by the forgotten men and women of this country. Yet Steve had everything to do with the loss of a Senate seat in Alabama held for more than thirty years by Republicans. Steve doesn't represent my base—he's only in it for himself."

The statement continued: "Steve pretends to be at war with the media, which he calls the opposition party, yet he spent his time at the White House leaking false information to the media to make himself seem far more important than he was. It is the only thing he does well. Steve was rarely in a one-on-one meeting with me and only pretends to have had influence to fool a few people with no access and no clue, whom he helped write phony books."

Bannon, who'd been in the doghouse before, did not initially grasp the severity of the storm, believing he could ride it out and worm his way back into the president's good graces. But Trump was

on the warpath, sending senior White House officials on TV to ex-
coriate Bannon and telling allies that they had to choose between him
and Bannon. They chose Trump.

None came as a greater blow than Rebekah Mercer, who, after
speaking with Trump, issued a statement of her own, cutting ties
with Bannon. "I support President Trump and the platform upon
which he was elected," Mercer said. "My family and I have not com-
municated with Steve Bannon in many months and have provided
no financial support to his political agenda, nor do we support his
recent actions and statements."

Five days later, another blow landed. Bannon was out at *Breitbart
News*. And then another: SiriusXM Radio announced he would no
longer host his show. Bannon had been planning to make a speech at
a South Carolina Tea Party rally later that month to publicly mend
the rift with Trump. That fell apart, too. Every avenue of influence
was suddenly shut off.

Bannon swore it was not the end of the nationalist project. He
had big plans for a nonprofit, and claimed to have lined up wealthy
donors, too. Even now, he still believed that the movement, on some
visceral level, remained loyal to him and his ideas. Trump, he always
told people, was "purely transactional" and would one day run into
trouble and reach out as if nothing had happened. That's just how
he was.

Already, Bannon saw dark clouds gathering on the horizon. A
movement was growing, infecting the culture, building into a wave.
If anyone understood the power of a political backlash, the primal
forces it unleashed that could upend the electoral process in a heart-
beat, it was Bannon. This time, however, the backlash was against
Trump and Bannon and the world they stood for.

It was already dark outside, and well below freezing, when Bannon plopped down on the couch in the back room of the Embassy and flicked on the TV. It had been a hell of a week—and it was only January 8!

A Hollywood guy at heart, Bannon switched over to the Golden Globe Awards, and in a rush it all came into focus. The black dresses. The Time's Up activism. The preening Hollywood egos dictating to the country. Only now, he noticed, the men—leading men, *movie stars!*—were silent and submissive, gelded by the female rage pulsing and throbbing right through his television set. This was real, he recognized, and profound.

It took only a moment for Bannon to summon the perfect historical allusion. "It's a Cromwell moment!" he practically shouted, invoking the seventeenth-century Puritan zealot Oliver Cromwell. "It's even more powerful than populism. It's deeper. It's primal. It's elemental. The long black dresses and all that—this is the Puritans! It's anti-patriarchy." Bannon snorted at the image of The Rock, all movie-star muscle and presidential ambition, gazing impotently as Oprah Winfrey commanded the stage. "He's ruined his career," Bannon declared. "If you rolled out a guillotine, they'd chop off every set of balls in the room."

Bannon thought Oprah might represent an existential threat to Trump's presidency if she decided to campaign for Democrats in 2018. She'd flip the House and they'd race to impeach him. But the movement was bigger than Oprah. "The anti-patriarchy movement is going to undo ten thousand years of recorded history," he said. "You watch. The time has come. Women are gonna take charge of society. And they couldn't juxtapose a better villain than Trump. He *is* the patriarch. This"—the Golden Globe Awards—"is a definitional moment in the culture. It'll never be the same going forward."

He raced ahead, imagining out loud how the forces would clash.

The 2020 election, he was suddenly sure, wouldn't be merely the Democrats versus the Republicans, but the Patriarchy versus the Matriarchy. And right now, Oprah was winning.

But all was not lost. Not by a long shot. Nationalism could still save Trump and the Republicans. Eventually, Bannon fell silent, sifting the elements of this new idea, and war-gaming how Trump should react. After that, there was nothing left to do but wait for the phone to ring.

PREFACE

In the late spring of 2011, I got a phone call from a publicist inviting me to a screening of a documentary film about Sarah Palin. At the time, I was a political writer for *The Atlantic*, and I'd just returned from a reporting trip to Alaska and published a long, somewhat contrarian article on Palin's aborted governorship. My piece argued that Palin had done more good than people realized—cleaning up a corrupt state GOP, raising oil taxes, fixing Alaska's budget—and that if she was going to run for president in 2012, which was a live possibility, then she should revert to her populist instincts. The filmmaker had read my article and loved it, the publicist told me.

A few days later, I showed up at a sound studio in Arlington, Virginia, and met the filmmaker. His name was Steve Bannon. His film, a soaring testimony to Palin oddly titled *The Undefeated* (she and John McCain lost the 2008 election), was forgettable. Bannon himself was unforgettable. Brimming with vigor in a military field jacket, he made an impassioned speech about the power of the Tea

Party movement, still a gathering force, and Palin's place in the vanguard of a new populist conservatism. He was clearly intelligent, had a manic charisma, and espoused a distinct and unusual politics. He also claimed to have been a Goldman Sachs investment banker and Hollywood producer, recently returned from running a video-game empire in Hong Kong.

I quickly sized him up as a colorful version of a recognizable Washington character type: the political grifter seeking to profit from the latest trend. No politician was hotter in 2011 than Palin. And Washington was rife with Tea Party con men. We agreed to stay in touch (grifters can be good sources). Later on, out of idle curiosity as much as anything else, I called Goldman Sachs to see if Bannon had really worked there. He had. A quick check revealed that he had also produced movies for Sean Penn and Anthony Hopkins. His story, in all its multifaceted oddness, checked out.

One of the joys of being a magazine feature writer is that you can collect interesting characters and find excuses to write about them later on. I decided right away that I would profile Bannon, but took years to get around to actually doing it. In the meantime, we hung out at political events or at the Capitol Hill headquarters of *Breitbart News*, which he took over in 2012. Through the years, I discovered seemingly endless new dimensions (and contradictions): his admiration for Rachel Maddow, whom he considered a master of fact-based partisan polemics; his controversial stint overseeing the Biosphere 2 Project in Arizona; his deep interest in Christian mysticism and esoteric Hinduism; and his particular fascination with an obscure, early-twentieth-century French intellectual, René Guénon, who became a Muslim and observed the Sharia—a jarring contrast to the bombastic Islamophobia Bannon often espoused. What also became clear was his sincere belief that right-wing Tea Party populism was a global phenomenon: Palin soon faded, but Bannon's conviction in his political ideas only grew stronger. And although I didn't know it at the time of the screening, he had recently met Donald Trump and begun informally advising him on this very subject.

In 2015, I finally found an angle for my profile. Bannon had spent two years masterminding an investigative book about Bill and Hillary Clinton, marshaling an entire research team at a Florida think tank to conduct a forensic examination of the Clinton Foundation's financial backers. He thought that the contributions the Clintons had solicited and received from foreign donors of dubious character and motivation posed a serious political threat to Hillary Clinton's designs on the White House. And he had devised what struck me as a rather ingenious plan to get the mainstream media to write about it (a plan I elucidate later in this book).

That summer *Clinton Cash: The Untold Story of How and Why Foreign Governments and Businesses Helped Make Bill and Hillary Rich*, by Peter Schweizer, was published and immediately upended the presidential race, sullying Clinton's image in a way that she never fully recovered from. My profile of Bannon explaining what he'd done appeared on the cover of *Bloomberg Businessweek* that fall.

Of course, that turned out to be only a piece of a much larger story—the story of the greatest political upset in modern American history, and one that ended with Donald Trump and Steve Bannon in the White House. As someone whose job it was the last three years to immerse himself in right-wing politics, as someone who had up-close access to many of the principals, I'd like to be able to say that I saw this coming. But that would be entirely untrue. Never did I imagine that Trump would win the Republican nomination, would install Bannon to run his campaign, or would defeat Hillary Clinton in the general election. Only in hindsight did it become clear that Bannon had a better feel for the American electorate's anxieties than almost anyone else in the arena, save perhaps Donald Trump.

This book is an attempt to go back and tell the story from the beginning, charting its unlikely origins and following the two men whose partnership was its epicenter—how they came together, how they triumphed, and how their relationship ultimately came apart. The seeds of this effort are the twenty-plus hours of interviews I conducted over eight months with Bannon and his associates in Washington and Florida while reporting my original profile. I've also drawn on dozens of conversations before that period and since, including reporting conducted for subsequent *Businessweek* feature stories on Trump, his campaign, and several of his top advisers. Shortly after he locked up the Republican nomination, Trump granted me a wide-ranging ninety-minute interview in his Trump Tower office. I've included some of that material here. During the campaign, and in some cases also the transition and early months of the Trump administration, I conducted interviews that inform this book with figures who include: Reince Priebus, Jeff Sessions, Sean Spicer, Stephen Miller, David Bossie, Kellyanne Conway, Newt Gingrich, Rudy Giuliani, Roger Stone, and Nigel Farage, as well as other Trump advisers and intimates who preferred not to be named.

Several provided e-mails, strategy memos, polling data, photographs, and notes, some of which are quoted or described herein. With help from participants, those they confided in, or contemporaneous recordings, I've reconstructed dialogue in a number of places. Wherever I've drawn on the work of other journalists, I've tried to include a citation, either in the text or in an endnote. Quotes that are not cited there are drawn from my own reporting.

While no work of this kind can hope to be a comprehensive

account of every twist and turn in a campaign that featured (by my count) twenty-two major candidates, what I hope I've done here is to better illuminate the core of the story. I also argue that an implicit bargain lay at the heart of the relationship between Trump and Bannon, the same one Bannon was hoping to strike with Palin when I first met him: that his hard-right nationalist politics could carry the right person to the White House—at which point the powers of the presidency would be marshaled to faithfully enact it. Trump sold this brand of nationalism with the same all-out conviction he brought to selling his own name. Whether he actually believed in it, he recognized that it was the key to closing the biggest deal of his life.

DEVIL'S
BARGAIN

ONE

"IT WILL TAKE A MIRACLE"

*F*ucking unbelievable, Steve Bannon thought, shaking his head in disgust as the "Breaking News" alert raced across the television screens in the Trump Tower war room. It was 7:22 p.m. on Election Night, the polls hadn't even closed, and yet here was CNN's Jim Acosta breathlessly touting a damning quote he'd pried out of an anonymous senior Trump adviser: "It will take a miracle for us to win."

Bannon didn't have to guess at the culprit. He simply assumed it was Kellyanne Conway, Trump's campaign manager, and how the hell would she know? Conway was a pollster by trade, but she tested messaging, not horse race, and the campaign had cut her off weeks earlier because Trump preferred to see her spinning on TV. If Bannon cared to—and right now, he did not—he could have watched Acosta's full report and looked for the Tell. That's what always gave her away. Because Conway was the only woman on Trump's senior staff, reporters avoided using gender pronouns when quoting her anonymously, lest an errant "she" slip out and reveal their source. Instead, they employed the awkward but gender-neutral "this adviser" or "this person," and by the third or fourth reference what they were doing became pretty obvious. That was the Tell. Some of Trump's advisers had long ago caught on and joked about it.

Sure enough, Acosta cited "a senior adviser from Donald Trump's inner circle," followed by a trifecta of "this adviser"'s, with nary a "he" or a "she" to be heard. Even before he'd finished talking, CNN—Trump's obsession and bête noire—had billboarded the "take a miracle" quote in a banner that stretched across the screen.

But Bannon had already moved on. He could never fathom why people like Conway worked so hard to win goodwill from reporters (most of whom, he thought, were idiots with no earthly idea what was really going on) or why they cared so much about appearances.

It took only a glance to see that Bannon himself cared not a whit for appearances—at least not his own. This was, in fact, one of his defining traits. He had spent most of his life donning the uniform of the various institutions to which he belonged: the cadet's uniform at Benedictine High School, the all-male Roman Catholic military school he and his brothers attended in Richmond, Virginia; the naval officer's starched whites during his eight-year stint aboard destroyers in the Pacific and the Persian Gulf; and the banker's expensive suits, a uniform of their own, which he'd worn during his tenure at Goldman Sachs.

But once he made real money and cashed out, Bannon gleefully threw off the strictures of the working stiff and adopted a singular personal style: rumpled oxfords layered over multiple polo shirts, ratty cargo shorts, and flip-flops—a sartorial middle finger to the whole wide world.

Even now, at sixty-three, having left a right-wing media empire a few months earlier to become Trump's chief campaign strategist, Bannon made only the tiniest concession to the Trump world's boardroom ethos by swapping the cargo shorts for cargo pants and tossing a blazer over his many layers of shirting. Although it was Election Night and television satellite trucks stretched for blocks around Trump Tower, Bannon hadn't bothered with a shave or a haircut, and he had a half dozen pens clipped to his shirt placket, like some bizarre military epaulet. "Steve needs to be introduced to soap and water," said Roger Stone, Trump's longtime political adviser. He looked for all the world like someone preparing to spend the night on a park bench.

But Trump needed him. Practically alone among his advisers, Bannon had had an unshakable faith that the billionaire reality-TV star could prevail—and a plan to get him there. "It's gonna be ugly," Bannon would tell anyone who would listen during the closing weeks of the campaign. "But there's a path."

Trump had turned to Bannon in August to rescue his floundering presidential campaign at a time when nearly everyone agreed that he was headed for a landslide loss. He had burned through two campaign chiefs already. First was the volatile Corey Lewandowski, a walk-through-walls yes-man whose blind devotion and willingness to defend any outrage was appreciated by Trump.

But Lewandowski had gotten crosswise with some important family members, in particular Trump's son-in-law Jared Kushner, and he lacked strategic vision. He was ousted in June. Next came Paul Manafort, a longtime Washington lobbyist with murky ties to foreign autocrats. Manafort had attempted to refashion Trump into someone who would be acceptable to the moneyed GOP establishment, an effort Trump had bridled against at every step. By the time reports surfaced in August that Manafort was the designated recipient of millions of dollars in cash payments from Russian-aligned politicians in Ukraine, Trump had all but signed his death warrant, tagging him with the dreaded "low energy" epithet he'd applied to the woeful Jeb Bush. "My father just didn't want to have the distraction looming over the campaign," Trump's son Eric explained to Fox News on the day Manafort was shown the door.

The surprise elevation of Bannon to head Trump's campaign on August 17 hit political Washington like a thunderclap—and, to most insiders, like a bad punch line. Bannon had never worked on a campaign; he was despised by Democrats and Republicans alike for his eagerness to attack them both; and he had a profile that guaranteed still more terrible headlines for Trump. He was executive chairman of *Breitbart News*, the crusading, racially charged, hard-right populist website that had helped spark the 2013 Republican-led government shutdown and then bullied House Speaker John Boehner into resigning. Bannon's personal motto was "Honey badger don't give a shit," a reference to the insouciant African predator of YouTube fame whose catchphrase became a viral sensation.

To Washington Republicans, Bannon was about the worst choice Trump could have made because it signaled that, rather than steer toward a gentlemanly defeat that might preserve Republican seats in the House and Senate, Trump was going to burn it all down en route to a loss so ugly it might destroy the party. Even on his best days, these Republicans agreed, Trump was never more than a hairsbreadth from blowing himself up and taking out the party with him. No one who had encountered Bannon or *Breitbart* doubted for a moment that he would encourage Trump's worst tendencies. He was a human hand grenade, an Internet-era update of the Slim Pickens character in *Dr. Strangelove* who rides the bomb like a rodeo bull, whoopin' and hollerin' all the way to nuclear annihilation. As one of his *Breitbart News* employees admiringly put it, "If there's an explosion or a fire somewhere, Steve is probably nearby with some matches."

But Trump, a honey badger himself, saw plenty to like. Bannon was nothing if not high-energy, a mile-a-minute talker who rarely slept and possessed a media metabolism to rival Trump's own. His first instinct was always to attack. Bannon's distinctive vocabulary, an admixture of Navy boiler room and '80s Wall Street, was another point of appeal. A blue-collar kid from a Navy family, Bannon gloried in the slights and scorn directed at Trump supporters, proudly insisting that elitist Clintonites looked down on them as "hobbits," "grundoons," and—co-opting Clinton's own ill-advised term—"deplorables." Anyone who thought otherwise was a "mook" or a "schmendrick." And Clinton herself was the subject of a steady stream of derision, carefully pitched to Trump's own biases and insecurities, and delivered with the passion of a cornerman firing up a boxer for one last grueling round in the ring. Clinton, Bannon would insist, was "a résumé," "a total phony," "terrible on the stage," "a grinder, but not smart," "a joke who hides behind a complacent media," "an apple-polisher who couldn't pass the D.C. bar exam," "thinks it's her turn," but "has never accomplished anything in her life"—and, for good measure, was "a fucking bull dyke."

Trump loved it. And he loved how Bannon, an avid reader of history and military biographies, fitted Trump's outsider campaign into the broader sweep of history. For years, Bannon had tracked, and occasionally abetted, the right-wing populist uprisings sweeping across Europe and Great Britain. Where others saw Trump's campaign as a joke or an ego trip, Bannon framed it as the inevitable U.S. manifestation of these same forces and Trump as the avatar of an us-versus-them populism that could galvanize an electoral majority to rise up and smash a corrupt establishment. He had a role for himself, too. On his office wall hung an oil painting of Bannon dressed as Napoleon in his study at the Tuileries, done in the style of Jacques-Louis David's famous Neoclassical painting—it was a gift from Nigel Farage, a nationalist-minded friend.

For all its shock, the choice of Bannon wasn't nearly as random as it seemed. He had first been brought into Trump's orbit years earlier by David Bossie, the veteran Republican operative, to provide informal counsel on a potential presidential bid. At the time, Bannon hadn't thought much of Trump's chances and regarded these visits as an adventure and a lark. He doubted that Trump would run. But this hadn't prevented him from imparting his nationalist worldview—particularly his hostility to illegal immigration—and long before Trump declared his candidacy, the billionaire was reading *Breitbart News* articles flagged by Bannon and then printed out on paper (Trump's preferred medium for reading) and delivered to him in a manila folder by his staff.

It was no accident that Trump's formal declaration of his candidacy, on June 16, 2015, took the form of a bitter paean to American nationalism that quickly veered into an attack on Mexican immigrants as criminals and "rapists." Nor was it coincidence that one of his first trips as a bona fide presidential candidate was a circus-like visit to the U.S.–Mexican border crossing in Laredo, Texas. Bannon, who established a *Breitbart* Texas bureau in 2013 to focus on immigration, had worked for weeks with sympathetic border agents to help arrange the trip. And while Trump's remarks were pilloried by the press and by many of his fellow Republicans ("extraordinarily ugly," Jeb Bush called them; House Speaker Paul Ryan said he was "sickened" by them), that wasn't what registered most with the candidate himself. By the time he left Texas, Trump had rocketed to first place in polls of Republican primary voters.

But that was more than a year ago. Now, as the first returns trickled in, Trump was brooding high above Fifth Avenue in his gilded Trump Tower penthouse with his wife, Melania, all too aware that it had been months since he last led Clinton in a reputable national poll. When his campaign brass gathered down below on Election Night, plenty of them thought their boss needed a miracle to win. Trump's team had access to three different sources of polling—its own, run by Conway and a trio of Republican pollsters; large-scale surveys conducted by the GOP firm TargetPoint that fed into the Republican National Committee's micro-targeting model; and another set of surveys by Cambridge Analytica, a London data science outfit contracted by the campaign to build a sophisticated model of its own. None of them pointed toward victory.

Outwardly, Trump's team kept up appearances by mercilessly flaying Clinton and insisting that their man could win. But behind the scenes, some advisers had already begun positioning themselves for the knife fight that would immediately follow a loss. The RNC had quietly summoned a group of top political reporters for a private presentation that laid out all that the committee had done on Trump's behalf. The purpose of this secret meeting was purely exculpatory. Reince Priebus, the RNC's put-upon chairman, and Sean Spicer, its indefatigable chief strategist, were sending a message: "Hey, Trump's loss won't be our fault—it'll all be on him and his team." In the days leading up to the election, Spicer met with top executives at the major networks to press this same message in person.

News of these assignations had traveled back to Trump and

members of his inner circle, many of whom regarded the RNC, the cradle of establishment Republicanism, with deep suspicion and even contempt. Although Spicer and Priebus had both gone to extraordinary lengths to publicly defend and support Trump—at a steep cost to their personal reputations because many Republicans now viewed them as boot-licking enablers—word raced across the Trump war room when Priebus and Spicer were spotted packing up their personal belongings early on Election Night, apparently anticipating a swift loss.

Privately, even Bannon had moments of doubt. In the depths of Trump's worst scandal, after *The Washington Post* broke news of an *Access Hollywood* tape that captured his lewd comments about women and how he liked to "grab them by the pussy," Bannon admitted to an associate that Trump might be done for. Yet he wasn't despondent, nor did he seem to view the possibility as a fatal setback to the broader movement. "Our back-up strategy," he said of Clinton, "is to fuck her up so bad that she can't govern. If she gets 43 percent of the vote, she can't claim a mandate." Psyching himself up to the task, he added, "My goal is that by November eighth, when you hear her name, you're gonna throw up."

In the weeks that followed, Trump rigorously carried out his part of the job, going so far as to call Clinton "corrupt" to her face, as she sat on the dais with him at an October 21 bipartisan charity dinner. A week later, FBI director James Comey's decision to reopen the investigation into her private e-mail server delivered an even greater blow. Out on the stump, Trump ratcheted up his criticism of Clinton to a degree that was almost unhinged. "A vote for Hillary is a vote to surrender our government to public corruption, graft, and cronyism that threatens the survival of our constitutional system itself," he thundered at an Arizona rally on October 29. "What makes us exceptional is that we are a nation of laws and that we are all equal under those laws. Hillary's corruption shreds the principle on which our nation was founded."

And Trump didn't stop there. In speeches and in ads, he channeled Bannon's conspiratorial worldview by implicating Clinton in a dark web of moral and intellectual corruption that encompassed the entire global power structure—the banks, the government, the media, the guardians of secular culture, as well as financial titans including the billionaire investor George Soros, Federal Reserve chairwoman Janet Yellen, and Goldman Sachs CEO Lloyd Blankfein. "It's a global power structure that is responsible for the economic decisions that have robbed our working class, stripped our country of its wealth, and put that money into the pockets of a handful of large corporations and political entities," Trump warned in a controversial ad that the campaign saved for the eve of the election. "The only thing that can stop this corrupt machine is you."

The sinister allusions to international financial conspiracies, and the fact that Soros, Yellen, and Blankfein are all Jewish, set off alarm bells at the Anti-Defamation League, whose CEO, Jonathan Greenblatt, blasted Trump for propagating "painful" anti-Semitic stereotypes and "baseless conspiracy theories." Trump's campaign rejected the attack and criticized the ADL for involving itself in partisan politics. "Darkness is good," Bannon counseled Trump. "Don't let up."

By this point, the campaign had curtailed most of its polling. But it wasn't quite flying blind. A few days earlier, Trump's team of data scientists, squirreled away in an office down in San Antonio, had delivered a report titled "Predictions: Five Days Out," which contained stunning news that contradicted the widespread assumption that Clinton would win easily. It was suddenly clear that Comey's FBI investigation was roiling the electorate. "The last few days have proven to be pivotal in the minds of voters with the recent revelations in reopening the investigation of Secretary Clinton," the report read. "Early polling numbers show declining support for Clinton, shifting in favor of Mr. Trump." It added: "This may have a fundamental impact on the results."

The report's authors further detected plummeting support for the Democratic candidate among early voting African Americans (down 18 percent from 2012) and "a reduction of turnout in Urban areas relative to Rural areas," which together were shifting the electoral demographics sharply toward Trump in the key swing states of Ohio, Virginia, and North Carolina. The deeper you dove into the data, the more it appeared that the "hidden" Trump support postulated by Trump and ridiculed by most analysts was, in fact, quite real—and heading to the polls.

Yet these voters weren't being accounted for in public polling or even those conducted by Trump's pollsters and the RNC. So the scientists, in their stilted jargon, modeled what the electorate might look like if "turnout includes a simulated increase in low-propensity voters that has been apparent throughout this election cycle"—what they dubbed a "Trump Effect." This exercise illuminated a clear electoral path for Trump—ten different paths, in fact, most of which entailed winning Florida, Pennsylvania, and Ohio—that now looked entirely plausible. It gave Bannon hope that no miracle would be necessary.

Like its namesake, Trump Tower is given to hyperbole. Its southwestern facade folds, accordion-style, so that the building magically produces dozens more corner offices and apartments than a typical glass slab. Although the top floor is labeled as the sixty-eighth, this is an illusion—a flight of stairs outside Bannon's fourteenth-floor office leads down one level, directly to the fifth floor. Trump skipped over numbers when labeling the floors, which is how a building that the city records as having only fifty-eight floors was able to sell the more exclusive and expensive (but fictitious) floors fifty-nine through sixty-eight.

It was on the unfinished fifth floor, once used as production offices for Trump's reality-TV show *The Apprentice*, that the campaign had set up its Election Day operations a week earlier. By late in the afternoon, lawyers, political operatives, and assorted Republican officials and hangers-on were anxiously buzzing about the rows of folding tables as they awaited the results. The most exclusive among them—a rotating cast of Bannon, Conway, Spicer, and Priebus, along with Trump's spokeswoman Hope Hicks, his running mate Mike Pence, and assorted Trump offspring and their spouses—squeezed into a ten-by-fifteen-foot storage room built from makeshift drywall partitions. Bossie dubbed it "the crack den." Its walls were plastered with bumper stickers and posters bearing chest-thumping declarations of purpose ("DONALD TRUMP: HE WILL GET THINGS DONE"), along with, incongruously, a painting of a teddy bear and a blue butterfly smiling at a potted sunflower.

Bill Stepien, a hard-bitten former top aide to New Jersey governor Chris Christie who was Trump's national field director, set up a projection TV that beamed an electoral map from his laptop onto a wall. The laptop contained an RNC dashboard that automatically populated the Associated Press's county-level election results as they rolled in.

There had been a sudden scare. Just after five p.m., the first exit polls splashed across the *Drudge Report*, showing that voters were deeply dissatisfied and longing for "change"—but they also showed that Trump was tied with or trailing Clinton in nearly every critical swing state. Bannon pulled Kushner out of the crack den so no one would register their panic.

"What do you think?" Kushner asked.

"Well, the numbers tell two different stories," Bannon replied. "If you believe one set, we're killing it, it's a change election, and everything lines up exactly like we thought. But, man, if you believe the other one, we're getting crushed."

It was a moment of truth—and a dilemma. The Cambridge Analytica model had picked up a late shift in the electorate toward Trump. But it was only a model. These exit polls were based on thousands of interviews with actual voters, and they were telling a much different story.

Not knowing what else to do, Kushner and Bannon called Matt Drudge to ask what he thought.

"Fuck the corporate media," Drudge told them. "They've been wrong on everything. They'll be wrong on this."

Solace came slowly at first, and then in a great gusher. On the wall of the crack den, Stepien was clicking through swing states, rattling off numbers like an auctioneer. The campaign had prepared a list of bellwether counties that it thought would provide the earliest indication of its fate. These included not only the traditional swing counties that cable news pundits always puttered on about—places such as Loudoun County, Virginia, and Jefferson County, Colorado—but also areas brimming with older, white, working-class "Trump Republicans": places like Okaloosa County in Florida's panhandle and Mahoning County in eastern Ohio. The campaign's thinking was that if counties like these broke decisively for Trump, then so, too, would the vast swaths of the upper Midwest that they were depending upon to forge a path to victory.

On TV, the cable networks had for several days focused obsessively on the surge of early votes in Latino-heavy counties, such as Florida's Miami-Dade and Nevada's Clark, all but promising a Clinton victory and a humiliating comeuppance for Trump. Stepien's projector showed a different surge. The numbers in Okaloosa County were through the roof, certain to surpass the 2012 Republican totals by a mile. "This is beyond where we need to be!" Stepien enthused. The dead heat that exit polls showed in Ohio also proved to be a mirage: it soon became clear that Clinton didn't have a prayer of winning the Buckeye State. And while Wolf Blitzer made great drama on CNN about the large Democratic counties in Florida (Broward, Miami-Dade) that were still outstanding, Trump's brain trust had already determined that he'd won the state based on the extraordinary turnout in the panhandle. Furthermore, they knew that if Florida fell into their column, the Cambridge model—grandly dubbed the "Battleground Optimizer Path to Victory"—put Trump's odds of winning at around 80 percent.

But it was the states Trump *wasn't* supposed to win that told the story in the end. Bannon was fixated on Michigan, constantly urging Stepien to click back over and zoom in on bellwethers like Macomb County—and with 30 percent, 40 percent, then 50 percent of precincts reporting, Trump's lead was holding steady. Or growing. As the night wore on, he even led in Wisconsin, a scenario none of Trump's data scientists had ever imagined.

Later on, several of those crammed into the room would recall a moment when Stepien's manic patter flagged for just a second and the room fell quiet. Then somebody—no one could remember who—muttered, "Holy shit. This is happening."

Drudge was right. The corporate media blew it.

And they knew it. The calls and texts came pouring in. At 9:05 p.m. a frantic reporter e-mailed Bannon: "Can't believe what

I'm seeing. You guys are gonna win, aren't you?" His curt reply:
"Yes." In newsrooms everywhere, pre-written "Clinton Wins Presidency" stories were being frantically updated or simply trashed.

Sensing, suddenly, that history was unfolding in their midst, a couple of Trump's advisers whipped out their phones and began snapping pictures. As word of what was occurring spread through the building, more and more people crammed into the room. Chris Christie showed up and squeezed in next to Ivanka Trump.

Then Ivanka got a phone call from her father. He and Melania were coming down from the penthouse. Donald and Melania Trump were not, it was instantly understood, going to wedge themselves into the filth and stink of the crack den. No, Trump was headed for the fourteenth-floor war room with its thirty-foot-long wall of televisions. All at once, the room emptied out, as operatives and family members began scrambling for the elevators or the stairs. Only Stepien paused on his way out the door, to scoop up his laptop and projector.

By ten p.m., Trump had stationed himself at the center of the war room, where he stood facing the five big-screen televisions bolted to the wall and taking in the full spectrum of the cable news meltdown he was presently precipitating. Mike and Karen Pence sidled over to join him, and soon dozens of staffers and family members surrounded them to watch as the networks called a steady procession of states for Trump. Stepien set up his projector around the corner, in an alcove near the desk of Trump's senior policy adviser and speechwriter, Stephen Miller. A junior aide was dispatched to race back and forth from the projector to the war room with the latest electoral tallies, like a marathon runner carrying news to the emperor in ancient Greece. Spicer hurriedly summoned a video crew from the fifth floor to begin documenting all that was happening up above.

Before long, the room was packed. Trump remained riveted to the television screens, and while his aides obsessed over each incoming bloc of voters added to the map—Which part of the state did they come from? Which areas were still outstanding?—Trump hit upon a simple metric that cut through the minutiae and went straight to his odds of winning. "How did Obama do there in 2012?" he would ask, each time a county's numbers were updated. By and large, the answer was that the key counties in states like Michigan, Pennsylvania, and Ohio that had produced narrow victories for Obama in 2012 were now showing narrow—and sometimes not-so-narrow—Trump leads. On TV, the cable anchors were working hard to keep up the level of drama, but the scenarios they were spinning for how Clinton could win were becoming narrower and more far-fetched with each passing minute.

No one was quite sure of the moment when Trump realized that he was going to be the next president. Although he was surrounded by friends, aides, and family members, there seemed to be a hidden force field around him that discouraged a direct approach. So instead of approaching Trump, most well-wishers began congratulating a beaming Mike Pence, whom they high-fived and saluted as "Mr. Vice President."

After a while, Trump, perhaps needing to absorb the gravity of what was happening, went and sat down. A moment later, Christie burst through the force field and sat next to him.

"Hey, Donald," he said. "The president talked to me earlier." Christie knew Obama from their work together in the aftermath of Hurricane Sandy.

"If you win he's going to call my phone, and I'll pass it over to you."

Trump flashed a look of annoyance, clearly resenting the intrusion. He was also, his aides knew well, a fanatical germaphobe who would not want Christie's cell phone pressed to his face—not even for the deep satisfaction of hearing Barack Obama congratulate him on having defeated Clinton.

Still, onlookers were startled when Trump snapped, "Hey, Chris, you know my fucking number. Just give it to the president. I don't want your fucking phone." Christie's move was, one witness later recalled, "the ultimate mistake." It was one from which he wouldn't recover.

Finally, Trump stood up and began to circulate among the crowd. Word had gone around earlier in the day that Trump probably wouldn't attend his victory party a few blocks away at the Hilton Hotel unless he was certain of the outcome. Now, Bannon informed the team, his decision had been made. "He's going to the Hilton," Bannon said. "But first he's going to go upstairs."

Spicer realized that this meant they would all be going over to the Hilton. Somehow, that made Trump's victory feel official. As Trump headed toward the elevator to return to the penthouse and collect himself, Spicer ventured forth to pay his respects to the man who would soon become the next president of the United States. "Congratulations," Spicer said.

Trump just stared at him and uttered two words: "Not yet."

It was Bannon who finally delivered the news, although by then it could hardly have been a surprise. "Hey, look, we're gonna win this thing," he said. Trump nodded, sensing where his chief strategist was going, and replied, "Let's go get this done."

Trump was alluding to his victory speech: he didn't have one. Nor had he prepared a concession speech. Aware that his boss was deeply superstitious—so much so that journalists had witnessed Trump tossing salt over his shoulder before meals for good luck— Bannon had intuited that he wouldn't respond well to the hoary political tradition of writing out two speeches ahead of time, and so had simply never raised the subject with him. Trump wouldn't want to jinx himself, he was sure. Truth be told, Bannon loved this part of Trump—his easy willingness to say "fuck that" to any number of venerable traditions without so much as a moment's thought. Pure honey badger. He sometimes wondered whether Trump would even bother to take the stage in the event of a loss, and half suspected that he wouldn't.

But that scenario no longer applied.

When they arrived in the penthouse, Trump, Bannon, and Miller gathered in the kitchen, along with Ivanka and her husband, Jared, to decide how Trump should address himself to a shell-shocked nation—a shell-shocked *world*. Trump made clear that he wanted a speech that would bring the country together, something "presidential" that would salve the wounds of the bitter campaign and at least crack open a door to millions of stunned Clinton supporters struggling to get their bearings. When he got up onstage, he'd surround himself with his family, too, to give Americans a fuller, softer glimpse of the man who would be leading them. Miller roughed out some lines about how it was "time for America to bind the wounds of division" and "time for us to come together as one united people."

As midnight struck and Clinton's carriage turned into a pumpkin, the penthouse started filling up with VIPs: Trump's sons Don Jr. and Eric and their wives, Melania and ten-year-old Barron, Conway and communications adviser Jason Miller, Rudy and Judith Giuliani, the Pences. Then, loudly and boisterously—inevitably—Chris Christie emerged from the elevator, eager as ever to join the party. He made a beeline for Trump. "It's one of the main reasons he got fired," one attendee later insisted. "Trump hates being smothered, and Christie just got under his skin." Trump and his writing team moved to the dining room.

Eventually, thirty or forty people were milling around, excitedly buzzing about the upset they were witness to and waiting for the president-elect to head to his victory party. There was no longer any doubt that he would prevail or do so by a comfortable electoral margin. But Trump decided that he wasn't going to leave for the Hilton until the Associated Press called Pennsylvania, thereby slamming the door on even the one-in-a-million shot Clinton had left.

The AP's call came at 1:39 a.m., and a roar went up in the penthouse. It was time to go.

The Secret Service ushered Trump and his family toward the awaiting motorcade, with Bannon and Miller in tow. Down below, Spicer and several of his RNC colleagues threw on their jackets and decided to walk the four blocks to the Hilton. Although by now they were certain of victory, they wondered what Trump would say—there had still been no word from the Clinton campaign.

A week earlier, Clinton's campaign manager, Robby Mook, had reached out to Conway to choreograph the Election Night formalities. Mook had informed her that if Clinton lost, she would call and concede fifteen minutes after the AP called the race—but should Clinton win, he added, "if we don't hear from you after fifteen

minutes, she's going to go out onstage and give her victory speech."
Bannon thought the message was arrogant—a veiled threat that
Trump had better fall in line—and told Conway to ignore it.

Trump was just preparing to take the stage at the Hilton when
the AP made the call. At 2:34 a.m., the news flashed across the
wire: "BREAKING: Donald Trump is elected president of the
United States." Quickly, Bannon and Priebus huddled with him to
figure out what he should say. And then, just as Mook had promised, the call came from Clinton. Her prompt, graceful concession
was, even Bannon had to admit, "very classy." And with that last,
outstanding bit of business put to rest, Trump and his family took to
the stage and made it official.

From the far left end of the stage, half eclipsed by Conway,
Bannon stood gazing out over the raucous crowd still absorbing the
news of the AP's call. *Total shit show*, he thought, approvingly. It was
true, and not least because the audience was filled with Bannons.
More than twenty of his relatives, including his ninety-five-year-old
father, Martin, were on hand for the celebration. One relative even
became a minor icon of sorts, when the next day's *Bloomberg Businessweek* chose for its cover an image of a stereotypical "Trump bro"
in a red "Make America Great Again" baseball cap grinning like a
jackal and pointing at the camera—it was Bannon's nephew Sean, a
"total fucking hammerhead," as he put it, affectionately.

After the Hilton shut down and the revelers spilled out onto
Sixth Avenue, Spicer, still unable to process what had just happened,
found himself roaming the streets of Manhattan alone, not ready for
the historic evening to end. He wandered north for a while until he
hit Central Park, then he turned east. Finally, realizing the chaos
that dawn would bring, he decided to head back to his hotel and
turned south.

His path took him down Fifth Avenue, right past Trump Tower. As he was about to cross Fifty-sixth Street, he noticed flashing lights and looked up. Trump's motorcade was just pulling up to the tower's residential entrance. As it rolled to a stop, a door flew open and a grizzled, grinning, disheveled figure with two pens still clipped to his shirt placket hopped out and enveloped him in a bear hug. Spicer, grinning wildly, reached out an arm and snapped a selfie—and it was at that moment, at exactly 3:27 a.m., standing with Bannon in the pitch black outside Trump Tower, that the magnitude of what they had accomplished finally sunk in. They had just carried off the greatest political upset in U.S. history and sent Donald J. Trump to the White House.

In the days after the election, the world wondered: *How could this happen?* Many people still wonder. No shortage of scapegoats and malefactors were offered up by way of explanation: James Comey, the Russians, the media, "fake news," sexism—the list went on and on. Yet none was entirely satisfying, or big enough to encompass the scale of the shock, or capable of unwinding the sense of dislocation so many people felt when they awoke to the realization that something so seemingly unlikely—*so utterly extreme*—as Trump's election could happen in plain view of everyone, without anyone really seeing it coming. It was like the opening scene of a Hollywood thriller, the sudden jolt that makes you sit upright in your seat, and after which some remarkable, winding backstory is gradually revealed. But the revelation never arrived. Even now, there's a sense that some vital piece of the puzzle is missing.

That piece is Steve Bannon.

From Machiavelli to Karl Rove, politics has a rich history of the genius figure whose plots and intrigues on behalf of a ruler make him the hidden hand behind the throne, the wily strategist secretly guiding the nation's affairs. So familiar has this story become that it's a trope of American political journalism: if you're a presidential candidate without a brilliant strategist, the media will often take it upon themselves to anoint one you never knew you had. The strategists, aware of this narrative compulsion, openly jockey to win the position.

Although he's been cast in the role, Bannon is no such figure—or in any event, he doesn't fit the typical mold any more than Trump fit the mold of "typical presidential candidate." What Bannon is instead is a brilliant ideologue from the outer fringe of American politics—and an opportunistic businessman—whose unlikely path happened to intersect with Trump's at precisely the right moment in history.

For years, Bannon had been searching for a vessel for his populist-nationalist ideas, trying out and eventually discarding Tea Party politicians such as Sarah Palin and Michele Bachmann. At the same time, he was building an elaborate machine designed to destroy the great enemy whose march to the White House posed the biggest threat to those ideas and to everyone whose beliefs hewed to the right of center: Hillary Clinton. In 1998, when Clinton first posited a "vast right-wing conspiracy" bent on ruining her and her husband, she was widely ridiculed. But she wasn't wrong. By the time she launched her 2016 campaign, Bannon was sitting at the nexus of a far-flung group of conspirators whose scope and reach Clinton and her campaign didn't fathom until far too late.

At first, Bannon didn't understand that he'd found the figure he'd been looking for. Trump wasn't a serious candidate and would never deign to let some Rove figure govern his behavior—that much was clear from the outset. But Bannon soon discovered that Trump's great personal force could knock down barriers that impeded other politicians. And Trump, for his part, seemed to recognize that Bannon alone could focus and channel his uncanny political intuition with striking success. Bannon didn't make Trump president the way Rove did George W. Bush—but Trump wouldn't be president if it weren't for Bannon. Together, their power and reach gave them strength and influence far beyond what either could have achieved on his own.

Any study of Trump's rise to the presidency is therefore unavoidably a study of Bannon, too. It's a story Trump won't like, because he isn't always the central character. And because, contrary to his blustery assertions, his victory wasn't a landslide, didn't owe solely to the force of his personality or his business savvy, and happened only due to a remarkable confluence of circumstances. This confluence occurred in large part because Bannon had built a trap that snapped shut on Clinton, and the success of this, too, was an incredible long shot. In fact, the whole saga of Bannon is every bit as strange and unlikely as that of Trump. He's like an organism that could have grown and blossomed only under a precise and exacting set of conditions—a black orchid.

This book is the backstory of how those conditions came to be—it's the part of the movie you haven't seen. To understand Trump's extraordinary rise, you have to go all the way back and begin with Steve Bannon, or else it doesn't make sense.

TWO

"WHERE'S MY STEVE?"

The Trump-Bannon partnership, like so much else in Trump's life, has a bizarre and winding lineage that traces back to a lawsuit. In the mid-1990s, Steve Wynn, the Las Vegas casino mogul, was looking to move in on Atlantic City, New Jersey, a possibility that threatened the livelihoods of the Trump Plaza Hotel and Casino, the Trump Taj Mahal, and other gambling establishments along Atlantic City's Boardwalk. Unable to make headway, Wynn's Mirage Resorts, Inc., filed an antitrust suit against Trump's company and Hilton Hotels, setting the stage for an epic showdown. At the time, Trump and Wynn were both in their fifties, both graduates of the University of Pennsylvania, both fiercely competitive giants of the casino industry, possessed of healthy egos, and operating at the peak of their powers. And perhaps because they shared so much in common, they were bitter enemies. "They hate each other's guts," a casino analyst told the *Philadelphia Inquirer*. "It's like poison."

Right away, things had gotten very strange. A private investigator working for Trump's defense team had gone off to dig up dirt on Wynn and Mirage, only to switch allegiances partway through his assignment and secretly defect to his target. The resourceful sleuth—whose tradecraft included using a "modified jock strap" with a hidden tape recorder and microphones concealed in a belt— turned over to Wynn the secrets he had purloined for Trump, later claiming that he was moved to do so by a crisis of conscience (and not, as Trump's lawyers suggested, a $10,000-a-month consulting deal with Mirage).

Wynn and Mirage sued again, this time claiming that Trump's company had engaged in a conspiracy to steal its trade secrets— including a list of high-rolling Korean gamblers about whom, Wynn's suit alleged, it spread dark rumors of money laundering and mob ties, in hopes that Wynn Resorts would be denied a New Jersey casino license. (The lawsuit revealed, among many other colorful details, that the investigator had given his counterintelligence mission the code name "Operation Seoul Train.") An attorney for Trump likened the investigator, not unreasonably, to Judas Iscariot. Wynn shot back that the case exemplified "the most outrageous misconduct, the most flagrant violations of law and decent behavior in the history of the resort hotel industry."

It was all about to explode into open court—until, on February 23, 2000, the case was abruptly settled. A week later, the reason became clear: MGM made an offer to buy Mirage Resorts that eventually netted Wynn, its largest shareholder, around $300 million. Wynn's designs to build a casino in Atlantic City never came to fruition. In the aftermath, with both men having effectively "won" their battle, Trump and Wynn became friends.

And that is how, several years later, at a fund-raiser for Children's National Medical Center in Washington, D.C., Steve Wynn called his friend Donald Trump over and introduced him to a man who would soon set the course for his unlikely political rise: David Bossie.

By the time he met Trump in the late 2000s, Bossie, then still in his early forties, was already a hardened veteran of Washington's political wars. Smitten with Ronald Reagan as a teenager growing up in Boston, he became youth director of Bob Dole's 1988 presidential campaign, and then a foot soldier in Newt Gingrich's Republican revolution when the GOP took back the House of Representatives in the 1994 election. Not long afterward, the beefy, buzz-cut, hyperintense Bossie (who still resembles a *Dick Tracy* villain) landed a job as chief investigator for the House Government Reform and Oversight Committee.

The job put Bossie at the beating heart of the Republican anti-Clinton movement that was then still picking up steam, and in the employ of perhaps its fiercest prosecutor, Representative Dan Burton of Indiana, the committee's new chairman. Even before Burton took the gavel in 1997, his unhinged zeal to take down Bill Clinton was the stuff of legend. A few years earlier, convinced that the 1993 suicide of Clinton's deputy White House counselor, Vincent Foster, was in fact a cold-blooded murder, Burton had re-created the event by shooting a watermelon with a pistol in his backyard in an effort to prove his theory. (He didn't convince too many people, but he did earn the enduring nickname "Watermelon Dan.")

When he became Oversight chairman, Burton quickly laid waste to the committee's tradition of august bipartisan restraint and seized on its considerable legal powers—in particular, the power to issue subpoenas—to torment the Clintons, often by dispatching his chief investigator to hound anyone he suspected of abetting them.

Bossie required no special encouragement. He routinely evinced a zealousness that matched, or even eclipsed, that of his boss. *The New York Times* once described him, in a news story, as "a relentless ferret." He cut a strange figure. A volunteer firefighter, he lived in a firehouse in Burtonsville, Maryland, where he slept in a bunk bed and responded to emergency calls when he wasn't racing off in pursuit of real and imagined Clinton perfidies. But some of those Clinton scandals were legitimate. And Bossie, who was often first to document them, was a favorite source of political reporters, to whom he reliably leaked the latest incriminating details about the first family—even if his methods rubbed some of his own colleagues the wrong way. Not long after Bossie's arrival, the Oversight Committee's counsel abruptly quit, blast-faxing to reporters a letter of resignation that attacked "the unrelenting self-promoting actions of the Committee's Investigative Coordinator."

Relentlessness and self-promotion were no sins in Gingrich's Washington. But Bossie's fanatical desire to fell the Clintons at any cost eventually did him in. Burton's committee developed a troubling reckless streak that led to unconscionable errors. In their determination to prove that Clinton was illegally taking money from Chinese donors, Burton's staff fired off hundreds of subpoenas, sometimes targeting the wrong person. In 1997, for instance, his investigators mistakenly subpoenaed the telephone and financial records of an elderly Georgetown University professor named Chi Wang, who happened to share a name with a major Democratic donor, and yet, when Bossie was apprised of the error, he still wouldn't relent. "Whether he deserves a subpoena or not, we haven't decided," he said of the innocent professor. "If you make a mistake—and we're not sure we made one—you want to look into it."

But it was Bossie's recklessness in a *different* Clinton investigation—this one involving the jailed former White House associate attorney general Webster Hubbell, once a partner at Hillary Clinton's Little Rock, Arkansas, law firm—that finally brought about his downfall. In 1998, Burton released some transcripts of prison recordings of Hubbell's private telephone conversations. (Hubbell had been convicted of fraudulently billing his law firm.) Burton went on *Nightline* and *Meet the Press* to announce that the conversations implicated Clinton herself in the fraud. The media, by now conditioned to tout Burton's charges, went into overdrive on what looked to be a major new scandal. Burton didn't know it, but he was about to walk into a trap.

His Democratic counterpart on the Oversight Committee, Henry Waxman of California, was a legendary investigator himself, with a clever and sharp-eyed staff alert to Bossie's recklessness. (At the time, Waxman's Oversight investigation of the tobacco industry was being made into the Oscar-nominated Al Pacino–Russell Crowe film *The Insider*.) While conducting its own forensic examination of the Hubbell transcripts, Waxman's team discovered that the excerpts Burton had released to the press had been doctored in such a way as to appear to incriminate Clinton, when the full transcript plainly did not. They had a good idea of who the culprit was.

Rather than simply issue a press release, Waxman devised something far more attention-grabbing and dramatic. The following Sunday, Burton was booked for an encore appearance on *Meet the Press*. The show's host, Tim Russert, was quietly made aware of the discrepancy between the two sets of Hubbell transcripts.* On Sunday, when the cameras began rolling, Burton became an unwitting captive as Russert, the dean of Washington journalism and a maestro of the prosecutorial interview, confronted the chairman on air with evidence of the doctored transcripts.

The uproar was immediate and intense. Gingrich, humiliated, condemned Burton's committee as "the circus." Republicans fumed at the embarrassment Burton had brought on them and demanded he atone for it. *The Washington Post* splashed the story across its front page: "Burton Apologizes to GOP." The whole edifice of probity and professionalism that Republicans had painstakingly constructed to give themselves license to go after the Clintons seemed to come crashing down at once. "The Burton investigation is going to be remembered as a case study in how not to do a congressional investigation and as a prime example of investigation as farce," declared Norman Ornstein, a respected congressional scholar at the conservative American Enterprise Institute.

The fallout landed heaviest on Bossie, who was very publicly fired from his job. Once a feared and respected figure who operated in the innermost sanctum of Republican power, he was now cast far, far outside it, to the fringes of the conservative world. The subsequent collapse of the Republican power structure (including Gingrich's resignation as House Speaker) brought about by the backlash to Bill Clinton's impeachment only ratified Bossie's status as persona non grata among respectable mainstream Republicans.

Bossie, however, did not disappear or even leave Washington,

---

*Political hit jobs like the one on Burton are always disguised in order not to divert focus away from the target. The public story of Russert's triumph, detailed afterward in *New York* magazine, was that Russert himself discovered the divergent transcripts. He did not. He was a fine journalist, but here he had some help.

D.C. Nor did he abandon his obsession with taking down the Clintons. Instead, he became president of the conservative group Citizens United, a position that gave him rein to become what he was probably best suited to being all along: an uninhibited, full-time, generously compensated anti-Clinton warrior, whose plots and intrigues could now be funded by wealthy conservative ideologues.

The job made Bossie a big deal in a small but intense universe of rabid Clinton haters. He arrived at a pivotal moment. By and large, the public rejected what this group's members regarded as their great triumph—Clinton's impeachment—and punished Republicans such as Gingrich, whom they deemed responsible for it. For those who had fought so long and hard to damage Clinton, this unexpected turn of events only deepened their animosity and drove them further from the mainstream of the GOP. Their influence waned. A new Republican president, George W. Bush, got elected by championing a different, more "compassionate" conservatism, while holding the right-wing fire-breathers at bay.

Bossie's ilk continued nursing their obsession, blasting out fundraising appeals, making overheated political films, propagating dark conspiracy theories that revolved around the Clintons, and gathering at the sorts of conferences where intense adherents to far-right-wing causes set up tables to lure new recruits, and vendors hawk merchandise pitched to the politics of the crowd, such as Hillary Clinton nutcrackers, and bumper stickers that read "Life's a Bitch. Don't Vote for One." Yet for all its fevered efforts, this group rarely made a ripple outside its own insular bubble—its members were mostly cranks who wound up speaking mainly to one another. Republican politicians were happy to receive their votes. Many, in fact, depended upon them, even as they privately held the cranks in low esteem. As one campaign manager for a Republican presidential candidate described them, "They're the stuff you scrape off your shoes. Bad people."

Yet in one instance the Clinton-haters did manage to break through in a big way—and Bossie was the man responsible. In 2007, in anticipation of Hillary Clinton's run for the White House, Citizens United produced a scalding documentary film that purported to detail a thicket of nefarious Clinton scandals, although it consisted mainly of interviews with off-kilter conservative commentators such as Dick Morris and Ann Coulter maligning the former first lady. Bossie's plan was to release *Hillary: The Movie* as a cable television video on demand in January 2008, just as the Democratic presidential primary was getting underway. In truth, it was more of a fund-raising ploy than a serious effort to sway Democratic voters, who would be unlikely to seek out a film attacking their leading presidential candidate, much less be turned against her by the opinions of the right-wing talk-radio hosts who were its central characters.

But Bossie didn't get very far. The Federal Election Commission prohibited Citizens United from advertising the film on the grounds that *Hillary: The Movie* constituted a campaign ad. The new McCain-Feingold campaign finance law restricted so-called issue advertisements that mentioned federal candidates from airing within thirty days of a primary and sixty days of a general election. Bossie sued, claiming his film was protected commercial speech and therefore exempt from campaign laws. A three-judge panel of the U.S. District Court for the District of Columbia denied his request for an injunction, stating that his film was effectively a ninety-minute campaign ad "susceptible of no other interpretation than to inform the electorate that Senator Clinton is unfit for office, that the United States would be a dangerous place in a President Hillary Clinton world, and that viewers should vote against her."

Yet in 2010, the Supreme Court disagreed and sided with Bossie in *Citizens United v. Federal Election Commission*, a landmark decision that said political spending is protected speech under the First Amendment, and corporations and other organizations can therefore spend unlimited amounts of money to support or denounce candidates in an election. Republicans were ecstatic.

The Supreme Court case briefly turned Bossie into a conservative *cause célèbre*, not because Republicans thought his film would have any effect on Clinton, who had already been dispatched by Obama, but because it was the vehicle that eliminated campaign spending restrictions, opening the floodgates for more corporate money to pour into electoral politics. It bestowed upon Bossie a temporary glow that made him seem like a big deal and a consequential player in Republican circles at the very moment when Donald Trump was getting serious about running for president and casting about for advice. Trump had few connections to the political world, where no one took him seriously, even though (and in part because) he was kicking up a shit storm by claiming that Obama had faked his birth certificate and wasn't really born in the United States.

And yet Trump was hardly dissuaded. His habit always was to quiz anyone and everyone about what they thought, whether or not that person could claim any expertise on the topic at hand. In Trump's mind, then, Steve Wynn's opinions about politics and how to shape it were every bit as valid and worth listening to as those of a seasoned political consultant—and maybe more so because Wynn had traveled a path so similar to Trump's own, not just in business but also in politics. Wynn, too, had once been a Democrat and even claimed to have voted for Obama in 2008. But he turned sharply against the president and the Democratic Party after the election, and would later get into a tabloid-friendly fight over the subject with the actor George Clooney, who once stormed out of Wynn's dinner party after the casino magnate called Obama an "asshole." For Trump, who was trying to figure out how to navigate national politics, Wynn's imprimatur of Bossie, and Bossie's own post–*Citizens United* celebrity, both counted for a lot. Trump brought Bossie into the fold, later describing him this way: "Solid. Smart. Loves politics. Knows how to win."

By March 2011, employing a style that would soon become familiar, Trump had orchestrated the "birther" crisis over Obama's citizenship, roiling the political world and making himself a central figure in the national conversation. Now he faced a dilemma: Wynn had invited him to be a guest at his three-day, celebrity-studded Las Vegas wedding on April 30, where Clint Eastwood was going to be the best man. But *The Washington Post*, eager to capitalize on Trump's sudden political notoriety, had invited him to be a guest at the White House Correspondents' Association dinner that was being held the same night. Trump had accepted both invitations.

In the end, he decided to attend a Friday night party in Las Vegas honoring Wynn and his fiancée, Andrea Hissom. Trump mingled poolside with Sylvester Stallone and Hugh Jackman. Then, early the next morning, he jetted off to Washington, D.C., where the comedian Seth Meyers was going to emcee the Correspondents' Dinner. Trump had no idea that Meyers and Obama were anticipating his arrival and preparing to make him a national laughingstock. And none of them knew that this elaborate humiliation would be the catalyst that put Trump on a path to the White House.

It was a setup from the beginning. Trump had been invited to the Correspondents' Dinner by Lally Weymouth, the daughter of *The Washington Post*'s legendary publisher Katharine Graham and someone who routinely courted stars and celebrities as guests to the annual event held at the Washington Hilton. Trump's invitation had caused grumbling in the *Post* newsroom. Was it really appropriate, reporters wondered, for the paper to embrace the purveyor of a racist conspiracy theory directed at the nation's first black president—who would, not incidentally, be the dinner's featured speaker?

But ever since 1987, when, in the wake of the Iran-Contra scandal, the journalist Michael Kelly brought one of its central figures, Fawn Hall, the document-shredding secretary to Lieutenant Colonel Oliver North, to the event, there had been an unspoken competition among prestige media outlets to land the most notorious and newsworthy guests. In the social context of elite Washington, the *Post*'s nabbing Trump as a guest was a coup. And Trump was, by all accounts, delighted to be among the actors, starlets, and television personalities who flock to the A-list dinner each year. Knowing that the dinner speakers typically single out members of the audience for roasting, and that Trump was a ripe target, a couple of *Post* reporters asked him if he was prepared for some ribbing. Trump waved them off. "I'm fine with this stuff," he replied.

Trump was seated in the very center of the Hilton ballroom, his confection of blond hair aglow in the bright lights, his star wattage eclipsing the graying eminences of journalism and politics who craned their necks to get a look at him. No one confronted him about his outrageous slander or questioned why he was so intent on humiliating Obama, because doing so would have run counter to the spirit of the evening. Instead, Trump schmoozed and flattered his fellow guests, and they in turn schmoozed and flattered him.

Nobody knew it yet, but the president and his staff would not be so solicitous. They had, in fact, been eagerly awaiting Trump's arrival in Washington from the moment the news became public, recognizing the occasion as the perfect opportunity to exact a humiliating revenge. Obama's writing staff even brought in a ringer, the comedian and director Judd Apatow, to help its most comedically gifted speechwriter, Jon Lovett, compose a devastating takedown of Trump. The White House Office of Digital Strategy had agreed to produce a video complement.

Toward the end of the evening, when the lights dimmed for Obama's remarks, giant screens throughout the ballroom broadcast a blaring music video of Rick Derringer's cheesy rock anthem "Real American" that the digital-strategy team had crammed full of over-the-top patriotic imagery—rippling American flags, screaming eagles, Uncle Sam—and then Obama's long-form birth certificate came dancing across the screen. The White House had just released it three days earlier, after months of Trump's haranguing suggestion that Obama couldn't produce it because he hadn't really been born in Hawaii.

As the lights came up, Obama stood at the lectern grinning broadly and looking right at Trump. "My fellow Americans, Mahalo!" he said. "As some of you heard, the State of Hawaii released my official long-form birth certificate. Hopefully this puts all doubts to rest. But just in case there are any lingering questions, tonight I'm prepared to go a step further. Tonight, I am releasing my official birth video."

Now the screens showed a clip of Disney's *The Lion King*

bearing a time stamp that read August 4, 1961—Obama's birthday. The crowd hooted and laughed.

"Donald Trump is here tonight," the president announced. "Now, I know he's taken some flack lately. But no one is happier, no one is prouder to put this birth certificate matter to rest than the Donald. And that's because he can finally get back to focusing on the issues that matter, like . . . Did we fake the moon landing? What really happened in Roswell? And where are Biggie and Tupac?"

The crowd laughed louder. Trump sat frozen in a rictus grin.

Obama kept after him: "All kidding aside, obviously we all know about your credentials and breadth of experience, um . . ." Here Obama paused to let the laughter die down. "No, seriously, just recently, in an episode of *Celebrity Apprentice*, at the steakhouse, the men's cooking team did not impress the judges from Omaha Steaks. There was a lot of blame to go around. But you, Mr. Trump, recognized that the real problem was a lack of leadership, and so ultimately you didn't blame Lil Jon or Meat Loaf—you fired Gary Busey."

Obama started cracking up, but kept on going: "These are the kinds of decisions that would keep me up at night." The crowd roared. "Well handled, sir! Well handled."

Meyers was up next. After methodically working through the field of 2012 Republican presidential hopefuls, he arrived at his real target. "And then, of course, there's Donald Trump," Meyers said, with a devilish grin. "Donald Trump has been saying that he will run for president as a Republican—which is surprising, because I just assumed that he was running as a joke."

Trump reddened.

"Donald Trump often appears on Fox," Meyers continued, "which is ironic, because a fox often appears on Donald Trump's head. If you're at the *Washington Post* table with Trump and can't finish your entrée, don't worry: the fox will eat it."

More laughter.

"Gary Busey said recently that Donald Trump would make a great president. Of course, he said the same thing about an old, rusty birdcage he found."

Gone from Trump's visage was any pretense that he was enjoying this. He did not seem to possess the ability to laugh at himself, nor even the politician's ability to smile broadly and pretend to. Trump was plainly humiliated—and it showed.

When Meyers was finished with him, Trump, looking shaken, beat a hasty retreat. He had been "incredibly gracious and engaged on the way in," Marcus Brauchli, the *Post*'s executive editor, would later say, but after his drubbing Trump had departed the dinner "with maximum efficiency."

To all outward appearances, Trump had just been brutally dispatched—his dignity snatched away from him, his foray into politics swiftly cut short, the preening, grasping interloper who had barged into a world where he didn't belong sent crawling back to his rightful station: a tawdry world of bimbos, pink marble, reality TV, and "*Page Six.*" This is what all of Washington understood to have happened, for years afterward: Trump had made another of his absurd periodic displays of pretending to contemplate a run for president, ventured too far in his quest for publicity, and suffered a terminal humiliation. Now the universe had snapped back into balance and ejected him.

Only that wasn't what had happened at all.

Trump had indeed toyed many times before with running. The

first time, in 1987, he was about to publish his book *The Art of the Deal* when a Republican activist in New Hampshire launched a presidential draft campaign. One day that fall, Trump, then forty-one, disembarked from a black helicopter onto an airfield in Hampton, New Hampshire, and gave a speech to five hundred people at the local Rotary Club, many of them waving "Trump in '88" and "Trump for President" signs. Striking notes that could have been sounded in his 2016 campaign, Trump claimed that the United States faced "disaster" because it was "being kicked around" by the likes of Japan, Iran, and Saudi Arabia, countries that were "laughing at us." He added, "It makes me sick." Trump never entered the race. But people responded. He drew headlines. His book became a bestseller.

In 1999, he went a step further, quitting the Republican Party and actively campaigning for the Reform Party nomination. Ross Perot had founded the Reform Party to fight the North American Free Trade Agreement (NAFTA) and push a balanced budget, mounting a pair of White House bids in 1992 and 1996. While the Reform Party has faded from memory, in 1999 it represented a serious political vehicle because it assured its nominee access to all fifty-one ballots and money from the Federal Election Commission. Those said to consider pursuing its nomination included everyone from Oprah Winfrey and Cybill Shepherd to Warren Beatty and Pat Buchanan. Trump, sizing up Winfrey as the biggest star, declared her his dream running mate. While he reveled in the attention that came with his presidential flirtation, Trump also seemed to absorb some of the ideas and tactics that had animated Perot's success. He rushed into print another book, *The America We Deserve*, that railed against NAFTA and aped Perot's famous warning about "a giant sucking sound" of American jobs heading south to Mexico.

Perot was a kind of ur-Trump. In an era before Twitter, he used unconventional methods to organize his followers and draw attention to his campaigns, including an 800 number and frequent appearances on Larry King's CNN show. Although Trump, with characteristic braggadocio, vowed to spend $100 million, he took a page from Perot and relied mostly on a blitz of free media to win Reform Party primaries in Michigan and California, before eventually dropping out (during a *Today* show appearance).

Trump briefly toyed with challenging George W. Bush in 2004, this time sensing that his opportunity lay on the left. "You'd be shocked," he told CNN's Wolf Blitzer, "if I said that in many cases I probably identify more as a Democrat." As public sentiment soured on Bush after his reelection, Trump stepped up his criticism, hinting to the *New York Post* that he might run in 2008, although he never took steps beyond orchestrating suggestive leaks to newspapers.

Each of these episodes coincided so obviously with some other angle Trump was pursuing at the time—either hawking a book or promoting *The Apprentice*, which began airing on NBC in 2004— that people in politics grew inured to them, rolling their eyes as each new self-promotional campaign got underway. So nobody paid much attention when, after Obama's election, Trump became more active in politics.

In February 2011, he was a late addition to the roster of speakers at the Conservative Political Action Conference, his first ever appearance at the annual cattle call for Republican presidential hopefuls held every year in Washington, D.C. To fan interest in this latest feint at the White House, one of his lawyers had created a website, ShouldTrumpRun.com. "While I'm not at this time a candidate for the presidency," Trump announced grandly at CPAC, "I will decide by June whether or not I will become one." Reporters soon realized that his announcement timeline just happened to coincide with sweeps week and dismissed it as a ratings stunt, the usual Trump-presidential-hype cycle cranking up again.

That's why it didn't register as particularly significant when Trump, in the same speech, deployed a curious line of attack against Obama, one previously confined mostly to the fever swamps of far-right websites. "Our current president came out of nowhere. Came out of nowhere," Trump said, shaking his head. "In fact, I'll go a step further: the people that went to school with him, they never saw him; they don't know who he is. It's crazy!"

In the weeks that followed, Trump traveled the talk-show circuit making explicit what he'd merely hinted at in his CPAC speech: his contention that Obama hadn't been born in the United States, had somehow forged his birth certificate, and therefore was an illegitimate president. "I want him to show his birth certificate," Trump said, in March, on ABC's *The View*. "There's something on that birth certificate that he doesn't like." A week later on Fox News he went further: "People have birth certificates. He doesn't have a birth certificate. He may have one, but there's something on that—maybe religion, maybe it says he is a Muslim. I don't know. Maybe he doesn't want that. Or he may not have one. But I will tell you this: if he wasn't born in this country, it's one of the great scams of all time."

Trump was plumbing the depths of latent racist hostility toward the president and discovering that there was a lot of it there. Everybody in politics knew this sentiment existed, but the long-standing consensus had been that it should be kept out of the public arena. In the 2008 presidential campaign, John McCain had quickly upbraided a woman at his rally who prefaced a question to him about

Obama by stating, "He's an Arab." The crowd booed McCain for correcting her.

Trump, who has an uncanny ability to read an audience, intuited in the spring of 2011 that the birther calumny could help him forge a powerful connection with party activists. He also figured out that the norms forbidding such behavior were not inviolable rules that carried a harsh penalty but rather sentiments of a nobler, bygone era, gossamer-thin and needlessly adhered to by politicians who lacked his willingness to defy them. He could violate them with impunity and pay no price for it—in fact, he discovered, Republican voters thrilled to his provocations and rewarded him. National polls taken in mid-April, two weeks before the White House Correspondents' Dinner, showed Trump leading the field of 2012 GOP presidential candidates.

Privately, what amused him the most, he later told a friend, was that no party official in a position of power dared to stand up to him. In his first nationally televised interview, on C-SPAN, the new chairman of the Republican National Committee, Reince Priebus, was confronted about Trump's possible candidacy and his birther attacks on Obama. "Is the birther debate good for the party?" Jeff Zeleny, a reporter for *The New York Times*, asked him. "I think all these guys are credible," Priebus replied, looking slightly nauseated. "I mean, I think it's up to the primary voters to decide that. I mean, obviously, people are going to have different opinions. And, you know, you're going to have a lot of different candidates that are running, they're gonna talk about different things at different times. . . . I think having a diversity of opinion is fine."

The lesson Trump took away was that the party gatekeepers, who were privately appalled at his behavior and did not want him in the race, would pose no threat to him at all if he decided to run.

Obama's humiliation of Trump at the Correspondents' Dinner appeared to smother the hype that had been building around Trump for months. Years later, when Trump won the Republican nomination, analysts seeking to understand his rise and how they had missed it would look back at the evening as the catalyst that launched his subsequent climb to the pinnacle of American politics. Essentially, they understood Trump's pursuit of the presidency to be a revenge fantasy exacted upon his tormentors to establish, with sweeping certainty, his dominance over all who had mocked him.

Trump himself has rejected this view (in no small part, one suspects, because accepting it would involve an un-Trumpian admission that he had indeed been humiliated). "It's such a false narrative," he complained in 2016. He added, less convincingly, "I had a phenomenal time. I had a great evening." Trump also could have pointed out that he had long ago developed many of the themes that became hallmarks of his eventual campaign—everything from the evils of Chinese currency manipulation to the economic damage that NAFTA inflicted on a broad swath of U.S. workers.

What is clear in hindsight, however, is that Trump's interest in politics intensified right after the dinner, instead of quickly melting away, as it had after each of his presidential flirtations in the past. "I realized," he said, "that unless I actually ran, I wouldn't be taken seriously." For years, Trump had sought political advice from Roger Stone, a junior Richard Nixon henchman turned lobbyist and a notorious self-promoter, whose carefully cultivated image as a master of the political dark arts often seduced wealthy naïfs like Trump (*The New Republic* once dubbed Stone a "state-of-the-art Washington sleaze ball" for his ability to fleece credulous newcomers). Now

Trump decided to broaden his circle of advisers. He turned to Bossie to school him in the rudiments of preparing for a presidential campaign.

Trump's decision to reach out to Bossie was consequential in ways that he probably couldn't appreciate because it immediately plunged him deep into the anti-Clinton milieu in which Bossie was a chieftain. The match might have been more or less inevitable. Trump also sought meetings with more mainstream Republican consultants, some of whom had experience in presidential campaigns. But none took him seriously or envisioned any future for him in high-level politics, particularly not after his public comedown from the birther attacks. As he had with Obama and Meyers, Trump registered with them mainly as a punch line.

The connection to Bossie, however, brought entrée to a whole menagerie of characters who were eager to advise Trump and would figure prominently in his future. Most of them belonged to a distinct subcategory within Republican politics: professional anti-Clinton operatives. As Bossie's own résumé testified, Bill and Hillary Clinton had been prominent Democratic fixtures on the national political scene for so long—two decades, at this point—that it was possible for a conservative to build an entire career out of specializing in devising ways to oppose and attack them. No equivalent job category exists on the left. A liberal simply couldn't sustain himself professionally by developing a specialized capacity for attacking, say, Romneys or Bushes. Either there wasn't sufficient continuity across election cycles or, as in the case of the dynastic Bushes, they didn't inspire the kind of visceral loathing among the opposition that is necessary to maintain a permanent counter-operation. The Clintons, on the other hand, registered to most conservatives as the primary and ever-present enemy.

Through Bossie, Trump forged a connection with people such as Kellyanne Conway, who first rose to cable news fame in the late nineties as part of a trio of blond conservative "pundettes" (along with Ann Coulter and Laura Ingraham) who became anti–Bill Clinton fixtures during the Monica Lewinsky scandal and Clinton's subsequent impeachment.* Conway's husband, George T. Conway III, helped to impeach Clinton by drafting the Supreme Court brief when Paula Jones sued the president. The court agreed with Conway's argument that a sitting president could be subjected to a civil lawsuit. (Clinton's denial under oath that he'd had sexual relations with Lewinsky eventually led to his impeachment.) George Conway earned a special place in conservative lore by reportedly e-mailing Matt Drudge an infamous tip, which Drudge quickly published, about the shape of the president's penis. Even Roger Stone, sensing opportunity, had begun fashioning himself into an author of heated anti-Clinton polemical books.

All of these influences helped shape Trump's view of politics and steer it in a sharply anti-Clinton direction just as Trump was starting to think seriously about running for president. In 2012, he surprised Mitt Romney's campaign by repeatedly and forcefully offering his endorsement. Somewhat reluctantly, Romney's team agreed to accept it at a Trump hotel in Las Vegas two days before Nevada's GOP caucus, though not before taking steps to minimize the association by hanging blue curtains around the ballroom where the endorsement would take place, so that Romney wouldn't appear to be standing "in a burlesque house or one of Saddam's palaces," a Romney aide, Ryan Williams, later recalled. (They missed the

---

*Conway and her husband did know Trump socially because they had lived in one of his buildings, Trump World Tower, for a period in the 2000s. She began polling for Trump in 2013.

gold-emblazoned "Trump" lectern at which both men spoke.) Another adviser was surprised by Trump's expectation that the campaign would want him to barnstorm the country on Romney's plane. "We finally had to tell him: it's not gonna happen," the adviser said. "He couldn't believe that we were saying no." Trump seemed to imagine a role for himself that would have amounted to a kind of dry run for his own campaign four years later.

No one whom Bossie brought into Trump's orbit would exert a greater influence than Bannon would. Not long after the fateful Correspondents' Dinner, Bossie, who knew Bannon from fringe conservative circles, brought him along on a trip to Trump Tower to offer advice about how Trump might prepare for a run. By all accounts, the two men clicked right away. Like Trump, Bannon had cycled through multiple marriages and was rich, brash, charismatic, volcanic, opinionated, and never ruffled by doubt. He, too, was a businessman and a deal maker, and he had faced down moguls ranging from Ted Turner to Michael Ovitz. Fluent in the argot of Wall Street and Hollywood, Bannon specialized in media, having moved from financing television shows and films to making movies himself. He had plenty of experience maneuvering among the outsize egos of aggressive billionaires such as Trump and seemed to possess a sixth sense about how to connect with them.

Perhaps owing to this background, Trump, whose habit was to surround himself with obsequious lackeys, took Bannon's counsel more seriously than he did that of other advisers. "[Steve] was the only alpha male in his universe," said a Trump associate. When Trump began visiting conservative conferences, such as the South Carolina Freedom Summit, which Bossie hosts each year, he would make a point of seeking out Bannon. "I remember Trump at the Freedom Summit going, 'Where's my Steve? Where's my Steve?'"

said Sam Nunberg, an ex–Trump aide. "He loved the guy." It was clear the connection was genuine, said Roger Stone, "because Steve is a slob, and Trump hates slobs."

Initially, Bannon was no more inclined to take Trump's presidential ambitions seriously than anyone else who wasn't on Trump's payroll. He also met with more plausible candidates, such as Ted Cruz, Rand Paul, and Ben Carson. Always on the lookout for a new adventure, Bannon viewed the meetings with Trump as a lark and a chance to possibly conscript him into one of his many enterprises.

To prepare for one meeting, Bossie conducted some cursory opposition research, mostly combing through public records, in order to give Trump a sense of where he might be vulnerable to attack. Bannon and Bossie traveled up to New York City to present what they'd found. Trump was astonished when the pair informed him that he had bothered to vote only sporadically and had given money to Democratic politicians. "How did you get that information?" he asked them, unaware that it was readily available in public records.

According to a former Trump adviser, Bannon was also behind a needling stunt Trump pulled two weeks before the 2012 election. Having badgered Obama into releasing his birth certificate the year before, Trump had started insinuating that his passport and college transcripts may also be forged or missing. "I'm very honored to have gotten him to release his long-form birth certificate—or whatever it may be," Trump said in a blurry video he posted to YouTube. "I have a deal for the president, a deal that I don't believe he can refuse, and I hope he doesn't. If Barack Obama opens up and gives his college records and applications, and if he gives his passport applications and records, I will give, to a charity of his choice . . . a check, immediately, for $5 million." Bannon told an associate he had lined up a donor willing to supply half the sum.

The media, chastened by the birther episode, didn't bite on this
one. But by now, Trump and Bannon had forged a connection, and
Trump's thoughts were already shifting to 2016. "I knew Trump was
running in 2013," said Nunberg, an aide to Trump at the time. "I
knew because he got a taste of it in 2012—he was surprised that
he was number one [in the polls]." Nunberg called Bannon to make
sure he knew they weren't screwing around. "I remember telling
Steve, 'We're going to rage against the machine,'" said Nunberg.
"And Steve just loved it. I still remember his reply. He goes, 'That's
amazing, brother.'"

Although neither of them could have had any inkling of where
they would end up, Bannon would provide Trump with two great
services in the years ahead—services without which Trump probably wouldn't be president. First, he supplied Trump with a fully
formed, internally coherent worldview that accommodated Trump's
own feelings about trade and foreign threats, what Trump eventually dubbed "America first" nationalism. One aspect in particular
that preoccupied Bannon—the menace of illegal immigration—was
something Trump would use to galvanize his supporters from the
moment he descended the Trump Tower escalator on June 16, 2015,
to declare his candidacy. By then, Bannon had left banking and
Hollywood to take over the combative right-wing populist website
Breitbart News after the death of its founder, Andrew Breitbart, in
2012. *Breitbart's* fixation on race, crime, immigration, radical Islam,
and the excesses of political correctness—as well as the site's dark
and inflammatory style—did much to shape Trump's populist incli-
nations and inform his political vocabulary. (An analysis of his
Twitter feed conducted after the election showed that *Breitbart* is far
and away Trump's primary source of news.)

The second service Bannon provided Trump was to conceive

and create over several years an infrastructure of conservative organizations that together would work, sometimes in tandem with mainstream media outlets, to stop the woman everyone believed would become the 2016 Democratic nominee: Hillary Clinton. What Bannon built was in essence the very thing Clinton herself was mocked for invoking in 1998: a "vast right-wing conspiracy" designed to tear her down. Bannon didn't set out to do this specifically for Trump. Rather, Trump was the fortunate beneficiary of an elaborate plot to discredit his opponent—and then, either through luck or foresight, he put the architect of that plot in charge of his campaign for the critical final stretch before the election, producing a result that shocked the world.

How did this happen? Why did no one see it coming? And why did conservatives succeed in stopping a Clinton this time, when they had failed so badly to stop one before?

Many of the answers trace back to the Oz figure of Bannon. Though he befriended Bossie and other veterans of the anti-Clinton movement, he was not a part of their world when Bill Clinton was president. Watching from afar, he developed a perceptive critique of why they failed. "In the 1990s," he explained, "conservative media couldn't take down Clinton because most of what they produced was punditry and opinion, and they always oversold the conclusion: 'It's clearly impeachable!'" Stunts like Dan Burton's watermelon murder theory and Bossie's doctored tapes cost conservatives the public's trust—and they didn't even recognize it, until voters took their power away. Bannon's diagnosis of their chief flaw was simple and direct: "They wound up talking to themselves in an echo chamber."

To be effective, he believed, a conservative effort to thwart Clinton would need to be based on facts, not punditry, and reach beyond the conservative bubble to turn liberals and independents against her. The insular world of anti-Clinton conspiracists was ill equipped to mount such a campaign, of this Bannon had no doubt. So instead, he drew upon the lessons of his own strange and peripatetic career, which had equipped him with a set of skills and a grand theory about how he could pull it off.

THREE

BILDUNGSROMAN

annon was born into a blue-collar, Irish-Catholic family of Democrats in 1953, within sight of the naval base in Norfolk, Virginia. He was the third of five children born to Martin Bannon, a telephone linesman, and his wife, Doris, a homemaker. Soon afterward, the family moved to a leafy neighborhood in North Richmond, Virginia.

Bannon's upbringing was steeped in traditionalism at every turn: at church, at school, and at home, in the working-class identity forged by his parents' Democratic politics. In 1953, the South was still solidly Democratic, and Virginia was dominated by the Byrd Organization, the political machine led by former governor and U.S. senator Harry F. Byrd, Sr., a conservative Democrat bent upon stopping the advance of the civil rights movement. Although the Byrd machine was well into its decline by the time Bannon was growing up, and never had the same strength in urban centers such as Richmond that it did in rural areas, it still shaped the tenor of the local politics. Yet the Bannons, like many conservative Irish-Catholic families, were captivated by a different Democrat, John F. Kennedy. "We were Kennedy freaks," said Chris Bannon, Steve's younger brother. "My dad knocked on doors for Kennedy. Every Irish kid thinks he wants to be Jack Kennedy, right?"

Their parents' views and infatuation with Kennedy filtered down to the Bannon children less as a politics than as a class identity and self-conception. They were raised with a clear understanding of the value of hard work and the expectation that they would do their part. Steve mowed lawns and delivered newspapers before graduating to a job at a local junkyard. "He would come home looking like a coal miner," said Chris. "Mom would make him strip down to his boxers and spray him off with a hose before he could come in."

Martin and Doris Bannon were serious Roman Catholics who insisted that the family attend Sunday Mass, and they sent all three of their sons to Benedictine, the private Roman Catholic military academy in Richmond. As the Roman Catholic Church took steps to modernize after the Vatican II reforms of 1962–1965, the Bannons were drawn in the opposite direction, toward a deeper connection with Church tradition and the mysteries and beauties of its ancient rituals. After Pope John Paul II permitted limited use of the Latin-only Tridentine Mass, which was banned by the Second Vatican Council, the elder Bannons became Tridentine Catholics. "When [the Roman Catholic Church] first started allowing it in the mid-eighties," Steve Bannon recalled, "we left our parish that we'd been in for years and went and joined St. Joseph's in Richmond, which offers a Tridentine Mass."

By the time he graduated from high school in 1972, the Byrd machine had withered, but Benedictine stood as a bulwark against a liberalizing world. "We were a right-wing military Catholic high school," said John Pudner, a childhood friend of the Bannons who grew up two blocks away and attended Benedictine. "We were very small, just four hundred kids at a time. It was a very close-knit community."

Bannon received an education steeped in classics and history. The Benedictine curriculum was traditional Western Civilization presented in a context of Catholicism. "We were all taught that Western civilization was saved five hundred years ago in Spain, when Ferdinand and Isabella defeated the Moors," said Pudner. "The lesson was, here's where Muslims could have taken over the world. And here was the great stand where they were stopped. We were taught a worldview: 'This is how Catholicism survived.' I think that shaped all of us. But what Steve took away, I think, was a belief that you've got to be willing to identify the threat. When we were growing up, the threat was the atheist, communist Soviet Union. . . . Now Muslims are trying to blow us up."

Even though the Benedictine student body was overwhelmingly white, very few cadets came from wealthy families, and the school itself was located in a polyglot neighborhood of whites, blacks, and Jews. Benedictine cadets thought of themselves as working-class and cultivated rivalries with a pair of rich preparatory schools in the Richmond suburbs, Collegiate and St. Christopher's. "We'd battle them in sports; we'd fight with them at parties," said Pudner. "We were the blue-collar guys. They were the rich snobs. They'd always do the employer-employee joke at us: 'When you grow up, you'll work for us.' And we'd punch 'em in the nose."

By every account, Bannon prized—even relished—this class identity, a born believer with a quickness to take passionate sides.

More often than not, he was the one who would throw the first punch in any showdown with a group of rich prep schoolers. But he was also taken with the much larger idea, imparted at Benedictine, that Western civilization had to be constantly and vigilantly defended against shadowy, shape-shifting enemies, and he was prone to viewing contemporary struggles, even minor ones, as critical junctures of historical significance. This fed a grandiose image of himself as someone galloping to defend not just a class but Western civilization itself.

Bannon would go on to work and thrive in a succession of elite, cosmopolitan institutions—Harvard Business School, Goldman Sachs, Hollywood—a fact that has caused many observers to puzzle over just how it is that he emerged as an apocalyptic, fire-breathing conservative populist. Those who have known him the longest see no mystery at all. The Bannon they witness in the White House is a recognizable extension of the teenage go-getter they knew in Richmond, and his political views, though now more fiercely held, are rooted in the same beliefs that were instilled in him at Benedictine.

"Look at the three legs of conservatism today," said Pudner, who went on to become a Republican political consultant. "There's military and foreign affairs—Steve went to military school. There's social conservatism—he's a pro-life Catholic. And there's economics, which for us didn't mean rich guys protecting their tax breaks. It meant, for all of us who were working-class, that you worked a job. It was that kind of conservatism that we believed really helped the average worker. And when you think about it that way, there's really no jump at all from Steve Bannon at Benedictine in 1972 to 2016 and Donald Trump."

Growing up, Bannon had designs on a military career. He wanted to become an officer. But he also wanted a break from the rigors of military discipline that was part of life at Benedictine, so rather than follow the dozen or so Benedictine graduates who headed straight into the Virginia Military Institute, he followed a different group of classmates and enrolled at Virginia Tech. Some people go to college and are immediately transformed by the exposure to new people and new ideas. This wasn't Bannon's experience at all. College seemed to make him a more vivid and intense version of the person he was when he arrived.

In an early display of the pugilistic style that would become his hallmark, Bannon, having previously evinced no interest in student politics, decided during his junior year to launch an insurgent campaign for president of the student government association. His preferred mode of politicking, then as now, was the all-out populist attack. He chose a female running mate, an uncommon move at the time, and printed up flyers charging his opponents with offering only "Platitudes, Promises and Slogans," implying that they were in league with a distant, elitist university administration. Against this, Bannon's flyers promised that he would "create change" through his own brand of "dynamic leadership." His opponents in the race, veterans of student government, were taken aback by the ruthless upstart who had suddenly thrust himself into their midst. "It just wasn't fun," Marshall DeBerry, who ran against Bannon, recalled recently. "It was very negative stuff. . . . Upon reflection, Trump's campaign seemed somewhat similar to the student body presidential campaign I faced in 1975."

How Bannon's opponents responded to his provocations also

prefigured criticisms that would be widely directed at him later on, even by frustrated allies. "Don't be fooled by Bannon. He has immense charisma, but lacks the ability to keep his head geared in any one particular direction long enough to accomplish anything," Gary Clisham, the sitting SGA president, warned in a letter to the student newspaper, the *Collegiate Times*. "Mr. Steve Bannon has run amok every assignment given him."

The letter outraged hot-blooded Bannon partisans, including his roommate Darrell Nevin, who shoved Clisham during a subsequent debate. ("Scuffle Occurs at Great Debate" read the headline in the *Collegiate Times*.) "I was young. I just thought, well, let's push him off the stage," Nevin recalled, with some embarrassment. "It was a bitter campaign."

Bitter but, for Bannon, victorious: he carried more than 60 percent of the vote and found himself the insurgent class president.

After graduating from Virginia Tech in 1976 with a degree in urban planning, Bannon was finally ready to join the military. He signed up for the Naval Reserve straightaway. The life that he imagined for himself as a junior naval officer—one that revolved around duty, honor, and patriotism—was nothing like what he encountered when he showed up at the Navy's training center in Rhode Island in 1977. Bannon, not one given to modest ambitions, had visions of one day becoming secretary of defense. "When I got into the Navy," he said, "I thought my shit didn't stink because I'd been president of the student body at college. I get there, and it's the [beginning of] the all-volunteer force, and I get assigned to the engineering department. I walk in and my entire division, my entire gang, basically looked like they had been given a choice between jail and the Navy."

He laughed. "They turned out to be great guys, but the all-volunteer force was just a different deal back then."

Bannon expected his naval career to roughly resemble Richard Gere's in *An Officer and a Gentleman*—a series of character-building trials and affirmations that would instill strength and valor, and reward him with the full measure of military prestige that he assumed he would merit. What he got instead more closely resembled Bill Murray's experience in *Stripes*. But he readily adapted to the Navy as it was, prizing the camaraderie that develops among shipmates at sea and thriving amid the towel-snapping, chauvinistic naval culture of that era. Later on, Bannon would frequently express deep nostalgia for the wardroom culture of the Navy, and it is something that he would seek to re-create at every stage of his life afterward.

Bannon was billeted to the USS *Paul F. Foster*, a Spruance-class destroyer designed for antisubmarine warfare. Assigned to the Pacific Fleet and operating out of San Diego, the ship was deployed in 1978 and spent much of the next two years in the western Pacific and Indian oceans. The job of an antisubmarine destroyer is to trail aircraft carriers and protect them from enemies. Bannon spent his first deployment uneventfully in the Pacific, working as an auxiliary engineer. Sometimes, Soviet vessels would test the ship with cat-and-mouse games, but more often life at sea was filled with long stretches of tedium. He passed the time reading books on Zen Buddhism and playing basketball, where his ball-hogging style of play earned him the nickname "Coast to Coast."

During Bannon's second deployment, when he had become a navigator, the *Paul F. Foster* was ordered to the North Arabian Sea. Just past midnight on March 21, 1980, he was piloting the destroyer off the southern coast of Iran when it rendezvoused with the super-carrier USS *Nimitz*, which it was assigned to shadow.

The previous November, Iranian revolutionaries belonging to the Muslim Student Followers of the Imam's Line, an Iranian student group that backed the Ayatollah Khomeini, had stormed the U.S. Embassy in Tehran and seized fifty-two American hostages. The crisis dominated American headlines and roiled the latter stages of Jimmy Carter's troubled presidency. The *Paul F. Foster* and the *Nimitz* sailed to the Gulf of Oman, where they began preparations for the secret mission that was to become Carter's response. The *Nimitz* carried eight RH-53D Sea Stallion helicopters that were supposed to swoop into Tehran with Delta Force soldiers, who would free the American hostages in a lightning blitz code-named Operation Eagle Claw.

"We were there for the workup, day after day," Bannon said. "There were two battle groups, one Camel Station, one Gonzo Station. The U.S. Navy had never really been there before, so we have aircraft carriers, submarines, destroyers, cruisers, helicopters, just going everywhere." Bannon's faith in the capacity of his commanders had diminished throughout his time in the Navy, and the preparations he was witness to left him with an uneasy feeling about the mission's prospects. "You could tell it was going to be a goat fuck," he said.

It was. On April 24, 1980, Operation Eagle Claw commenced to almost immediate disaster. The eight Sea Stallions were supposed to fly to a staging area called Desert One in the remote Dasht-e Lut desert under cover of darkness. There the helicopters would refuel, wait out the day, and then ferry the Delta Force soldiers 260 miles further inland to Desert Two, just outside Tehran, the following evening. From there, the soldiers would drive into Tehran, storm the embassy, and rescue the hostages, whom they would spirit across the street to a soccer stadium, where helicopters would whip everyone back to the desert, and on to freedom. AC-130 gunships would blanket the sky over Tehran to provide supporting fire. Carrier Air Wing Eight, established at Gonzo Station, which was Bannon's operating area, would take off from the *Nimitz* and provide air protection.

Almost nothing went according to plan. On the way to Desert One, one of the Sea Stallions was grounded in the desert when sensors detected a cracked rotor blade. The seven remaining helicopters pressed on, only to hit an unexpected sandstorm, causing two more of them to have to abandon the mission. At this point, commanders disagreed about whether to abort the rescue attempt. Eventually, Carter called it off. But as the team was pulling out of Desert One, one of the helicopters struck the tail of an EC-130 aircraft that had brought fuel to the staging area. The fiery explosion killed eight servicemen and badly burned two more. The remaining Sea Stallions had to be abandoned in the desert. The White House, humiliated, revealed the failed rescue operation the next day.

Bannon was not a part of the Desert One debacle. To the disappointment of its crew, the *Paul F. Foster* was ordered to Pearl Harbor several days before Carter launched the ill-fated mission. Bannon and his shipmates learned about what happened while they were at sea. "We felt defeated," said Andrew Green, who served aboard Bannon's destroyer.

Bannon blamed Carter, whom he regarded with undisguised contempt. It was enough to shake him free of the loose affiliation he'd felt with his parents' Democratic politics. "When I was in the service, I wasn't really that political," he said, "but then you see a guy like Carter, how fucked up things can get. My political views were formed by seeing how a weak leader like that could get America into the middle of a Middle East debacle." Bannon felt as if he were waking up to fundamental truths about the world, truths that alarmed him. The motley assemblage of enlisted men who made up the all-volunteer force had disabused him of his romantic notion of naval life. Serving aboard the *Paul F. Foster* in the gulf, his darkening view of the wider world grew to encompass his civilian commanders—above all Carter, whose pusillanimous hesitancy, and failure of leadership when he did finally act, Bannon held directly responsible for damaging American prestige.

Bannon's experience as a naval officer in the gulf did more than sour him on Democratic politics. It pushed him into a different party. He became enraptured with a hawkish, outspoken, confrontational, and struttingly pro-military Republican, Ronald Reagan, whose searing critique of Carter's weakness matched his own views. Bannon's years abroad also opened his eyes to what struck him as a gathering threat. It was not the sort of immediate, existential danger posed by the Soviet Union. Rather, this was a more distant menace that loomed just over the horizon: Islam. Anyone seeking to trace the pathogenesis of the Islamophobia that would grip Bannon thirty years hence can follow it back to Tehran and his time in the Middle East. The hostage crisis, he came to believe, was just the first hint of a hostility that could grow into something that would one day threaten the West—something that, he would finally conclude thirty-five years later, urgently necessitated "a global war against Islamic fascism."

"It was not hard to see, as a junior officer, sitting there, that [the threat] was just going to be huge," said Bannon. "We'd pull into a place like Karachi, Pakistan—this is 1979, and I'll never forget it—the British guys came on board, because they still ran the port. The city had 10 million people at the time. We'd get out there, and 8 million of them had to be below the age of fifteen. It was an eye-opener. We'd been other places like the Philippines where there was mass poverty. But it was nothing like the Middle East. It was just a complete eye-opener. It was the other end of the earth."

In fact, he could hardly comprehend that places like Pakistan and Iran were terrestrial at all, so otherworldly was this strange and forbidding place whose sudden aggressions had summoned the full might of the U.S. military, flawed though its civilian leaders might have been. "The only way I can describe Iran," Bannon recalled, "is that it looked like the moon. You're literally months away from home, steaming across the ocean, these vast expanses, you get to this place and it was like you'd landed on the moon. It was like the fifth century—completely primeval."

After the *Paul F. Foster* arrived back in San Diego, Bannon decided that he had had enough of sea duty. Energized by Reagan's election and eager to join the new administration, he transferred to a job in the Pentagon. On the same day that Reagan was sworn into office, Bannon began serving as an assistant in the office of the chief of naval operations. "I came back to the U.S. and saw how Reagan inspired the country," he said. "I was just a huge Reagan admirer." As disillusioned as he had become under Carter, Bannon was thrilled by Reagan's steep increase in the military budget, and though he held a low-level position, he had a front-row seat and a security clearance to watch as the Navy figured out how to distribute this largesse and strengthen its forces.

To get ahead in the administration, he started working toward a master's degree in national security studies at Georgetown University in the evenings. "We were all very involved in the Navy budget, working with the senior admirals," said Peter Harris, who worked alongside Bannon in the Pentagon and attended the same Georgetown program. "It was a good time to understand how the Navy formulates its policies and looks at the force structure twenty years out."

Somewhere along the way, however, Bannon began to chafe at the limitations of his junior position and the sluggishness of the military hierarchy. He realized that it would be years—perhaps even decades—before the possibility of becoming an important decision-maker would even open up to him. "It was pretty evident at the time that as a uniformed officer, there was only so far that you could go," he said. "You could work your entire career and really not have a job that gave you the freedom and flexibility to do something big."

Throughout his seven-year tenure in the Navy, Bannon was a faithful reader of *The Wall Street Journal,* and had enough success as an amateur speculator in commodities such as gold and silver that shipmates sought out his investment advice. Still intoxicated by the go-go Reagan eighties, his restlessness mounted as he began to sense that the real action lay not in Washington but on Wall Street, which, by the fall of 1982, was beginning to boom as the economy began pulling out of a deep recession. "I decided I wanted to go to Wall Street," he recalled, "and somebody told me, 'If you want to go to Wall Street, then you've got to go to Harvard Business School.'" Harvard accepted him, and Bannon, at twenty-nine, matriculated in 1983.

———

By the time he arrived in Cambridge, the Dow Jones Industrial Average was flat-out soaring—up 50 percent in just eighteen months. To Bannon and his Harvard Business School classmates, Reagan made capitalism feel vital and newly alive, while Wall Street held the glittering allure of the riches that the sizzling economy could bestow on an elect few—many of them HBS graduates—who won positions at the leading financial firms. Almost overnight, the once sleepy profession of investment banking came to seem exciting, central, and valorous in a way that nobody had quite anticipated. It was the job that encapsulated the zeitgeist of the eighties.

For some students, Wall Street's boom fueled fantasies of the full-on, debauched eighties-investment-banker lifestyle. Not for Bannon, who wouldn't permit himself the distraction. Although he dressed the part of a rich preppy, in khakis and yellow Polo sweaters, he mostly forswore partying and resolved to become a grind. "He was not a rebel looking for a cause," recalled Scot Vorse, his friend and classmate. "You don't go to Harvard Business School to be a rebel and cause problems. You go to Harvard Business School because it was the most prestigious school to get in at the time." Ever alert to signifiers of class, Bannon understood that he differed from most of his HBS peers: he was several years older, married (he'd wed Cathleen "Susie" Houff, a young woman from Richmond who'd gone to Virginia Tech), had blue-collar Irish roots, and had made it to Harvard by way of the Navy rather than an elite university that might have endowed him with useful friendships and business connections.

The brass ring for HBS students was a summer associateship at one of the big investment banks, typically the prelude to a coveted job offer upon graduating. Competition was fierce. Bannon, who made friendships easily, was warned by his more well-bred classmates that he would probably have to stand out academically to have a hope of landing one. "They told me, 'Hey, since you were in the Navy and didn't really come up with us, you've got to become a first-year honors guy,'" he said. He took the advice to heart. "I was really focused on getting first-year honors, getting really great grades."

It helped to be hyper-competitive and driven, which Bannon was, and to have a healthy dose of charisma, which he certainly did. HBS divided its first-year students into sections of about ninety people and then pitted them against one another to determine their grades. Half of their grade was based upon class participation. Adding to the pressure, the program was designed to fail 7 percent of the class, in order to foster competition. Bannon was assigned to Section H and quickly distinguished himself as "the leader of the pack," said Vorse.

He had a knack for expository speaking and a self-confidence that bordered on arrogance, both attributes that lent themselves to the performative demands of the business school curriculum. "Most of the time, there is not a right answer," Vorse said. "These are cases where part of succeeding in business is figuring out what's important and what's not. . . . Steve is as good as anybody at getting through the noise, deciphering the issue, and deciding what's relevant."

For all that he studied, however, Bannon was no apple polisher. He invariably chose a seat in the back of the classroom, among a group of friends who sneered at the grasping, overeager "tire biters" in the front row. He felt comfortable doing this not only because it was entirely in his nature, but also because he felt increasingly sure of his academic primacy. "In my view, Steve was certainly top three in intellectual horsepower in our class—perhaps the smartest," recalled David Allen, who sat with him in the back of the class. "But he combined horsepower with logical, well-structured arguments. Whenever Steve spoke, my advice was to 'listen for understanding.'"

When he returned to Richmond over the Christmas holiday, Bannon mailed out dozens of letters requesting interviews for summer associateships. Goldman Sachs was, for him, an especially sought-after target, as it was for most of his classmates. Each year, hundreds of HBS students applied for what usually numbered fewer than two dozen Goldman slots. Bannon, having succeeded in earning first-year honors and fancying himself "a pretty hot runner," figured he had a better shot than most at landing one.

Yet weeks went by without an interview invitation, then months. Bannon was stunned. The firms that replied turned him down. Many didn't reply at all. "I thought it would be a very simple process," he said. "Everyone would want me because I'm a superstar, right? Nope. All rejections. One hundred percent."

In the spring, chastened, he resolved to make a good showing for the recruiters who filtered onto campus to tout their firms and select the next class of associates. "I remember going up to the guy from Dillon, Read & Co.—a classic investment bank with a great name on Wall Street—and I said, 'Hey, look, I sent in a request for an interview,'" Bannon recalled. "He goes, 'Lemme check . . . Bannon . . . Oh yeah, you were rejected.'" Bannon flushed, as some of his classmates looked on. Worse still, the Dillon, Read recruiter confirmed what his friends had warned him about. "He goes, 'Look, I'm sure you're a great guy and you're probably gonna be a rock star somewhere,'" Bannon recalled being told. "'But we're a small investment bank. You're older, you've been a naval officer. I need a guy who does finance, and I can't make a mistake. We're not the Dallas

Cowboys—we don't draft talent. We're looking for a position player.'"
Bannon walked away convinced that, despite his grades and class
standing, he might not get an interview anywhere, much less get
a job.

He had little choice but to keep trying. A short while later, a
team from Goldman Sachs arrived on campus. Bannon dutifully
attended a presentation delivered by Kevin Kennedy, a young vice
president who would go on to become a senior partner at the firm.
Thirty years later, Bannon could still summon the details of Kennedy's no-bullshit pitch to the HBS students for a Goldman Sachs that
was then still a close-knit, privately held partnership. "He says,
'We're a very hard-working place. There are no stretch limos outside. We're very middle class. We work very hard. It's all about the
firm. It's about partnership. It's about teamwork. What we're going
to do is have an open bar, and we'd like all of you to come and have
a drink with us.' It sounded perfect to me. It wasn't Gordon Gekko.
I thought to myself, *I gotta do this*."

The next day, Bannon put on his best suit and headed over to
the Goldman recruiting party, hoping to somehow inveigle his way
into getting an interview. "I get there, and there's like seven hundred people jammed into this tent," he said. "I said, 'Fuck it. There's
no chance.'" With practically his entire class jockeying to make an
impression on the recruiters, Bannon calculated that the odds were
impossible for him. He grabbed a beer and stood, discouraged, on
the periphery of the crowd. Social animal that he was, however, he
soon struck up a conversation with a pair of strangers who were
milling nearby. "I'm there with my drink and these two other
schmendricks standing next to me," he said. "I start talking to these
guys, and we have the greatest conversation about baseball, and I
find out after about half an hour that it was John Weinberg, whose

dad runs the firm, and a guy named Rob Kaplan, who became a senior partner"—and, later, chairman of the Dallas Federal Reserve Bank.

At the time, Kaplan and Weinberg were both young associates. They came away from their impromptu conversation entertained and impressed by the charismatic naval officer who had worked his way up from Richmond to Harvard. Bannon, an engrossing storyteller with a gift in the Irish comic tradition, had regaled them with tales of his exploits around the globe, as well as his thoughts on subjects ranging from Harvard to Reagan.

That evening, the Goldman executives gathered in a room to compare notes and begin winnowing the pool of applicants. One of them later recounted the scene.* They placed the names of prospective hires up on a board. When they got to Bannon, someone said, "I guess we're going to reject him. He's too old for a summer job." Kaplan and Weinberg leaped up. "And these guys say, 'Oh no, we talked to him—he's terrific,'" Bannon said. "It was literally a complete crapshoot. But I got a job."

---

*One of the Goldman executives in the room that evening confirmed these events as Bannon described them, but asked that his name not be used.

FOUR

"A DANGEROUS WAY TO LOOK AT THE WORLD"

After Bannon graduated from Harvard Business School in 1985, he parachuted into a war zone, landing in Goldman Sachs's New York office at the height of the hostile-takeover boom. The job thrust him into the kind of high-pressure situation he adored: a primal, intense, all-consuming struggle between two warring factions. Goldman Sachs put him on the front lines.

A few years earlier, in the late 1970s, a young bond trader named Michael Milken had quietly set the stage for a revolution on Wall Street when he discovered that, in the aggregate, bonds of former blue-chip corporations that had fallen on hard times—known as "fallen angels"—consistently outperformed those of current blue chips with better creditworthiness. Because struggling corporations held a higher risk of failure, fallen angels had to offer higher interest rates than blue-chip bonds to attract customers. These higher interest rates meant that a portfolio of fallen angels, even though some would go bust, would almost invariably beat a portfolio of blue-chip bonds. Yet most investors shunned them as "junk." Milken's insight was that junk bonds were undervalued assets because investors, who feared seeming imprudent, didn't want to own them. An enormous opportunity awaited someone less constrained by appearances.

Milken made himself rich by trading junk bonds. Then he made himself vastly richer by becoming the chief evangelist for their cause. Along the way, he upended U.S. corporate finance. By convincing other investors that junk bonds were a shrewd bet, Milken almost single-handedly created a market for them. The demand he created meant that two types of businesses considered too risky to lend to by commercial bankers—new, smaller businesses and large, struggling corporations—could suddenly gain access to capital by floating junk bonds. Some of them failed. But many junk-fueled corporations, such as MCI and Chrysler, hit it big. And even though he won extraordinary wealth and renown, Milken had the chutzpah to style himself a populist, conjuring up capital for businesses that were looked down on and refused by established lenders.

By the time Bannon graduated from HBS, Milken's revolution had generated tens of billions of dollars in junk bonds, enough to fund all the companies shut out of the credit markets. So Milken and his firm, Drexel Burnham Lambert, devised an ingenious new use for them: they used junk bonds to finance raids on undervalued blue-chip corporations. Milken and Drexel would fund these hostile takeovers by pledging the assets of the target corporation as collateral, in the same way that a home buyer obtains a mortgage by pledging the collateral of the home against the loan. This practice gave rise to an army of corporate raiders, men such as Ron Perelman, Carl Icahn, T. Boone Pickens, and Nelson Peltz, who became rich selling junk bonds through Drexel Burnham to finance predatory raids on such Fortune 100 companies as TWA, Disney, Revlon, and Phillips Petroleum. So fearsome did Milken's reputation become that sometimes the mere rumor that a company might come under siege was enough to send it scrambling toward a defensive merger.

Hostile takeovers became a hugely profitable business for Milken and Drexel. By 1986, Bannon's first full year on Wall Street, Milken had become Wall Street's most notorious villain and Drexel Burnham its most profitable investment bank, clearing $545.5 million on revenues of $4 billion. More important for Bannon and Goldman Sachs, Milken and his army of raiders had struck terror in the hearts of the chief executives of America's finest corporations. "Everything in the Midwest was being raided by Milken," said Bannon. "It was like a firestorm."

The attacks by Milken had a corollary effect on the companies he targeted: they needed help staving off the barbarians at the gates. This, too, created profitable new business opportunities. Goldman Sachs, not yet evolved into the money-grubbing "vampire squid" it would later become, was a white-shoe firm that wouldn't deign to represent corporate raiders in hostile takeover bids. Instead, Goldman developed a specialty in raid defense for blue-chip companies targeted by the likes of Drexel Burnham and First Boston. Bannon landed in the firm's mergers-and-acquisitions department, the SWAT team that companies called in to advise and protect them when the raiders came calling.

Ensconced on the twenty-third floor of Goldman's old headquarters at 85 Broad Street, Bannon spent his first few years at Goldman working one-hundred-hour weeks and clocking in every day except Christmas. "You'd get a call at seven a.m. on Sunday from a partner wanting to go over your work schedule for the day," he said. Goldman's M & A department was led by Geoff Boisi, the fanatically driven "Mastermind of the Mega-Deals" (as *The New*

York Times dubbed him), and Mike Overlock, who had served in a long-range reconnaissance patrol in the Vietnam War. "I was just a junior grundoon," said Bannon. "But we got to work with Hank Paulson [the future treasury secretary], who was the new-business guy in the Chicago office and the most intense guy in humanity." It was a grueling life, but one that he loved. "The environment was intense, but the camaraderie was amazing," he said. "It was like being in the Navy, in the wardroom of a ship."

At the time Bannon arrived, Goldman Sachs was the last major partnership on Wall Street. "Goldman then was a very different place than it is today," he said. "A very small partnership and an enormously conservative place at the time." Goldman's caution was dictated by its ownership structure. Not only did the partners have their own money on the line, but they held unlimited liability if an investment went wrong. "If Milken came in and did a raid," said Bannon, "and you were going in to tell the board of directors that you could get a better price, it was like going to argue before the Supreme Court: you had better be able to back it up. Because if it turned out you were wrong, shareholders would come back and sue the partnership for bad information." These circumstances instilled a rigor that Bannon, like Michael Lewis and other Wall Street veterans turned critics, believes was lost when investment banks became publicly traded companies that felt free to gamble with shareholders' money.

"Goldman in the eighties was like a priesthood," said Bannon, "a monastic experience where you worked all the time but were incredibly dedicated to client services, to building and growing companies." The firm thought of itself as "long-term greedy," meaning that it was devoted to the well-being of its clients, who, over years and decades, would reward that devotion by giving Goldman their business. "It was a calling, like joining the Jesuits," he said, "to build and grow companies. Somebody once told me, 'The river of history runs deep through Goldman's M & A department, because you're at the forefront of helping the country restructure into a post-industrial economy.' We believed that."

Yet even as Bannon was imbibing the lore of Goldman's high priests, the firm was headed down a path that would destroy this careful balance of interests, when the partners cashed out their stakes in Goldman's public offering a decade later. Without the restraining force of their liability, Goldman began to emulate the behavior of other publicly traded investment banks, whose collective excesses ultimately precipitated the 2008 financial crisis. "Cut to twenty years later," Bannon said, "and Wall Street is a casino that taxpayers have to bail out. I soured on Wall Street for the same reason everybody else did: the American taxpayer was forced to cut mook deals to bail out Wall Street. It was totally unfair."

Even in the eighties, long before Wall Street's collapse, Bannon harbored an admiration for the villain whom he and his colleagues were often matched up against in his early Goldman days. Milken, a Jew who wore an ill-fitting toupee, was initially shunned, and later despised, by the old-money firms with their WASP lineage and culture of restraint. But it was Milken who ultimately prevailed by storming their fortresses and upending their businesses. Eventually, they wised up and began doing what Milken had been doing all along: taking big stakes in the companies for themselves. Bannon had the brains and the social intelligence to pass as a Harvard preppy and a Goldman whiz kid, but deep down he identified more with Milken, a swashbuckler and rogue who struck fear in his adversaries. "The strengths that Milken had—the aggressiveness, the creativity, the hard work—those are all traits Steve admires," said a former Goldman colleague. Whether he recognized it or not, Bannon was better suited to the other side.

Later on, when Milken went to prison for insider trading, Bannon did a deal to roll up one of his companies. After Milken was freed and had begun rehabilitating his image, Bannon appeared as a featured speaker at one of his conferences. More than anything, Milken was a kind of spirit animal who fired the imagination and showed just how far you could go if you stopped worrying about appearances and seized opportunity. His lesson was never forgotten. If you took Michael Milken and Drexel in 1985 and teleported them from Wall Street to Washington, D.C., in 2015, what you'd wind up with would look a lot like Stephen Bannon and *Breitbart News*: a band of outsiders laying siege to a comfortable, fattened, and vulnerable establishment.

Two big things were going on at Goldman Sachs in the late 1980s. The globalization of world capital markets meant that size suddenly mattered. Everyone realized that the firm, a private partnership, would eventually have to go public to keep pace with its competitors. Bankers also could see that the Glass-Steagall Act separating commercial and investment banking was going to fall, setting off a flurry of acquisitions. Young bankers like Bannon were trained to be generalists. In the world to come, specialists would command a premium. After spending a year in Goldman's London office, Bannon shipped out to Los Angeles to learn the media and entertainment businesses.

Throughout the 1980s, big media companies were expanding and becoming more valuable. Some of this was due to the growing audience for TV shows and movies. But it was also because the federal government under Reagan had relaxed antitrust restrictions, which meant that the media and entertainment industries—like the oil-and-gas, retail-clothing, and pharmaceutical industries—were taking a page from Wall Street and embarking on an orgy of mergers and acquisitions. Some of these media mergers, such as Time Inc.'s $14 billion merger with Warner Communications in 1989 to create the world's largest entertainment conglomerate, were defensive in nature, intended to make companies large enough that they wouldn't fall prey to corporate raiders. Others were strategic acquisitions, like General Electric's 1985 takeover of RCA and its NBC division for $6.3 billion, a deal Bannon worked on for Goldman in its capacity as an adviser to GE. "A lot of people were coming from outside buying media companies," he said. "There was just huge consolidation going on."

The frenzy to acquire TV and film companies posed a particular challenge for investment banks like Goldman Sachs that profited by facilitating these deals. Hollywood movie studios were notoriously fickle, boom-and-bust affairs whose value was often tethered to whether or not they had recently churned out blockbuster hits. A steadier source of value—at least, in theory—was contained in the vast libraries of movie titles many studios controlled, because there would always be an audience for classics such as *Gone with the Wind* and *The Godfather* and therefore television channels willing to pony up to broadcast them. The trouble was how to value these films: they were closer to intellectual property than to tangible assets such as broadcast networks. Most investors preferred hard assets that could be easily measured—factories, airplanes, real estate— and avoided things like movie studios and film libraries, which were much harder to price with precision.

Bannon and some colleagues figured out how to do it. By

drawing on hard data such as VHS cassette sales and television ratings, they came up with a model to value intellectual property in the
same way as physical assets. Removing this obstacle made it as easy
to value Columbia Pictures as it was to value American Airlines or
Chrysler Motors—which only added to the Hollywood merger
stampede. Bannon possessed a gift, a kind of x-ray vision, that let
him walk into a studio and quickly suss out not just top-line numbers
but the whole schema—how the interlocking pieces fit together, and
what they were really worth. "He understood the math completely,"
said a colleague. "He could walk in, take one look, and say, 'You're
fucked. You're going bankrupt.'"

Rather than keep working for a salary, Bannon and a fellow
Goldman vice president quit in 1990 to form their own boutique
investment bank in Beverly Hills that became Bannon & Co. Staked
to $100 million in financing from a Japanese trading house, Ban-
non started a production company, installed the ousted former head
of Universal Pictures Thom Mount as president, and executive-
produced Sean Penn's 1991 directorial debut, *The Indian Runner*.
Although the film's cast included Dennis Hopper, Benicio Del
Toro, and Viggo Mortensen, it was a box-office flop, grossing just
$191,125 in the United States and Canada. Mount, who worked
closely with Bannon and generally liked him, recalled a figure of
swashbuckling grandiosity who would be entirely recognizable to
someone who knew him today. "He was constantly telling stories
about great warriors of the past, like Attila the Hun, people who
had slain empires," Mount said. "It's one thing to be interested in
the triumphs of military history; it's another thing to obsess over
them. Victory at all costs is a dangerous way to look at the world."

The Wild West atmosphere of Wall Street in the eighties produced no small amount of chaos and financial carnage. The

prestige of owning blue-chip companies, the clashing egos of big-time financiers, and the enormous fortunes to be made attracted a rogue's gallery of ambitious frauds and hucksters who managed to blow up or bankrupt a whole roster of brand-name companies. Hollywood, with its star power and show-biz glamour, proved to be, if anything, an even greater lure for ambitious charlatans longing for fame and riches. The debt-fueled takeover of Metro-Goldwyn-Mayer Studios in 1990 followed soon after by its spectacular collapse still stands as the era-defining example of reckless stupidity—and the one that made Bannon rich.

In 1990, after bids from Ted Turner and Rupert Murdoch fell through, MGM's owner, Kirk Kerkorian, sold the historic studio to a shady, little-known Italian financier named Giancarlo Parretti, for $1.3 billion. Parretti, a producer of low-budget foreign movies, had started out in life as a petty crook in Sicily, where he earned a rap sheet for securities fraud, check kiting, and conspiring to commit bodily harm. Yet by the mid-eighties, he had gained control of an Italian insurance company and hotel and real estate firms, at which point a Roman Catholic organization asked him to supervise the production of *Bernadette*, a biographical film about a French peasant girl in the 1850s who saw visions of the Virgin Mary and became a saint. Parretti, enthralled by the movie business, arranged to buy the film's nearly bankrupt distributor, Cannon Group, with a $250 million loan from the French bank Crédit Lyonnais. Upon arriving in Hollywood, Parretti promptly reinvented himself as a Rolls-Royce–driving movie mogul, all the while cooking up a blizzard of bribes, shell companies, and fraudulent loans. He bought a yacht. He flew to the Vatican to screen *Bernadette* for Pope John Paul II. Finally, after bribing assorted high-level Crédit Lyonnais officials, Parretti persuaded the bank to lend him more than $1 billion to buy MGM

from Kerkorian, pledging the studio's film library as collateral (and
hiding some of the loans behind shell companies). On the day the
deal closed, Parretti threw a champagne party in MGM's offices
that featured a live four-hundred-pound lion. Then he set about loot-
ing the place, firing top financial executives, installing his twenty-
one-year-old daughter in their place, and, as court records would
later reveal, placing a harem of his mistresses on the MGM payroll.

By then, Crédit Lyonnais had quietly become the largest lender
in Hollywood, funding not only Parretti's MGM gambit but dozens
of independent production studios as well. Within eight months, all
of it came crashing down. MGM defaulted on its payments to several creditors, who attempted to force the studio into bankruptcy.
Alerted to Parretti's criminal history, the SEC and FBI started
snooping around. Crédit Lyonnais's fraudulent loans were exposed.
Parretti was arrested in Los Angeles on a French warrant charging
him with embezzlement and defrauding the French bank, indicted
by a Delaware grand jury on perjury and evidence-tampering charges,
and slapped with civil fraud charges by the SEC for misrepresenting
Crédit Lyonnais loans as equity investments in the purchase of
MGM. (Parretti and two associates eventually settled the charges.)
The French government, humiliated, fired Crédit Lyonnais's chief
executive, and the bank foreclosed on MGM, having lost somewhere in the neighborhood of $1 billion.

Even as it teetered on the brink of its own bankruptcy, Crédit
Lyonnais suddenly found itself in possession of MGM and thirty-
odd independent production houses that it had no earthly idea how
to value or sell. Bannon and his partners were brought in to clean
up the wreckage. "It was a disaster," said Scot Vorse, Bannon's HBS
classmate who became a partner in his new firm. "Every one of
these companies was flailing." As Bannon and Vorse pored over the

books, it soon became clear that the production houses were all going to go bust, a state of affairs that earned them the ignominious industry nickname "the Dirty Thirty."

Seduced by the glamour of the Hollywood lifestyle, corrupt French bankers had showered producers and distributors with more money than they knew what to do with. But the bankers never grasped the economics of the movie business. The industry's focus was on getting films made and collecting producers' fees—the glitzy stuff of stars, directors, red-carpet premieres, and *Variety* headlines. For investors, however, the real money was made on the back end, in licensing the rights to broadcast and distribute those films in the United States and abroad. In the same way that a collateralized-debt obligation is the sum of hundreds of individual mortgages, the real value of a film is the outstanding sum of its individual licensing deals: both products can quickly ruin investors who don't understand them. When Bannon dug into the financials, he discovered that many of the assets owned by MGM and the Dirty Thirty were toxic and had little value.

"Hollywood is a terrible, tough business to make money in," said Vorse. "Because of Crédit Lyonnais, huge amounts of money were lent to outfits with terrible business plans. All these producers and distributors were running around, and the bankers were all hanging out with them in swanky Hollywood hotels—it was a complete disaster."

Bannon loved it. "We got a ton of business," he said. "We were the only sane ones who knew what was going on." His firm represented the post-Parretti MGM management as it belatedly took stock of its assets, while providing the same services to the Dirty Thirty. Fortunately for Crédit Lyonnais, plenty of global media conglomerates still wanted to get into the film business. Now, however, with

MGM's implosion having underscored the value of understanding precisely what it was that they were acquiring, they had the good sense to seek out expert advisers who could tell them. When PolyGram decided to get into the film business, it hired Bannon & Co. to advise it on the purchase of the Dirty Thirty from Crédit Lyonnais. Then Seagram wanted into the business and bought Poly-Gram. Bannon & Co. advised PolyGram on the sale. When Seagram turned around and decided to sell those same assets, the company brought in the investment bankers who understood their value best: Bannon & Co. "We used to joke that we were like pilot fish," said Vorse. "We spent our lives at MGM, learned the microeconomics of the business, and sold the same properties again and again and again." In 1996, the story came full circle when Crédit Lyonnais sold MGM back to Kirk Kerkorian.

Bannon & Co. handled several other high-profile deals. They flew to Italy to advise Silvio Berlusconi, the founder of Fininvest and future prime minister, on the value of his firm's film library. They represented the Saudi businessman Prince Alwaleed bin Talal. They worked on the takeover of Orion Pictures by MGM. And, in 1993, they represented Westinghouse Electric in selling its ownership stake of Castle Rock Entertainment, the film and TV production company behind Billy Crystal's films, to Turner Broadcasting—a deal that unexpectedly pulled Bannon into the entertainment industry and handed him a winning lottery ticket.

Having failed in his quest to buy MGM three years earlier, Ted Turner was still itching to create an empire. "Turner was going to build this huge studio," Bannon said, "so we were negotiating the deal at the St. Regis Hotel in New York. As often happened with Turner, when it came time to actually close the deal, Ted was short of cash." Westinghouse wanted out. Bannon pleaded with them not to walk away from the bargaining table. "We told them, 'You ought to take this deal. It's a great deal,'" he said. "And they go, 'If this is such a great deal, why don't you defer some of your cash fee and keep an ownership stake in a package of TV rights?'"

Bannon had no interest in getting into the residuals business. But neither did Westinghouse. The company made clear that unless Bannon & Co. swapped its cash fee for residuals the deal was off. "So we took a residual," he said.

In lieu of a full adviser's fee, the firm accepted a stake in five Castle Rock television shows, including one in its third season that was regarded as the runt of the litter: *Seinfeld*. At the time, the show hadn't cracked the Nielsen Top Thirty. A year later, it became a hit. "We calculated what it would get us if it made it to syndication," said Bannon. "We were wrong by a factor of five."

The desire of large foreign banks to plunge into Hollywood did not abate—not even among French banks, who might've known better. But Société Générale was confident it wouldn't repeat the mistakes of Crédit Lyonnais because, in 1996, as part of a plan to move into the independent distribution business, it had struck a deal to acquire Bannon & Co. By the time the deal paid out, in 1998, Bannon was sitting pretty. (Société Générale . . . not so much—the independent distribution business had dried up by then.)

No longer needing a day job, Bannon dabbled in minor Hollywood moguldom. He became an executive producer of movies, including Anthony Hopkins's 1999 Oscar-nominated *Titus*. He rolled up a succession of small media properties from, among others,

Michael Milken, Terry Semel, and Doug Liman (the latter carrying residuals to Fox's prime-time teen soap opera *The O.C.*—"great intellectual property," Bannon boasted to *Variety*). "He loved doing deals," said Vorse. "He had his hands in everything." He invested in, or served on the board of, companies that made products ranging from homeopathic nasal spray to branded video games for Burger King.

He met a hard-partying talent manager named Jeff Kwatinetz, who had discovered the band Korn and managed the Backstreet Boys. Newly flush and eager for adventure, Bannon joined Kwatinetz's new management outfit, The Firm, as a partner and helped orchestrate its great coup, the acquisition of former Disney chief Michael Ovitz's company, Artist Management Group. Ovitz had spent $100 million building a behemoth he thought would conquer Hollywood. But AMG was hemorrhaging money. Selling to The Firm was a last-ditch bid to save face. Instead, Bannon showed up one day at Ovitz's Beverly Hills mansion to deliver a final humiliating blow: an offer for AMG of just $5 million, less than the value of Ovitz's home. "He didn't understand the fundamental math of the business," said Bannon. "We really ended up negotiating with his bankers, J. P. Morgan."

The acquisition gave The Firm a client roster that included Cameron Diaz, Leonardo DiCaprio, Ice Cube, and Limp Bizkit. "We were pirates, and Jeff was the King Pirate, shocking Hollywood," said Bannon. Kwatinetz and Bannon had grand visions of a sprawling, vertically integrated business that would "brand" its A-List artist-clients across a dizzying array of platforms: not only recording and film but also concerts, clothing, animation, video games, and television. Bannon was as effusive about clients such as the rapper/actor Ice Cube as he would later be about TV star/politician Donald Trump. "It's the beginning of a revolution," Bannon declared with characteristic brio to an entertainment reporter for *The Washington Post*. "We're in the Vin Diesel business, or the Fred Durst business." (Amid charges of cocaine use from ex-employees, which Kwatinetz denied, and unexplained absences, Kwatinetz eventually left The Firm.)

Bannon didn't stick around for the revolution. By 2005, he had left Hollywood for the other side of the globe, Hong Kong, where he became involved in what was undoubtedly the strangest business of any in his kaleidoscopic career—one that introduced him to a hidden world, burrowed deep into his psyche, and provided a kind of conceptual framework that he would later draw on to build up the audience for *Breitbart News*, and then to help marshal the online armies of trolls and activists that overran national politics and helped give rise to Donald Trump.

The business centered on a video game, *World of Warcraft*, a so-called "massively multiplayer online role-playing game" (MMO), whose 10 million subscribers competed against one another in the mythical realm of Azeroth, a fantasy world of elves, dwarfs, trolls, goblins, and dragons. Skilled players can win weapons, armor, and gold. These are, of course, *virtual* items acquired and used within the game. Yet ardent enthusiasts were willing to buy them for real money, in the real world, to help them conquer *World of Warcraft* and other MMOs—a practice known as "real-money trading." Soon, entrepreneurial gamers systematized the process of "gold farming," earning tens or even hundreds of thousands of dollars a year by selling digital loot. The Hong Kong company Bannon joined, Internet Gaming Entertainment, sought to take gold farming to industrial scale by building out a supply chain of low-wage Chinese workers who played *World of Warcraft* in continuous, rotating shifts, battling monsters and dragons to produce a steady stream of virtual goods that IGE sold to gold-hungry gamers in the West.

Founded by a former child actor, Brock Pierce, who starred in Disney's *Mighty Ducks* movies, IGE proved that real-money trading was a sizable market, one the company claimed was worth nearly $1 billion. Whether it was a *legal* market was less clear. *World of Warcraft*'s publisher, Blizzard Entertainment, frowned on real-money trading. Many gamers hated the practice and considered it a form of cheating. They flooded gaming boards with anti-Chinese vitriol to protest farmers and their sponsors. Pierce knew IGE needed legitimacy. So he enlisted Bannon to raise capital, hoping game publishers would eventually agree to license the practice. Bannon pitched the idea that the currency market for virtual gold wasn't all that different from its real-world counterpart—and landed $60 million from Goldman Sachs and other investors.

Their timing turned out to be terrible. Rather than agree to a licensing deal, Blizzard, under pressure from its customers, started shutting down the accounts of suspected gold farmers and sellers. Beset by competitors, IGE's profits turned to losses. Then the company was hit by a class-action lawsuit filed in U.S. district court in Florida by an irate *World of Warcraft* fanatic who claimed that IGE's gold-farming practices were "substantially impairing" the collective enjoyment of the game. In a bid to survive, IGE shed its toxic name, Pierce was forced out, and Bannon was installed as CEO of the newly christened Affinity Media.

In a financial sense, the push to build a third-party business around selling virtual goods inside a video game was a disaster for almost everyone involved. Inevitably, game makers began selling goods directly to their players. Yet Bannon was captivated by what he had discovered while trying to build the business: an underworld he hadn't known existed that was populated by millions of intense young men (most gamers were men) who disappeared for days or even weeks at a time in alternate realities. While perhaps not social adepts, they were smart, focused, relatively wealthy, and highly motivated about issues that mattered to them, their collective might powerful enough to wreck IGE's business and bend companies such as Blizzard to their will. As he would later confirm, this luciferous insight gave him an early understanding of the size and strength of online communities, along with an appreciation for the powerful currents that run just below the surface of the Internet. He began to wonder if those forces could be harnessed and, if so, how he might exploit them.

Affinity sold off its gold-farming operations to a competitor at a steep discount. But Bannon held on to a network of three large MMO gaming sites that the company had acquired (Wowhead, Allakhazam, and Thottbot) that were the hubs where these gamers congregated by the millions.

If you trace a line backward from Trump's election, it doesn't take long before you encounter online networks of motivated gamers and message-board denizens such as the ones who populate Trump-crazed boards like 4chan, 8chan, and reddit. During the campaign, users of these message boards were eager purveyors of racist, alt-right invective, such as the anti-Semitic Pepe the Frog images that the Anti-Defamation League declared a hate symbol. Trace the line back a little further and it leads to *Breitbart News* and Bannon, whose hiring of the anti-feminist internet troll Milo Yiannopoulos as *Breitbart*'s tech editor in 2015 greatly exacerbated these forces.

But Bannon's path would never have veered from Hollywood

and pointed him in that direction had it not been for a tragedy that re-inflamed his antipathy toward Islam and his conviction that Western civilization was under attack.

The September 11, 2001, terrorist attacks on the World Trade Center and the Pentagon functioned as a kind of echo for Bannon of the 1979 seizure of American hostages at the U.S. embassy in Tehran. The two decades in between, he realized, had done nothing to stanch the threat of radical Islam to the United States—in fact, Islamic terrorists had struck with greater force than anyone imagined they could and had chosen as a target of their attack the very Wall Street financial district where he had long toiled for Goldman Sachs.

The Iranian hostage crisis first impelled Bannon toward Ronald Reagan, whose strength he was certain was vital to preserving America's safety and influence in the world. Having long ago left the military, he didn't have any obvious outlet to respond to the new attacks—a middle-aged Hollywood investment banker can't exactly walk into a recruiter's office and reenlist. But the following year, Bannon, an avid reader of biographies and political histories, picked up a new book, *Reagan's War: The Epic Story of His Forty-Year Struggle and Final Triumph Over Communism*, by the conservative scholar Peter Schweizer. Drawing on newly available archives—including Reagan's KGB file—Schweizer drew a portrait of the president as he was seen by his enemies, arguing (rather effusively) that Reagan's steadfastness and foresight, along with his willingness to buck expert opinion, was almost single-handedly responsible for winning the Cold War.

Working in Hollywood all these years, Bannon had plenty of

up-close experience in the film business. But it was all on the financial side. He longed, like countless moneymen before him, to get involved on the creative side. Never wanting for ideas or conviction, he now had the means to indulge his passion. He optioned the film rights to Schweizer's book and wrote and directed a movie based upon it, *In the Face of Evil* (2004). "It was really a metaphor," Bannon said of his film. "It was just after 9/11, and I wanted to tell a story about how a democracy takes on a radical ideology." He persuaded Schweizer to collaborate with him on the project. "Peter and I worked on the film to tell the story of Reagan's sixty-year struggle with communism," he said, "and at the end, we connect the dots about how that was like America's struggle with radical Islam."

The film had a modest release and won glowing praise from conservative audiences ("A brilliant effort . . . extremely well done," said Rush Limbaugh). It won the Best Feature Film award at the Liberty Film Festival, a new film festival meant to establish a conservative beachhead in liberal Hollywood. It was here that Bannon first encountered Andrew Breitbart, the conservative impresario, and was drawn into his orbit. "We screened the film at a festival in Beverly Hills," Bannon recalled, "and out of the crowd comes this, like, bear who's squeezing me like my head's going to blow up and saying how we've got to take back the culture. I didn't really know who he was."

Breitbart, who also lived in Los Angeles, had an immediate and profound influence on Bannon. He became the kind of guru figure that the Maharishi was to the Beatles. When they met, Breitbart was just starting his eponymous website network, after having worked with Matt Drudge to publish the *Drudge Report* and having helped Arianna Huffington launch the liberal *Huffington Post*. Breitbart was a character after Bannon's own heart: loud, opinionated, cocksure, gleefully combative, and possessed of performative gifts that Bannon could only envy. "I'd never met a conservative who had this kind of huge persona," he recalled. Breitbart also shared a keen appreciation for, and a deep understanding of, online audiences and how to influence them—and not just audiences but also the media outlets that catered to them. Bannon marveled at how Breitbart was able to shape media coverage through the *Drudge Report*, which was raptly followed by television producers and news editors, and how he seemed to have a visceral feel for the news cycle. Breitbart also heightened his awareness of culture as an important front in the battle against secular liberalism and the weakness that both men felt it instilled. "Politics is downstream from culture," Breitbart liked to say. "I want to change the cultural narrative." What this meant was that Breitbart was less interested in trying to influence Washington directly than he was in going after the institutions (and the methods they employed, like "political correctness") that he believed shaped this narrative.

Bannon, recognizing a new Pirate King, helped Breitbart build out his new endeavor, lending financial acumen and office space. He had direct experience with media-focused Internet start-ups. "I had looked over the shoulders of some of the private-equity guys who had put the money into *The Huffington Post*," Bannon said. "The one thing they told me to explain the huge valuation is that it was not a content play but a technology play. They had Jonah Peretti—guy's a genius—[who] at the time was walking me through the tech side of the business [and told me], 'You're really not thinking about traffic, you're thinking about community.' That always stuck in the back of my mind."

The other thing Bannon gleaned from Breitbart was the

exhilarating, galvanizing power of being the bad guy, publicly despised by those whom you profess to oppose. "I realized I liked being hated more than I liked being liked—that's when the game began," Breitbart explained to *Time* in 2010. But where Breitbart's "hatred" of his enemies often had a twinkle, Bannon took a more literal view of his role in the opposition.

Over the next several years, as Barack Obama was elected and the Tea Party backlash arrived, Bannon continued making and producing documentaries—big, crashing, opinionated films with Wagner scores and martial imagery: *Border Wars: The Battle Over Illegal Immigration* (2006), on clashes at the U.S.–Mexico border; *Battle for America* (2010), celebrating the rise of the Tea Party; and *Generation Zero* (2010), examining the roots of the financial meltdown. By then he had become a full-blown populist critic of Wall Street. "Here's what changed," said Bannon. "What Goldman represented in the 1980s was that they were principal providers of capital formation. It was all about [fostering] growth. Growth is good. If you went to Goldman when I did, the elite branch of the firm was investment banking, and the most elite was M & A. The traders were guys from Queens. They were just beginning the quant age." Bannon claimed he could no longer recognize the world he had known and the values it embraced, and he was repelled by the new one that had taken its place. He thought there was a cinematic poignancy to the transformation. "It's like watching the movie *Wall Street* when Charlie Sheen first walks into the trading room," he said, describing his younger self. "Then cut to 2008, when I come back from Asia, and investment banks had become highly leveraged hedge funds. That's where they make all the money. And they wrecked the economy."

This is the standard populist critique of the financial crisis, routinely espoused by liberals and many conservatives alike. That Bannon's father lost a good part of his retirement savings gives it an especially personal gloss. But Bannon's diagnosis of the *cause* of the crisis is where he parts company with Michael Lewis and other mainstream critics of Wall Street. *Generation Zero* is a film suffused with Andrew Breitbart's influence: in it, Bannon blames liberal social policies for creating the culture of Wall Street permissiveness that ultimately led to the crash. "By the late nineties," a narrator intones, "the Left had taken over many of the institutions of power—meaning government, media, and academe. And it was from these places and positions of power that they were able to disrupt the system and implement a strategy that was designed to ultimately undermine the capitalist system."

As the 2010 midterm elections neared, Sarah Palin, still riding high from her star turn in the 2008 presidential campaign, approached Bannon to see if he would be interested in shooting videos for her. This struck Bannon as a near-perfect conjunction of timing, personality, and politics: Palin was the avatar of the Tea Party movement, a global phenomenon, and someone thought to be seriously considering a run for the presidency. Instead of just shooting video, Bannon made a full documentary movie about Palin, *The Undefeated* (2011), on which he reportedly spent $1 million of his own money. He went all-out.

In the Bannon repertoire, no metaphor is too direct. *The Undefeated* is peppered with footage of lions attacking helpless gazelles and seedlings bursting from the ground into glorious bloom. Palin ate it up, and she traveled with her family to the first-in-the-nation caucus state of Iowa, trailed by hundreds of reporters, to appear with Bannon at a June premiere in Pella that the press thought might signal her entrance into the 2012 race. Before the curtain lifted, Bannon praised Palin's rough-hewn prairie populism: "The hard-worn bricks outside the Pella Opera House are all the red carpet she needs." The atmosphere was charged. That same day, Palin's daughter Bristol told a TV reporter that her mother had made up her mind about a presidential run. Andrew Breitbart, who trekked to Pella to serve as ringmaster for the occasion, was as effusive in his praise of Bannon as he was Palin, remarking afterward that he considered Bannon to be "the Leni Riefenstahl of the Tea Party movement."

But Palin never took the plunge. And no other candidate struck quite the same chords. Instead, the locus of right-wing populism moved to the Internet, and to *Breitbart News* in particular. "Most conservatives are individualists," Breitbart said. "For years, they've been pummeled by the collectivists who run the American media, Hollywood and Washington. The underground conservative movement that is now awakening is the ecosystem I've designed my sites to tap into."

One big draw of Breitbart's underground movement was his flair for showmanship along with his embrace of stunt journalism, which occasionally broke through into the mainstream. Breitbart's signature maneuver was the elaborate trolling operation aimed at some liberal icon or institution that exposed the hypocrisy at the heart of its enterprise. His first hit came in 2009, when he posted video of an amateur sting operation run by two conservative activists, James O'Keefe and Hannah Giles, against the liberal community-activist group Association of Community Organizations for Reform Now (ACORN), a favorite bogeyman of conservatives. In the video, O'Keefe appears to solicit and receive advice from the group on running a brothel. Subsequent investigations found that the videos had been manipulated in the editing process to make ACORN look complicit, but Congress suspended the group's funding anyway.

The following year, Breitbart caused an even bigger uproar by posting video excerpts (once again furnished by a conservative activist) of a speech to the NAACP by a Department of Agriculture official named Shirley Sherrod. In the excerpts, Sherrod appeared to advocate anti-white racism. Within hours, she was fired, as the story blanketed cable news. But it soon became clear that the *Breitbart News* video was misleadingly edited—that Sherrod's point, as the full tape makes clear, had been the opposite of what was portrayed. Fox News, which aggressively promoted the Sherrod video, banned Andrew Breitbart as an on-air guest.

By then, Bannon was actively involved in the site and its business. When the Sherrod story blew up, he was out raising money to expand and relaunch *Breitbart News*. With the negative publicity, and the taint of racism, he suddenly encountered "nuclear winter." And yet Breitbart himself was immune to shame—or at least, to being shamed—and had no compunction about launching vicious personal attacks. Upon learning of Senator Ted Kennedy's death, Breitbart tweeted that Kennedy was a "villain," a "prick," and a "duplicitous bastard," adding: "I'm more than willing to go off decorum to ensure THIS MAN is not beatified."

The ostracizing of *Breitbart News* didn't last long. Less than a year later, the site caught Democratic representative Anthony Weiner tweeting pictures of his genitals. According to Bannon, the site helped to orchestrate his downfall: tipped to Weiner's proclivity for sexting with female admirers, he said, the site paid trackers to follow his Twitter account around the clock and eventually

intercepted the fateful crotch shot Weiner inadvertently made public.*
As if orchestrated by some higher power, the ensuing scandal cul-
minated in the surreal scene, carried live on television, of Breitbart
hijacking Weiner's New York press conference and fielding questions from astonished reporters. He was quickly welcomed back to
Fox News. The experience taught Bannon the power of real news
and how it could be exploited—a lesson he would soon have cause to
put into practice.

On March 1, 2012, with the relaunch of *Breitbart News* just four
days away, Bannon was in New York City pitching investors when
he got a phone call: Andrew Breitbart had been walking in his
Brentwood neighborhood that morning when he collapsed and died
of heart failure. He was forty-three. Feeling shell-shocked and duty-
bound, Bannon made the decision to formally join *Breitbart News*,
stepping in to become its executive chairman.

At the funeral, Matt Drudge asked Bannon what he planned to
do. Bannon replied: "We're going ahead with the launch."

---

*As the journalist Greg Beato has documented at Soundbitten.com, there is a fierce debate
about who caught Anthony Weiner and on whose behalf that person was operating. Bannon
told me in a 2015 interview that the site had used paid trackers. Beato notes that the person or
persons behind the Twitter account @PatriotUSA76 initially spotted and shared Weiner's
career-ending genital tweeting misfortune—that person claims his name is Dan Wolfe, but his
identity has never been independently verified. Andrew Breitbart maintained that he'd never
had any contact with @PatriotUSA76 before Weiner's tweet and never learned his true identity.

FIVE

NOBODY BUILDS WALLS LIKE TRUMP

Trump had been thinking about running for president for more than twenty years before he encountered Steve Bannon. During most of that period, they were not ideologically aligned. Trump did have long-standing impulses on certain issues that Bannon would have approved of—both believed, for instance, that the United States was constantly being victimized in foreign trade deals. But to the extent Trump expressed opinions on national affairs, they tended to reflect the views of a New York Democrat, which was, after all, the world that he inhabited. Then he met Bannon—and his views changed. Trump took up Bannon's populist nationalism, with its chesty blue-collar ethos and disdain for corrupt "globalist" elites. But just as important to Trump's path to the White House was what he chose to give up.

On January 8, 2004, viewers of NBC's prime-time television lineup got the first glimpse of a new show soon to become a cultural sensation. As a crow's-eye view of the Manhattan skyline floated across the screen, Donald Trump's unmistakable voice, all steely self-confidence, laid out the premise of his new series: "New York. My city. Where the wheels of the global economy never stop turning." The perspective jumps to the backseat of a limousine and a familiar figure: "My name is Donald Trump, and I'm the largest real-estate developer in New York. I own buildings all over the place, model agencies, the Miss Universe pageant, jet liners, golf courses, casinos." As he climbs out of the limousine toward a "Trump"-emblazoned helicopter that awaits him, Trump delivers the payoff: "I've mastered the art of the deal, and I've turned the name Trump into the highest-quality brand. As the master, I want to pass along my knowledge to somebody else. I'm looking for . . . *the apprentice.*"

Right out of the gate, *The Apprentice* was a hit. During its first season, the show drew an average of more than 20 million viewers a week. It was the dawn of the reality-TV era, and Trump's cartoonish persona lent itself perfectly to the new medium. Each week, Trump would preside from a luxe, walnut-lined boardroom high up in Trump Tower,* as sixteen contestants competed against one another by running business projects, after which they would all assemble in the boardroom and submit themselves to Trump's glowering judgment. Each week, at the end of the show, Trump would dispatch one of the contestants with his signature phrase: "You're fired!"

NBC executives were thrilled by the surprise hit on their hands. Until *The Apprentice*, the network had not managed to develop a successful reality-TV franchise, and it was falling behind its major competitors, CBS (*Survivor, Big Brother*) and ABC (*The Mole*).

---

*Actually, the boardroom wasn't high up in Trump Tower—this was an illusion created by the show's producers, who interspersed footage of the nervous contestants riding up in an elevator at the end of every episode before Trump's judgment was meted out. The boardroom used in the show was located on the fifth floor of Trump Tower, space that, as mentioned, was later gutted to serve as Trump's early campaign headquarters and housed the "crack den" on Election Night.

Trump's success was all the more important to NBC because the show aired in a critical time slot—Thursday prime time—that for years had boasted a powerhouse lineup, most recently anchored by the ensemble comedy *Friends*. But by the spring of 2004, *Friends* was finishing up its final season. To NBC's great relief, *The Apprentice* reached out and took the baton.

The show's fast success produced significant economic benefits for the network. It did so for Trump, too—but it also did something more. It indelibly established his national image. Mark Burnett, the show's creator, had originally sold the concept to NBC as one where Trump would host *The Apprentice* for only the first season, after which he would give way to a succession of iconic business moguls, such as Richard Branson, Mark Cuban, or Martha Stewart. That idea quickly fell by the wayside. "After the first episode," recalled Jeff Gaspin, who ran reality programming for NBC, "we said we want more Trump."

Trump's power to draw a mass audience during prime time was also vital to NBC because, by the mid-2000s, all of the major networks were beginning to lose audience share to cable television and other outlets. The fact that Trump could reliably hold huge swaths of viewers made it easy for NBC to line up major advertisers. And line them up it did: McDonald's, Pepsi, Home Depot, Visa, Ford, Capital One, Kellogg's, Panasonic, and many other blue-chip corporations advertised during *The Apprentice*, several of them continuing to do so for the show's entire decade-long run. The fact that Trump's 20 million viewers were tuning in on Thursday nights also made *The Apprentice* the perfect destination for Hollywood studios keen to advertise the new films they would be debuting over the weekend.

But there was an additional aspect of Trump's appeal that

received almost no mainstream media attention at all—and yet it was a key part of why advertisers found his show so desirable, and why Trump, even though he was politically dormant during this period, managed to build a national profile that was dramatically different from any other major Republican figure, then or since: Trump was extremely popular with minority audiences.

Because *The Apprentice* drew a mass audience that pulled in an especially high proportion of African American and Hispanic viewers, Fortune 500 companies seeking to reach these particular demographics could advertise on the show and get the best of both worlds. "First and foremost, advertisers are buying the absolute number—and he got really good numbers," said Eric Leininger, who was chief marketing officer at McDonald's in 2004. "Secondly, they're buying against particular demographics. And it's easier for a company like McDonald's to buy a program that has a big audience, as opposed to having to aggregate an audience by buying five smaller ones. If you can have a mass program that brings you a diverse audience, that's a beautiful thing."

Furthermore, it quickly became apparent that the appeal of *The Apprentice* to minority audiences was rooted not just in the manufactured drama of a business competition, but in Trump himself and the world he projected on his show. "As an active marketer watching the show, the beautiful thing about *The Apprentice* was that it was a wonderfully integrated program," said Monique Nelson, chief executive officer of UniWorld, an advertising agency focused on minority audiences with two clients, Home Depot and Ford, that advertised on *The Apprentice*. "There were always people of color, women, people from all different backgrounds—so it connects. The one thing we know about marketing is that when you see a character that reminds you of yourself, you get invested."

What's more, Trump and the show's creators featured their minority contestants in a role that departed from how minority characters were historically portrayed on television and in movies: *The Apprentice* presented them as striving, ambitious entrepreneurs. Although she was "fired" from the show in week nine, Omarosa Manigault-Stallworth, an African American graduate student at Howard University who had held a low-level White House job for Vice President Al Gore, was the breakout star of *The Apprentice*'s debut season, styling herself into what remains the epitome of the reality-TV villain. In the show's fourth season, which aired in the fall of 2005, Randal D. Pinkett, an African American business consultant and a Rhodes Scholar, won the overall title and became the Apprentice. People noticed.

"They did a wonderful job of showing America as it was even then: multiethnic, multiracial, and multigenerational," said Nelson. "[The show] appealed to companies looking to reach minority audiences, and it did it authentically, without trying too hard. That means everything in marketing. You always saw a nice swath of America through that business lens."

This popularity extended to Trump himself, who, according to private demographic research conducted at the time, was even more popular with African American and Hispanic viewers than he was with Caucasian audiences. "He was getting so much exposure from the prime-time show, and getting good ratings on NBC, that both his positive perception and his negative perception were well above average," said Henry Schafer, executive vice president of the company Q Scores, an opinion research firm that serves advertisers by measuring the familiarity and appeal of celebrities and television shows and distilling them into a "Q Score." "He was the kind of vivid character that I would put in the same category as the Kardashians,

Martha Stewart, and Howard Stern: celebrities you love to hate." At his peak in 2010, Trump's positive Q Score with black audiences was 27, while his positive score among English-speaking Hispanic audiences reached 18. Among nonblack audiences, however, Trump's positive Q Score was just 8. White audiences, along with everybody else, tuned in to watch Trump—but either they didn't particularly like him or they simply loved to hate him. Either way, said Schafer, "he definitely had a stronger positive perception among blacks and Hispanics."

This perception became even more valuable as the series continued because it dovetailed with a marketing strategy just then coming into vogue in corporate America that was known as "visual diversity"—the idea being that advertisers could run commercials designed to convey the message that corporate America was not merely "in touch" with a racially diverse country, but was itself an active (and inclusive!) participant.

Well into its run, *The Apprentice* was a show viewed by corporate America as the epitome of the forward-thinking, multicultural programming that all advertisers were increasingly seeking out, especially after the election in 2008 of a biracial president. "Going forward, all advertising is going to be multicultural by definition, because in most states, majority ethnic populations will no longer exist," Danny Allen, a top executive at the multicultural-focused ad agency Sensis, declared in 2009. Just as Obama symbolized the country's uplifting racial progress, Allen added, "advertisers are also tapping into that same yearning, particularly among younger Americans, to put racial divisions behind us and move forward in a more unified way."

As unlikely as it sounds from the vantage point of today, Trump and *The Apprentice*, up through the end of the decade, were considered by advertisers and audiences alike to be a triumph of American multiculturalism.

As a celebrity and a pop-culture icon, Trump was riding higher than ever. And yet, privately he was obsessing over politics. Nobody knew it yet, but soon enough they would—because Trump was about to do something that any ordinary Republican with an eye on the White House would consider reckless to the point of insanity: he was about to torch his relationship with minority voters.

Viewed through the lens of politics, Trump had achieved by 2010 what Republican politicians had struggled, without success, to accomplish for the better part of fifty years. He had made himself genuinely popular with a broad segment of blacks and Hispanics. This audience did not think of him as a politician, of course. Not yet. But as a starting point in a bid for high office, Trump was already out on the far horizon of where the Republican Party one day hoped to be.

Truth be told, the party was moving in entirely the wrong direction. Ever since 1964, when Barry Goldwater championed "states' rights"—understood to signify his opposition to the civil rights movement—minority voters had turned their backs on the Republican Party. Richard Nixon's "Southern strategy"—stoking white racism for electoral gain—had only cemented this state of affairs. In the eleven presidential elections that followed Goldwater's thumping loss, no Republican had won more than 15 percent of the black vote. And in the most recent election, in 2008, exit polls showed that John McCain had pulled a meager 4 percent of them. Republicans fared slightly better among the fast-growing population of Hispanic voters, with George W. Bush hitting a high point of 44 percent in 2004. But here, too, the GOP was backsliding: McCain had carried just 31 percent of Hispanics. Republican strategists looking toward the future were already growing nervous because the changing demography of the United States made perfectly clear that minorities would steadily increase as a share of the eligible electorate. Republicans needed to win more of them.

Trump was the furthest thing from a racial innocent. In 1989, after five black and Hispanic male teenagers from Harlem were accused of raping a white female jogger in Central Park, he had felt it necessary to spend $85,000 running full-page ads in the New York daily newspapers calling for the return of the death penalty. "Muggers and murderers," he wrote, "should be forced to suffer and, when they kill, they should be executed for their crimes." (Even after DNA evidence exonerated the Central Park Five, Trump refused to apologize and held fast to his insistence that they were guilty.) And yet, however improbable, he had managed to win the good favor of millions of minority voters.

What was it, then, that impelled Trump to suddenly launch his birther attack on Barack Obama? And not just air his suspicion that Obama was born in Kenya, but conduct a full-scale media blitzkrieg that took him from Fox News to ABC's *The View* to drive home this fantastical racist slur?

Trump himself would never say. The charge had been circulating for some time in the darker corners of the Internet, on right-wing conspiracy sites and e-mail chains. Only under great duress, when it was clearly hampering his presidential campaign, did he grudgingly withdraw the charge during a bizarre press conference, surrounded by ex-generals, that was staged in the lobby of his Washington, D.C., hotel two months before the election. As someone possessed of perhaps the best raw political instincts of any Republican in his generation, Trump had intuited, correctly, that a racist attack targeting a black president was the surest way to ingratiate himself with grassroots Republican voters. And so Trump, without even batting an eye, proceeded to destroy the goodwill he had built up with minority voters as a way of appealing to a new audience.

The effect was almost immediate, and the first place it showed up was in Trump's television ratings. In the spring of 2011, as his birther crusade took off in earnest, NBC was airing a new season of *The Celebrity Apprentice*. According to research conducted by National Media Inc., a firm that places political ads on television, the audience that tuned in to *The Celebrity Apprentice* was among the most liberal in all of prime-time television, owing in no small part to the large number of minority viewers that Trump attracted. As he broadcast his birther charge against Obama, Nielsen ratings for *The Celebrity Apprentice* took a sharp turn for the worse. "Given the downward trend of Trump's ratings among his current, liberal audience," joked one Republican media buyer, "maybe he's running as a Republican to add a little bipartisan diversity to his viewership."

The effect of Trump's attacks was even more pronounced on his personal image. His favorability rating with minority viewers began to collapse. Trump's positive Q Score among African Americans, which had reached a high of 27 in 2010, fell to 21 the next year, then to 10, and to 9, before bottoming out at 6 in 2014. That same year, his negative Q Score, which had floated in the 30s, skyrocketed to 55. Hispanics—not yet a Trump target—also soured on the *Apprentice* host. While his positive Q rating among English-speaking Hispanics roughly held steady in the teens, his negative rating soared up into the mid-40s.

"I think most people thought they really knew Donald Trump," said Schafer, of the Q Scores Company. "With his show, it was an emotional pact with the audience." When minority audiences perceived Trump to have broken that pact, their judgment was severe. The Q Scores Company doesn't measure the popularity of elected politicians; it rates only people whom it considers to be celebrities and entertainers. (It stopped measuring Trump after 2015, when he became a politician.) But among nonpolitical celebrities, Trump's favorability dropped to the bottom of the barrel. "We don't do folks like David Duke—not unless he had a show somewhere," said Schafer. "But toward the end, Donald Trump's negative rating with black audiences was the second worst of any celebrity we measured. Do you know who the only guy was they hated worse? It was 'The Situation' from *Jersey Shore*."

From a raw political standpoint, Trump's decision to adopt a set of views that offended and alienated minority voters, ugly though it was, turned out well for him. He would soon go further, broadening his attacks to include illegal immigrants. Trump did so at precisely the moment when Republican leaders, led by party chairman Reince Priebus (Trump's future chief of staff), released an "autopsy" of Mitt Romney's defeat that included a detailed plan for how the party could recover. Its most important recommendation was that Republicans embrace comprehensive immigration reform in order to broaden their appeal to minority voters. In so many words, Republican leaders were telling their rank and file that they needed to be more like Trump during his *Apprentice* glory days—while Trump was arriving at the opposite conclusion and, with Bannon's eager encouragement, doing everything he could to build a political movement around white identity politics.

A wily manipulator of public sentiment whose New York up-bringing taught him the power of racial resentment, Trump under-stood exactly what he was doing in leveling the birther attack. As he rose to the top of Republican primary polls in the spring of 2011, his instincts were borne out. But he never accepted the trade-off he had made. By the commutative property of Trump's exalted self-image, blacks and Hispanics still supported him with the same zeal they had during his *Apprentice* heyday—of this he was certain—and if the Nielsen ratings and poll numbers didn't back him up, then anecdotal evidence would suffice. A few days after locking up the GOP nomination in May 2016, Trump, sitting high up in his Trump Tower office, parried a question about his poor image with minority voters by insisting that he was as popular as ever: "A radio announcer, a Hispanic from New York, said, 'I don't know about these polls, because every listener that I have'—they call in Spanish—'they're all for Trump!' I think I'm going to do very well with Hispanics."

Whether or not he was deluding himself, Trump really *had* once looked poised to perform better among minority voters than any Republican since Dwight Eisenhower—at least on paper. His mul-ticultural appeal in 2010 raises the intriguing thought that Trump could have run an entirely different sort of campaign, one that drew on his strength with a set of voters Republicans don't typically com-mand and that sought to build on the diverse, entrepreneurial image of his TV show. "There was a time," Monique Nelson pointed out, "where he was talking to everyone." Had he been so inclined, Trump could have run a forward-looking campaign to "Make America Greater" rather than alluding to the past with "Make America Great Again." Instead, he plunged deeper into the racial morass.

After his excommunication at the 2011 White House Correspondents' Dinner, Trump fell off the mainstream political radar,
save for his periodic appearances on Fox News. Things settled
down. Despite the outcry over the birther issue, only a single corporate advertiser, Groupon, bailed on *The Apprentice*. For people who
read newspapers and watched the evening news, Trump appeared to
have left politics safely behind.

But he hadn't, really. Instead, he jumped the tracks to the parallel world of right-wing websites and talk radio. Here, his celebrity
could still garner him the validation and genuflection he constantly
craved. One of Trump's most faithful attendants during this period
was Christopher Ruddy, the publisher of *Newsmax* and a Clinton
conspiracy buff whose 1997 book, *The Strange Death of Vince Foster:
An Investigation*, darkly posited that the 1993 suicide of the associate White House counsel and longtime Clinton friend might have
been a murder. Ruddy, as the journalist Michael Isikoff memorably
described him, was "the Inspector Clouseau of the Foster case—a
determined, if bumbling, former *New York Post* reporter who has
virtually single-handedly spawned a cottage industry of conspiracy
buffs dedicated to the proposition that a foul and monstrous cover-up
surrounds the circumstances of Foster's death."

By 2006, Ruddy had built a successful right-wing publishing
empire near his home in West Palm Beach, Florida, where prominent Republican politicians would come to seek his favor. There he
befriended Trump, who extended an invitation that Ruddy accepted
to join his Palm Beach club, Mar-a-Lago. Ruddy's *Newsmax* supplied a steady stream of fawning testimony to Trump's supposed political power ("The Trump Effect") along with face-saving ego balm
when the GOP establishment denied him the respect he desired

("Trump Declines Prime-Time GOP Convention Speech"—he wasn't offered one). In a colorful burst of cross-promotional synergy, Ruddy even arranged for *Newsmax* to host a 2012 Republican presidential debate in Iowa that Trump himself was going to moderate. "Our readers and the grass roots really love Trump," Ruddy said, in announcing the event. Alas, Trump backed out when only Newt Gingrich and Rick Santorum agreed to participate. The debate was canceled.

Trump was still feeling his way toward a political identity when Mitt Romney lost the 2012 presidential election. Through *Newsmax*, Trump delivered a blistering critique of why Romney had failed, one that now feels disorientingly out of character because he attacked the former Massachusetts governor over his stance on immigration—but did so from the left. "He had a crazy policy of self deportation which was maniacal," Trump complained to *Newsmax*. "It sounded as bad as it was, and he lost all of the Latino vote. He lost the Asian vote. He lost everybody who is inspired to come into this country." Romney's approach was too "mean-spirited," Trump averred, and thus was always destined to fail.*

But as he navigated the fever swamps of the right, Trump quickly became attuned to the roiling grassroots anger over illegal immigration, which was very much coming from the right. "It was intuitive by him," said Sam Nunberg, the former Trump adviser, "to use immigration as a new wedge issue." Recognizing that his base

---

*One Trump adviser who wished to remain nameless suggested that Trump's seeming moderation on immigration here was driven by business concerns rather than politics. Trump had bought the Doral Resort and Spa in Miami out of bankruptcy in 2012 for $150 million and was in the process of renovating the 800-acre golf resort. Aware that Miami is "an epicenter of immigrants" and that he would need zoning variances, the adviser said, Trump took special care not to offend them.

of support would never come from genteel, country-club Republicans, Trump felt free to abandon niceties and embrace the same mean-spiritedness for which he had just criticized Romney. "He digests this stuff," said Nunberg. "He knew who his audience was going to be—it was not going to be people who want to have policy debates. It was going to be older people, people who work with their hands."

The political fault line Trump stumbled across was one that had lurked beneath the surface of Republican politics for a long time. Illegal immigration divided law-and-order conservatives, who wanted to see lawbreaking immigrants deported, from business-minded conservatives, who preferred to maintain a cheap source of labor, held more ecumenical views, and worried about the risks of alienating Latino voters. Periodically, these tensions flared up, as they had in 2007 when President George W. Bush, hailing the United States as "a nation of immigrants," tried to pass an immigration reform bill that would have allowed 12 million undocumented immigrants to become U.S. citizens. His effort was soundly defeated by conservatives in his own party who attacked the "amnesty" Bush was offering to people who had broken the law.

As the Republican Party turned once again to immigration reform following Romney's poor showing with Hispanic voters, these same tensions rose to a boil, even as leaders in both parties, including President Obama, agreed it was time to get something done. Trump positioned himself squarely against this effort, encouraged by his growing fixation with what was then still an unorthodox political technology: Twitter.

"That was our focus group," said Nunberg. "Every time Trump tweeted against amnesty in 2013, 2014, he would get hundreds and hundreds of retweets."

or a brief time after Barack Obama's reelection, it appeared as if a moment of reconciliation might finally be at hand. From its earliest days, Obama's first term had been marked by uninterrupted partisan fighting over everything from the $800 billion stimulus package to the new health-care law. Bitterly frustrated by that rocky experience, Obama had now won a second term and, he imagined, a chance to finally pursue bipartisan legislation. Always prone to applying Spock-like logical rigor to his analysis of a Republican Party that rarely hewed to this standard, Obama expected to encounter a new, more productive attitude from his opponents across the aisle.

"I believe that if we're successful in this election," Obama declared in a 2012 speech in Minneapolis, "that the fever may break, because there's a tradition in the Republican Party of more common sense than that. My hope, my expectation, is that after the election, now that it turns out that the goal of beating Obama doesn't make much sense because I'm not running again, that we can start getting some cooperation again."

The early signs were propitious, and they all centered on immigration. Stunned by a loss few of them had anticipated, most prominent Republicans concluded that passing comprehensive immigration reform was an existential imperative for the party. In early 2013, the vehicle to do so took shape in what became known as the "Gang of Eight" bill, a bipartisan reform measure led by eight senators that would provide a path to citizenship for the now 11 million immigrants living illegally in the United States, while enlarging guest-worker programs for low-skilled jobs in industries such as agriculture. In what seemed a positive omen, the Gang of Eight bill had the added designation of being a vehicle for the presidential ambitions of Senator Marco Rubio of Florida, the telegenic young Cuban American then considered to be the GOP's brightest rising star. With Rubio, the darling of Fox News, leading the charge, the bill appeared to have unstoppable momentum.

With the marquee conservative outlet Fox News foursquare behind immigration reform and the Democratic Party united in support, the locus of opposition to the Gang of Eight bill emerged in the conservative underworld: *Breitbart News*, the *Drudge Report*, and a far-flung network of allied radio talk shows. To Bannon, who was now running *Breitbart News* following Andrew Breitbart's death, killing the reform effort became a defining crusade, and to that end the website published a daily fusillade of alarmist fare about hordes of murderous illegal immigrants pouring across the southern border and the treasonous Republicans in Congress turning a blind eye to their menace. Having produced the film *Border Wars* on the subject, Bannon knew how to maximize his viewpoint for dramatic effect. At his urging, *Breitbart* opened a Texas bureau and developed a network of sources that included Immigration and Customs Enforcement agents stationed on the U.S.–Mexico border, who provided on-the-ground details that made these stories more vivid.

"Among those informed about immigration [the Gang of Eight bill] was shocking—a kick in the teeth to decent Americans," said Jeff Sessions, then a staunchly anti-immigrant Republican senator from Alabama, who would later become Trump's attorney general. An abiding frustration of right-wing populists such as Sessions and Bannon was that their views had little representation in the mainstream media, or even in conservative alternatives like Fox News. Rupert Murdoch, the CEO of News Corp., which owned Fox, and Roger Ailes, the network's president, were both strong advocates of immigration reform, and made sure the network reflected their preferences. "God bless Fox," gushed South Carolina senator Lindsey Graham, a Republican Gang of Eight member, soon after the bill was introduced. "Eighty percent of people [voting] in my primary get their news from Fox."

Instead, *Breitbart News* stories fed the opposition, suffusing right-wing radio. "They have an incredible eye for an important story, particular ones that are important to conservatives and Republicans," said Sessions. "They've become extraordinarily influential. Radio talk-show hosts are reading *Breitbart* every day. You can feel it when they interview you."

Trump felt it, too, and he responded almost immediately. "When I started putting him on conservative talk radio in 2013," said Nunberg, "Mark Levin's show and guys like that, they kept asking him about immigration. That opened his eyes." The issue also dovetailed with Trump's long-held view that the United States was being taken advantage of by hostile foreigners.

By the time Trump spoke at the Conservative Political Action Conference on March 15, 2013, less than four months after decrying Romney's "mean-spirited" attacks on immigrants, he was a fully recognizable incarnation of the candidate who would storm the White House three years later. "We have to make America strong again and make America great again," Trump told the CPAC crowd. "Because when it comes to immigration, you know that the 11 million illegals, if given the right to vote . . . every one of those 11 million people will be voting Democratic." Republicans who supported immigration reform, Trump warned, were "on a suicide mission."

Although it passed the Senate, the following summer the Gang of Eight bill died in the House of Representatives, done in by the conservative backlash. It was *Breitbart News* that put the final nail in the coffin. Tipped off by border agents, the website first drew attention to the child migrant crisis at the U.S.–Mexico border. The vivid scenes of helpless U.S. officials and detention facilities overrun by waves of Mexican and Central American children were widely picked up by the national media, killing any chance of Congress passing immigration reform. In the process, the backlash also took down Republican House majority leader Eric Cantor of Virginia. In June, after Cantor was blindsided in the GOP primary by an unheralded economics professor named David Brat, Trump gave an interview to *Breitbart News* that delighted conservative populists by blaming unchecked immigration for the party leadership's stunning loss.

Cantor's defeat was "a great signal because it tells them people want to get our house in order," Trump said in the 2014 interview. "If you look at what's happening in Texas right now, or other places, people are just flowing into this country just like it's an open-door policy. We're supposed to provide health care and we're supposed to provide education—we're supposed to provide everything. . . . We take care of everybody else before we take care of our own people."

Trump had transformed himself into a full-blown hard-right populist, a political persona he now projected like a cologne. He had made up his mind to run for president. "Donald told me on New Year's Day 2013, when I called to wish him Happy New Year, that he'd just trademarked the phrase 'Make America Great Again' and was definitely going to run," said Roger Stone. Yet few people noticed or cared. He was still a punch line. In fact, Republicans were soon celebrating. The midterm elections brought sweeping gains at every level of government, handing the party control of the U.S. Senate. As they looked ahead to the presidential election, Republican leaders were giddy at the presumed strength of the emerging GOP field, a distinguished roster of senators and governors—and perhaps even the more talented sibling in a Bush dynasty that had already produced two presidents.

Trump was no longer "talking to everyone." Now he was talking solely to the conservative grass roots and saying wildly polarizing things. It would not become clear until much later that Trump, the stridently anti-immigrant populist, was better able to address (and stoke) the fear and anger of Republican voters than anyone else in the vaunted GOP field.

Or rather, it wasn't yet clear to the wider world. Inside Trump's circle, the power of illegal immigration to manipulate popular sentiment was readily apparent, and his advisers brainstormed methods for keeping their attention-addled boss on message. They needed a trick, a mnemonic device. In the summer of 2014, they found one that clicked. "Roger Stone and I came up with the idea of 'the Wall,' and we talked to Steve [Bannon] about it," said Nunberg. "It was to make sure he talked about immigration."

Initially, Trump seemed indifferent to the idea. But in January 2015, he tried it out at the Iowa Freedom Summit, a presidential cattle call put on by David Bossie's group, Citizens United. "One of his pledges was, 'I will build a Wall,' and the place just went nuts," said Nunberg. Warming to the concept, Trump waited a beat and then added a flourish that brought down the house. "Nobody," he said, "builds like Trump."

In late 2013, Trump's march toward the presidency was nearly derailed by an idea that arrived out of left field: a handful of New York state politicians and a couple of advisers in his orbit wanted him to run for New York governor. Trump was intrigued.

To his advisers, Trump had long mused about his desire to run for political office. "I want to do it," he'd tell them. "I want to get this out of my system." Stone, Nunberg, and Trump's personal lawyer, Michael Cohen, had hoped he would seek the Republican presidential nomination in 2012. When he passed, the itch to run didn't subside.

In 2013, two Republican state assemblymen from New York, Bill Nojay and David DiPietro, approached Trump to see if he would be interested in challenging New York governor Andrew Cuomo in 2014. Michael Caputo, a Trump adviser who was a former employee of Stone's and managed Carl Paladino's 2010 gubernatorial race against Cuomo, also wanted Trump to run and pushed to organize meetings.

Although Trump had his eye on the presidency, running for governor offered a host of attractive benefits: it would be easier, it was local, it would entail less travel, and some of that could be done by helicopter. He also loved New York, knew the media, could sleep in Trump Tower, and—an adviser pointed out—would not have to worry about potential conflicts between the FCC and his role on *The Apprentice.*

Sensing that Trump's ultimate ambition was the White House, Nojay couched the New York governor's race as something that could vault him to the presidency. In a strategy memo he prepared for Trump, titled "Pathways to the Presidency," Nojay laid out a brief history of businessmen who'd sought political office, noting the risk of loss:

> *Capable, successful businessmen almost always conclude they can do better for themselves and their families by staying in the private business sector. Politicians, on the other hand, often have no alternative*

source of income or perceive their chances in politics are better than their chances in business (e.g., Harry Truman went bust as a men's clothing salesman and turned to politics to feed his family). . . . Businessmen are accustomed to taking risk, however business risk is often partially assigned, buffered, or diluted with partners, alliances, or vendors, insurance or legal shields such as the corporate veil, which reduce personal exposure. Political risk, on the other hand, is purely personal and almost impossible to allocate—the risk of loss is 100 percent on the candidate (blaming campaign managers or other outside factors is usually regarded as lame; the candidate is regarded by the public as solely responsible for his campaign).

But then Nojay made the (specious) argument that Trump would need New York State's electoral votes to win the presidency, and the even more farfetched claim that winning the governorship would make him the Republican presidential front-runner in 2016.

Trump thought enough of the idea to encourage his aides to explore his chances. "I want to do this," he told them. And he met with state party officials to discuss the possibility further. "He made it clear he wanted to run for president," said Daniel W. Isaacs, who was the Republican chairman in Manhattan at the time and attended a meeting with Trump. "Our pitch was if he runs for governor and makes it, he would be the presumptive front-runner."

As the prospect of Trump running for governor began to seem more real, a tug-of-war broke out among his advisers. Stone and Nunberg thought it was a terrible idea, given the state's heavy Democratic skew. A loss would tarnish Trump's image and kill any future presidential run. Cohen, however, spoke in favor of the idea. If the Republican Party would clear the primary field for Trump, he would have a straight shot to take out Cuomo. "One thing that's always dangerous is telling Donald he can't do something," said Stone, "because then he wants to do it."

Hoping to illustrate the futility of a run, Nunberg asked Bossie to commission a survey. In December, Bossie hired Kellyanne Conway to poll likely New York voters to get a clear picture of Trump's chances.

The results were as bad as Stone and Nunberg anticipated—but instead of highlighting the fact that her poll showed Trump losing to Cuomo by 35 points, Conway left out that information and produced an analysis suggesting that Trump could win. "She wrote a sycophantic memo telling Trump he was like the Kennedys," Nunberg complained.

Conway's memo read:

> *Heading into his re-election year, New York Governor Andrew Cuomo enjoys robust favorability and job approval ratings, but those belie some electoral vulnerability. Likely voters across New York who are upset with high taxes, poor business and economic climate, and the price tag associated with Medicaid expansion/Obamacare are open to real solutions and a job-creating governor with business leadership experience.*

Conway noted that while Cuomo's favorability ratings were high, the percentage of New Yorkers who wanted to see him re-elected was "at a dangerous low." She highlighted his vulnerability on Obamacare and taxes, adding, in bold, underlined text:

> Cuomo's re-elect score is positive in New York City (47%) and in the areas surrounding the city (45%), but a hypothetical "new person" wins the rest of the state by twenty points or more.

Most voters agree (70%) and a near-majority "strongly agrees" (49%) that New York needs "a Governor who has created jobs, balanced budgets, and run successful businesses in the private sector." Likewise, in a half-sample of voters (based off 298 interviews), almost 60% of voters thought it was "very important" that New York elect a Governor who has business leadership experience. Andrew Cuomo is not that Governor, but Donald Trump could be.

Having established Cuomo's supposed vulnerability to Trump, Conway cranked up the flattery:

NY loves its celebrity politicians and families: the Kennedys, Moynihans, Buckleys, Clintons, and even the Cuomos. Donald Trump fits that (loose) bill, and he has the money and moxie to compete if he chooses to enter the race. He may need to convince a skeptical electorate of his candidacy, given his very public consideration of running for POTUS before. When offered a choice between offices, New Yorkers are more than twice as likely to urge Trump to run for Governor of New York (27%) than President of the United States (12%). A plurality a third option: run for neither. Cuomo is not invincible. He can be toppled through a frontal assault that pierces his bravado and exposes the shortcomings of his tenure, as well as his lack of leadership. He presides over the corruption and lack of progress that is Albany. While there is plenty of good news here for Cuomo, there is little guarantee that he will escape the misfortunes of 2014 that may be visited on Democrats (thanks to Obamacare), and his own man-made problems plaguing New York (including high taxes and a poor business climate, and a "lack of frack").

Rather than kill off the idea of Trump running for governor, Conway's memo had the opposite effect. "She thought that it was possible for him to win New York," said Caputo. Stone called Conway's analysis "an enormous crock of shit," and Bossie a "major douchebag devoid of any political talent—and that's on the record." But that didn't stop Trump from moving ahead. He traveled to fund-raising events for local Republicans in Erie and Onondaga counties, and invited Westchester county executive Rob Astorino, a Republican who was also eyeing a run for governor, to meet with him.

At the meeting, Trump told Astorino that he would make him his lieutenant governor if he agreed to drop out of the primary. "He was serious," Nunberg said. "He would have run then." Astorino declined the offer. But for weeks, Trump's advisers feared that their boss might decide Astorino was bluffing and get in the race. Nunberg quietly called party officials and told them to encourage Astorino to speak frequently and publicly about his intention to run, in the hope that this would dissuade Trump.

Trump hadn't abandoned the idea of the White House. In early March, Kentucky senator Rand Paul, who was also eyeing a presidential run, asked Trump to go golfing in Florida to suss out his intentions. A few days later, Trump made his annual appearance at CPAC, delivering his anti-immigrant message to heavy applause. Then Astorino formally announced his candidacy for governor.

Trump, piqued that GOP officials had not pushed Astorino aside, tweeted his displeasure: "The top leadership of the New York State Republican Party is totally dysfunctional—they haven't won a major election in many years." In another tweet, he formally abandoned the idea of running for governor: "While I won't be running for Governor of New York State, a race I would have won, I have much bigger plans in mind—stay tuned, will happen!"

A few weeks later, on April 12, 2014, Trump appeared at the New Hampshire Freedom Summit in Manchester, an early presidential cattle call, with Rand Paul and Ted Cruz. In his speech, Trump attacked Jeb Bush, still considered a blue-chip presidential prospect, for his recent comments that illegal immigrants were motivated "by love"—and the crowd responded by booing Bush. Trump got an even bigger reaction from an off-the-cuff attack on politicians. "The problem with politicians," he said, "[they're] all talk and no action. It's true. All talk, it's all bullshit." Audience members stood up and cheered.

It was clear Trump had connected. He left New Hampshire in a glorious mood. He wanted to golf. "On the helicopter back from New Hampshire, we stopped at Briarcliff Manor in upstate New York, where he owns a golf course," Nunberg recalled. "We were shooting balls, and I printed out the press clippings from his speech. Everybody was writing about Trump and how Jeb Bush got booed. I said, 'You see? This is gonna work.'"

SIX

THE ALT-KOCHS

It was early December 2015, and Steve Bannon was wearing a full-on bombardier costume with leather jacket and goggles, and toting a goatskin flying helmet. He was dressed up as one of his favorite movie characters of all-time, Brigadier General Frank Savage, the tough-as-nails commander, played by Gregory Peck, who takes over a demoralized World War II bombing unit and whips them into fighting shape in the 1949 classic *Twelve O'Clock High*. Ordinarily, Bannon wasn't big into cosplay. But this was a special occasion: the annual Christmas party thrown by the reclusive billionaire Robert Mercer, an eccentric computer scientist who was co-CEO of the fabled quantitative hedge fund Renaissance Technologies.

As introverted and private as Bannon was voluble and outspoken, Mercer was nonetheless a man of ardent passions. He collected machine guns and owned the gas-operated AR-18 assault rifle that Arnold Schwarzenegger wielded in *The Terminator*. He had built a $2.7 million model train set equipped with a miniature video camera to allow operators to experience the view from inside the cockpit of his toy engine. He was a competitive poker player. He liked to relax by shaping gemstones. And he loved to dress up in costumes.

Each year, Mercer and his family threw an elaborate, themed Christmas party at Owl's Nest, his opulent waterfront mansion on Long Island's North Shore. Past themes had included "Cowboys and Indians" and "The Roaring Twenties." This year's theme was "The End of World War II." Mercer, styled as General Douglas MacArthur, had obtained an authentic World War II tank to park on his lawn and had flown in artifacts from the National World War II Museum in New Orleans: a piece of the USS *Arizona* recovered from the floor of Pearl Harbor, a parachute-silk wedding dress that once belonged to the French wife of an American GI, and the Medal of Honor given to PFC Arthur Jackson, a young Marine who single-handedly killed fifty Japanese soldiers on the South Pacific island of Peleliu in 1944. As guests mingled beneath tents spread across Mercer's sprawling twelve-acre lawn, a group of Andrews Sisters impersonators provided the evening's entertainment.

Mercer, who was then sixty-nine, had recently developed another late-in-life interest: politics. From a distance, his hard-line antigovernment views appeared no different from those of any number of financial-industry power moguls scattered throughout the country, whose collective fortune financed the Republican Party and its affiliated think tanks and pressure groups. Up close, however, Mercer was . . .well, he was different. He resembled the bloodless capitalist hero in an Ayn Rand novel. Mercer wanted to bring back the gold standard and abolish the fractional-reserve banking system upon which the modern economy is built. He funded an Idaho activist who foments legal challenges to environmental laws, claiming they are part of a United Nations plot to depopulate rural America. He was once overheard by a Renaissance colleague insisting that radiation from the atomic bombs dropped on Japan in World War II actually improved the health of people outside the blast zone. "He's a very independent thinker," said Sean Fieler, a fellow conservative hedge fund manager who has worked with Mercer to lobby for a return to the gold standard. "He's a guy with his own ideas, and very developed ideas."

Mercer's budding interest in right-wing politics was propitiously timed. He started to become active just as the Supreme Court was getting ready to hand down its decision in the 2010 *Citizens United* case—the case David Bossie had brought—opening the floodgates for wealthy individuals to take a larger and more active role in electoral politics. Mercer excited the Republican political world because, though he was a talented poker player, he didn't bluff about his intentions and he was willing, and even eager, to make an enormous ante to a candidate or a cause he believed in.

Of course, Mercer's eccentricity made it a bit difficult for ordinary Republican candidates to maneuver themselves into a position where they might catch the billionaire's eye. The first horse Mercer bet on in a big way was a candidate so far out on the right-wing fringes that simply to describe him is to invite disbelieving laughter (which it often did). In 2010, a sixty-eight-year-old research chemist named Arthur Robinson, who lived on a sheep ranch deep in the Siskiyou Mountains of southern Oregon, decided to challenge the longtime Democratic congressman, Peter DeFazio. Calling Robinson a "research chemist," while technically accurate, doesn't quite do justice to the exotic nature of the man's pursuits. A self-funded medical renegade, Robinson was consumed with extending the human life span and believed that the secret to staving off death and disease could be found in human urine. To that end, Robinson collected thousands upon thousands of urine samples, which he froze in vials and stored in massive refrigerators that stood among his wandering sheep. Robinson published a newsletter to share his findings and to periodically put out calls for more urine ("We need samples of your urine" read a typical house ad). Mercer was a subscriber to Robinson's newsletter (this was likely the source of his claim that exposure to atomic radiation can benefit human health, a theory known as "hormesis").

Robinson, who understandably had difficulty enlisting the backing of the National Republican Congressional Committee, did not appear to pose a threat to DeFazio. He had as little money to put toward a congressional race as he did for his urine research. Yet six weeks before the election, a wave of ads began appearing on local television attacking DeFazio as a tool of the Democratic House majority leader Nancy Pelosi. Robinson had no idea where the ads were coming from. When reporters discovered that Mercer had funded the group responsible for airing them, Robinson was surprised but appreciative. "I don't know him very well," he confessed. "If he's helping me in the campaign, then I'm grateful." While he didn't win, Robinson gave DeFazio his closest race in decades.*

In the years afterward, Mercer spread his political largesse

---

*As Zachary Mider of *Bloomberg News* has reported, Mercer's largesse wasn't limited to Robinson's congressional campaign. When Robinson made an appeal in his newsletter for funds to buy a powerful piece of research equipment called a "mass spectrometer," the Mercer family reached out to help defray the $2 million cost. Since then, tax filings show that the Mercers have sent Robinson's lab, which he calls the Oregon Institute of Science and Medicine, at least $1.6 million, which has allowed him to buy additional freezers to store his enormous stockpile of human urine—at last count up to fourteen thousand vials. Jane Mayer of the *New Yorker* has reported that after Trump's election, Rebekah Mercer pushed to have Robinson appointed to the position of national science adviser. She has not yet succeeded.

among a broad group of beneficiaries. Some of them fell closer to the mainstream of the conservative movement than did Arthur Robinson. They included Bossie's group, Citizens United, as well as groups such as the conservative Heritage Foundation and the Federalist Society. As a rule, Mercer distrusted the political establishment, just as he shunned the Wall Street financial establishment. Even so, he drifted close enough in 2012 to contribute $25 million to the dark-money network of wealthy conservative donors organized by Charles and David Koch, and he gave millions more to Karl Rove's Super PAC, American Crossroads, and to another that supported Mitt Romney. At around this time, Mercer's middle daughter, Rebekah, became more actively involved in the family's political giving. When Romney lost the presidential election and Rove's handpicked slate of Senate candidates was wiped out to a man, the Mercers became enraged and all but withdrew from their involvement in mainstream Republican politics. Led by Rebekah, the family members veered sharply to the right, establishing themselves as the alt-Kochs and using their fortune to back outsider candidates and causes of their own.

As the evening stars rose over Owl's Nest, friends and courtiers from all walks of life strolled across the Mercers' lawn, magically transported, if just for the evening, back to 1945. Jack Hanna, the khaki-clad celebrity zookeeper, came wandering by (the Mercers gave $100,000 to his zoo). But the evening's buzz was all about politics. With the presidential election less than a year away, Rebekah Mercer, who was dressed as Rita Hayworth, stood to be a figure of consequence. Texas senator Ted Cruz, dressed as Winston Churchill, was especially solicitous of her. As everyone gathered on the lush grounds of Robert Mercer's estate was keenly aware, the

Mercer family had given away more than $77 million to conservative politicians and organizations since 2008.

You didn't have to be a brilliant scientist to see the joy Bob Mercer derived from his annual Christmas pageant, or to understand that anyone hoping to curry favor with him would be wise to play along. This is how it came to be that adults who never imagined themselves dressing up in costumes—adults like Steve Bannon—wound up hunting for just the right period-appropriate accoutrements to make a positive impression. The effort could pay off handsomely. In fact, for Bannon, it already had. Over the past three years, the Mercers had become the key financial backers of a far-flung network of interlocking political and media groups that Bannon either had conceived of or had come to control. Bob Mercer was going to be vitally important to the presidential race. He was a man you'd dress up for. Bannon called him "the Godfather."

For years before he joined Trump's presidential campaign, Bannon had been a Washington figure of no particular distinction who tended to inhabit the far fringes of Republican politics, where he felt most at home. Sometimes, he drifted so far out on the fringe that he and his compatriots were shunned by mainstream right-of-center outfits such as the American Conservative Union, which throws the annual Conservative Political Action Conference. Bannon not only didn't mind the slights, he reveled in the minor notoriety, playing up his image as the skunk at the garden party.

In 2013, when CPAC banned a number of speakers for incivility and anti-Muslim animus, Bannon had *Breitbart News* organize a nearby counter-conference that he dubbed "The Uninvited" and personally emceed.* Featured guests included the blogger Pamela Geller, who called Muslims "savages"; Frank Gaffney, a former Reagan official who claimed that the Muslim Brotherhood had infiltrated the Obama administration; and Robert Spencer, the founder of Jihad Watch and Stop Islamization of America. (Geller and Spencer were later banned from entering the United Kingdom out of concern they would spark "inter-community violence.")

Bannon, in other words, was about the least likely candidate anyone could imagine to wind up being the recipient of millions of dollars from a wealthy conservative benefactor intent on radically reshaping American politics.

And yet one donor thought otherwise.

The reason Bannon appealed to Mercer and almost nobody else is that Mercer's odd, charmed life had taught him to reject ordinary ways of thinking and reflexively seek advantage in places other people didn't look or couldn't see. It shaped his way of viewing the world and made him extravagantly rich. And the particular way in which Mercer had taken this worldview and applied it at Renaissance Technologies—by stringing together a series of models that functioned in tandem—was the same way that Bannon thought about politics and hoped to attack the system.

The model that Mercer believed in so fiercely was devised by a

---

*It's worth noting here that of the many extreme and offensive beliefs Steve Bannon and the editors of *Breitbart News* have been accused of harboring, they have never advocated "birtherism"—the false claim that Barack Obama wasn't born in the United States. One of the oddballs who was not invited to CPAC in 2013 or to "The Uninvited" counter-conference was the most outspoken birther of all, a Moldovan-American dentist and lawyer named Orly Taitz. During this period, Taitz, an inveterate publicity seeker, was a frequent guest on low-rent TV and radio shows, and she actually crashed "The Uninvited" conference and made a big scene by getting into a heated argument with Bannon during the question-and-answer session following a panel discussion. It took some doing, but Bannon eventually shut her down, reiterating that he and the editors of *Breitbart* never had any doubts that Obama was born in the United States.

mathematician and former code breaker for the Pentagon's secretive
Institute for Defense Analyses named Jim Simons. In the late 1970s,
Simons was chairman of the math department at Stony Brook University on Long Island and an avid amateur speculator in commodities (he spent his wedding money trading soybean futures). Believing
that he could bring mathematical rigor to the gut-driven practice of
commodities trading, Simons began recruiting some fellow mathematicians and code breakers to help him automate the process of
finding the best trades. These esoteric skill sets were more applicable to finance than they might at first seem. The job of a military
cryptographer is to devise systems through which to send and spot
signals amid a sea of noise, ideally signals so faint that others don't
detect them. Finding the patterns that constitute the signal, Simons
realized, was not all that different from spotting hidden patterns
coursing in a sea of seemingly random market data—patterns that
might prove to be predictive and therefore profitable trading
opportunities.

What made Simons and his code breakers iconoclasts in the
realm of Wall Street's financial world is that the hidden patterns
they were looking for were not supposed to exist. The prevailing
view among academic economists at the time was that prices were
efficient, and if it was possible to know ahead of time that stocks
or soybeans were going to rise or fall, the valuations would have
changed already—all relevant information was thought to be priced
into the omniscient mind of the market. Money managers might get
lucky for a spell and outperform a benchmark index. But efficient-
market theory held that over the long term, they couldn't consistently beat the market.

Simons thought they could, if only they applied the right sort
of expertise. With professional code breakers to detect systemic

patterns in equity markets and mathematicians to write sophisticated algorithms, Renaissance Technologies, which Simons founded
in 1982, built a program that traded on the basis of computer-
generated signals. Before long, the firm was consistently outper-
forming discretionary traders. As his company flourished, Simons
recruited additional mathematicians, astronomers, and computer
scientists—but never economists or people with experience working
on Wall Street. Simons considered them, in effect, to be intellectu-
ally corrupted by what he thought was the narrow and incurious way
in which Wall Street trading houses approached financial markets.
He himself had come from the academy and prized the independence of mind this background had instilled in him. And he believed, correctly, that his ability to think differently from the major
Wall Street firms was the wellspring of his success. Struck by the
limits of establishment thinking, he sequestered Renaissance on a
campus on Long Island, far from Manhattan's financial district,
and hired only academic specialists trained in abstract thought. One
of them, in 1993, was Bob Mercer.

Mercer and a colleague, Peter Brown, were recruited mid-career
from IBM's research center, where they had revolutionized the field
of computer translation. All his life, Mercer had romanticized computers. As a teenager growing up in New Mexico, he had taught
himself programming by reading books. Having no access to a computer himself, he wrote programs in longhand in a wire-bound
notebook. In high school, he finagled a job in a nearby Air Force
weapons lab writing programs in Fortran. Mercer, who almost never
grants interviews and rarely speaks, even in private company, once
described with feeling the sense of bliss that overcame him in the job.
"I loved everything about computers," he recalled in a 2014 speech to
a gathering of linguists. "I loved the solitude of the computer lab late

at night. I loved the air-conditioned smell of the place. I loved the sound of the discs whirring and the printers clacking." After earning a Ph.D. in computer science at the University of Illinois at Urbana, he joined IBM's Thomas J. Watson Research Center in Yorktown, New York, where he became part of a team that was trying to teach computers to translate human language.

At the time, the field of computer translation was dominated by linguists. The agreed-upon approach was to teach computers the rules of syntax and grammar, so that they might develop sufficient "linguistic intuition" to be able eventually to translate, say, English to French. That is, after all, how people learn language. Mercer and Brown took an entirely different approach, chucking any concern about grammar and instead relying on a tool called an "expectation maximization algorithm"—a tool code breakers would use to find patterns. The pair got hold of Canadian parliamentary records, which are cross-published in English and French, and fed them into an IBM computer, which they instructed to look for correlations. Outside IBM, their unorthodox approach to translation was greeted with hostility ("the crude force of computers is not science," huffed one linguist at a professional conference who reviewed their work). But pattern-hunting worked. A computer could learn to recognize patterns without regard for the rules of grammar and still produce a successful translation. "Statistical machine translation," as the process became known, soon outpaced the old method and went on to become the basis of modern speech-recognition software and tools such as Google Translate.

At Renaissance, Mercer and Brown applied this approach broadly to the markets, feeding all kinds of abstruse data into their computers in a never-ending hunt for hidden correlations. Sometimes they found them in strange places. Even by the paranoid standards of black-box quantitative hedge funds, Renaissance is notoriously secretive about its methods. But in 2010, one intriguing example of the patterns it turns up became public. As the author Sebastian Mallaby details in his history of the hedge-fund industry, *More Money Than God*, a group of scientists at the firm's flagship Medallion Fund discovered a correlation between weather patterns and market performance. As Mallaby writes: "In one simple example, the brain trust discovered that fine morning weather in a city tended to predict an upward movement in its stock exchange. By buying on bright days at breakfast time and selling a bit later, Medallion could come out ahead."

Many of these signals were modest at best, difficult to detect and even harder for most people to profit from. But for Renaissance they held two great advantages. Stronger signals meant that other quantitative traders would be more likely to pick up on them, too, causing the market inefficiency to correct. The subtler and stranger the correlation—like the relationship between sunny weather and rising markets—the less likely that others would spot it and cause it to go away. "The signals that we have been trading without interruption for fifteen years make no sense," Mercer explained to Mallaby in a rare interview in 2008. "Otherwise someone else would have found it."

The other advantage Renaissance held was its ability to exploit these faint patterns, even if they were individually modest. Because trades were made algorithmically by computers, it didn't require much human effort to make hundreds or thousands of quick trades to capture small profits. Collectively, those profits added up. Where human ingenuity came into play was in building the infrastructure that tied all these programs together into a seamless, humming machine. The system's architecture and scope were Mercer's constant, preoccupying concern. "I spent all my time thinking about the problem of coordinating everything," he said in 2014.

This openness to odd correlations and skepticism toward received wisdom paid enormous dividends for Renaissance and its employees. In 2016, *Bloomberg* dubbed the firm's Medallion Fund "perhaps the world's greatest moneymaking machine," having by that point produced about $55 billion in profits during the twenty-eight years of its existence. Much of the firm's success was driven by Mercer and Brown, who took over as co-CEOs when Simons retired in 2009.

When Mercer's interest in right-wing politics began to blossom two years later, his instincts didn't lead him to seek out the wisdom of the GOP establishment—wisdom that had, not incidentally, produced the disastrous loss of the White House and both houses of Congress by 2008. They led him instead to charismatic, peripheral figures with dramatic, world-changing ideas—people such as Andrew Breitbart, whom Mercer met in 2011 at a conference held by the conservative group Club for Growth. And they led him to Steve Bannon, whom he met shortly afterward. As a glance across Mercer's lawn at Christmastime would confirm, his interests, and his generous sponsorships, were broad-based and varied. But by every account, both he and Rebekah were thoroughly captivated by Breitbart's zany, outsider approach to upending politics. The fact that most members of the Republican power structure viewed Breitbart as a loudmouth and a jester (and would come to view Bannon the same way) did not, in Mercer's eyes, detract in any way from his appeal, and probably counted as a mark in his favor. What good was the collective opinion of the establishment, anyway?

Through Bannon, the Mercers agreed to invest $10 million to help finance *Breitbart News'* long-planned relaunch. The rollout was scheduled for the spring of 2012, but Breitbart didn't live to see the result. After his sudden death a few days before the relaunch, the Mercers gave their blessing for Bannon to step in and take over the site. But *Breitbart News* was only a piece of a much larger system that Bannon wanted to build. There were other parts, too, and they would all work in harmony. Bob Mercer and his family became their eager benefactor, because to him such an approach made intuitive sense.

The Mercer family was not Trump's largest donor, but they were without a doubt the most important in helping Trump to win the presidency. There is no small irony in this fact, because Trump was not the candidate whom the Mercers initially backed in the 2016 Republican presidential primary. Ted Cruz was their first choice. The Mercers admired how Cruz had taken on the Republican establishment, going so far as to drive the shutdown of the federal government in October 2013 in an effort to slash government spending on health care. Republican leaders loathed Cruz, and yet he persevered in his criticism of them and in his strident right-wing politics. The Mercers gave $11 million to a Super PAC they established to support Cruz's candidacy, hiring Kellyanne Conway to run it, and they organized other wealthy donors to do the same.

Although the Mercers later switched their allegiance to Trump after Cruz dropped out, and gave millions more in support of his candidacy, their greatest impact on his behalf was indirect and aimed at helping Cruz. Through Bannon and his interlocking groups, the Mercers bankrolled the effort to discredit Trump's eventual opponent, Hillary Clinton, who everyone in politics had long assumed would wind up the Democratic presidential nominee. (The Mercers had simply expected that Cruz would be her opponent.)

To Bob Mercer, the plot to tear down Clinton may have held greater appeal than his support for a Republican alternative because, according to former Renaissance employees, he had long been convinced of the Clintons' treachery. Nick Patterson, a computational biologist who worked with Mercer in the 1990s, claims that at a Renaissance staff luncheon during Bill Clinton's presidency, Mercer declared that Clinton, while governor of Arkansas, had been involved in a CIA-backed drug-running scheme based out of the Mena, Arkansas, airport—a conspiracy theory that circulated in extreme right-wing circles at the time. "Bob told me he believed that the Clintons were involved in murders connected to it," Patterson said.

Bannon's plan to stop Hillary Clinton was multifaceted and years in the making. It was built primarily on four organizations, each of which the Mercers funded or had a stake in (they also compensated Bannon directly). The first was *Breitbart News*, whose staff and audience grew rapidly after the Mercers' $10 million investment in 2012. Although much of the site's energy was devoted to attacking establishment Republicans, such as former House Speaker John Boehner and his successor, Paul Ryan, *Breitbart*'s constant stream of outrageously critical stories about the Clintons made it a natural rallying point for conservative readers and a steady source of material for high-profile Clinton-hating sites like the *Drudge Report*.

The second organization was the Government Accountability Institute, a nonprofit research group based in Tallahassee, Florida, that was established in 2012 to serve as a home for Peter Schweizer, the conservative researcher whose book on Ronald Reagan had been the basis of Bannon's filmmaking debut in 2004. In the years after his book was published, Schweizer had become increasingly consumed with the issue of Washington cronyism, and his interests turned toward exposing this culture. In 2011 he published an investigative book, *Throw Them All Out: How Politicians and Their Friends Get Rich Off Insider Stock Tips, Land Deals, and Cronyism That Would Send the Rest of Us to Prison*. The book had a real effect, catching the attention of *60 Minutes* and leading Congress to pass a law, the STOCK (Stop Trading on Congressional Knowledge) Act, which aimed to curb the abuses Schweizer documented. Bannon told him that he ought to focus next on the cronyism endemic to the Clintons, and that financial help would be forthcoming if he was to agree. "He told me, 'I know people who will support this kind of work,'" Schweizer said. In 2013, the Mercer Family Foundation contributed a million dollars to GAI, which hired Schweizer as its president. Rebekah Mercer took a seat on the board. The following year, the foundation contributed another million dollars, and in 2015, it upped that amount to $1.7 million, which constituted the overwhelming majority of GAI's budget. The investment paid off. That year, Schweizer's book *Clinton Cash: The Untold Story of How and Why Foreign Governments and Businesses Helped Make Bill and Hillary Rich*, was published by HarperCollins, just as Clinton was preparing to launch her candidacy. The book dominated the national political conversation for weeks on end, doing more to shape Clinton's image in a negative way than any of her Republican detractors could.

The third Mercer-backed group was a film production company called Glittering Steel, which Bannon and Rebekah Mercer established to make movies and political advertisements. According to Bannon, Glittering Steel had ambitions not only to influence politics but also to become a commercially successful producer of Christian-themed movies, an endeavor that greatly excited Rebekah, who home-schooled her four children. It held allure for Bannon as well. During his Hollywood years, he was part of a discreet network of religious conservatives in the film industry that was loosely organized by the Wilberforce Forum—an evangelical group chaired by the reformed Watergate felon Chuck Colson—whose mission was to "shape culture from a biblical perspective." This network included the actor and director Mel Gibson, whose 2004 film *The Passion of the Christ* had been an unexpected hit, as well as a producer of that film with whom Bannon briefly teamed up to make a documentary on Pope Benedict XVI. Although Glittering Steel didn't turn out any commercially successful films, it did produce a movie version of *Clinton Cash* that appeared in 2016, just as the general election race was kicking off. The film debuted during the Cannes Film Festival,* on the French Riviera, where Rebekah Mercer entertained guests, including Bannon, aboard the family's 203-foot luxury super yacht, *Sea Owl*.

The fourth Mercer-funded outfit was a business after Robert Mercer's own heart, the U.S. offshoot of a British data analytics company, Strategic Communication Laboratories, that advised foreign governments and militaries on influencing elections and public opinion using the tools of psychological warfare. The American affiliate of SCL, of which Robert Mercer became principal owner, was christened Cambridge Analytica. (Bannon, too, took an ownership stake and a seat on the company's board.) The purpose of acquiring a major stake in a data company was to equip the Mercer network with the kind of state-of-the-art technology that had been glaringly absent from Mitt Romney's campaign. It also allowed the Mercers to build out an infrastructure for sophisticated messaging and strategy that would be independent of the institutional

---

*Although the movie *Clinton Cash* was screened in Cannes, France, in May 2016, it was not a part of the Cannes Film Festival. Instead, it was shown at a screening arranged for distributors.

Republican Party (an impulse shared by their fellow billionaires, David and Charles Koch, who also spent tens of millions of dollars building an alternative party structure, so disillusioned were they by the ineptitude of the GOP). Rebekah Mercer, who gained a fast reputation for aggressively involving herself in the campaigns of politicians she backed, made clear that as a condition of her financial support, she expected that campaigns would hire Cambridge Analytica to do their data work. Whenever necessary, Bannon played the role of heavy.

By the time Clinton launched her presidential campaign in April 2015, all four of these groups were up and running like the machine they were envisioned to be. But the collective power of the Bannon-Mercer project wasn't obvious to many people at the time. Trump was still considered a carnival sideshow, *Breitbart News* a site for trolls and crazies, and Bannon a fringe figure who wouldn't possibly factor into something as large and important as a presidential race. These were all assumptions the Clinton brain trust would come to bitterly regret. "One of the realities that I don't think was truly appreciated by our campaign," Brian Fallon, Clinton's communications director, admitted after the election, "was just how profound the Breitbart effect was in cultivating a standalone ecosystem in conservative media that very aggressively and successfully promoted certain stories and narratives we had a blind spot for during the campaign."

The Mercers cut a higher profile, as is typically the case when billionaires—especially eccentric ones—decide to direct part of their fortune toward influencing electoral politics. The family's public image as sinister masterminds of Republican politics has only mushroomed since Trump's victory. What's most interesting about the Mercers, however, is that their true role in the election belies this breathless coverage. After all, their preferred candidate didn't win. And yet their virtually limitless resources wound up working on behalf of the man who did win: the candidate preferred by Steve Bannon. It's standard practice for ultrarich people with an interest in politics to hire an adviser to counsel them on where to direct their money. What's so unusual about the relationship between Bannon and the Mercers is that it reversed the normal power dynamic. Typically, the adviser is a well-paid employee, a kind of political maître d' who oversees campaign donations and arranges meetings with Washington heavyweights. That person functions as a clear subordinate to his wealthy benefactor. In Bannon's case, the relationship was inverted. Instead of the help, he became the Svengali. And the Mercers, whether or not they fully appreciated it, became the merchant bankers funding Bannon's broad-ranging ambitions.

SEVEN

A ROLLING TUMBLEWEED OF
WOUNDED MALE ID AND AGGRESSION

I
t was nearing midnight as Bannon pushed past the bluegrass band
in his living room and through a crowd of Republican congressmen, political operatives, and a few stray *Duck Dynasty* cast members. He was trying to make his way back to the SiriusXM *Patriot*
radio show, broadcasting live from a cramped corner of the fourteen-
room town house a stone's throw from the Supreme Court that
served as the Washington headquarters for *Breitbart News*. It was
late February 2015, the annual Conservative Political Action Conference was in full swing, and Bannon, as usual, was the whirlwind
at the center of the action.

Earlier that day, Trump had made his annual CPAC speech to
only middling applause, going on for so long that many people in
the audience drifted away. When he finished, Sean Hannity of
Fox News, wearing a bright red Trump-branded necktie, strode
out to the lectern where Trump stood and awkwardly interviewed

him about the likelihood that he would run for president. "One to a hundred, I would say 75 and 80 [percent]," Trump replied. "I want to do it so badly. You know, I have the theme. It's my theme. It's 'Make America Great Again.' That's what I want to do."

But Trump didn't even rate as the day's most popular reality-TV star—Bannon outdid him. He'd spent the day at CPAC squiring around an unlikely pair of guests: Nigel Farage, the leader of the right-wing UK Independence Party, and Phil Robertson, the bandanna'd, ayatollah-bearded *Duck Dynasty* patriarch who was accepting a free-speech award. CPAC is a beauty contest for Republican presidential hopefuls. But Robertson, a novelty adornment invited after A&E suspended him for denouncing gays, delivered a wild rant about beatniks and sexually transmitted diseases that had upstaged them all, to Bannon's evident delight. Afterward, everyone piled into party buses and headed for the *Breitbart* town house.

Ordinarily, the town house was crypt-quiet and felt like a museum, as it was faithfully decorated down to its embroidered yellow silk curtains and painted murals in authentic Lincoln-era detail. Bannon slept in an upstairs bedroom when he was in town, while down below, the *Breitbart* newsroom operated out of the chilly basement. On this February night, however, the furniture was gone, a makeshift bar had been installed to serve "moonshine"—his wink at the *Dynasty* guests—and the party was jam-packed and roaring. Bannon was in high spirits. Along with his CPAC triumph, the Clinton book he had secretly conceived with Peter Schweizer, a full two years in the making, was almost finished being vetted by his lawyers. Bannon was certain it would upend the presidential race. "Dude, it's going to be epic," he insisted to a guest.

Somewhere, Hillary Clinton was carefully charting her path to the White House. Six weeks hence, on April 12, she would formally announce her presidential run and then steel herself, as she always did, for a barrage of attacks from the right. Clinton had long ago identified a "vast right-wing conspiracy" bent on tearing down her and her husband. Still, she could not possibly have imagined quite what she was about to encounter—or that the person at the nexus of the vast new conspiracy against her was, just then, surrounded by drunken, sweaty members of a reality-TV dynasty who were hooting and making duck calls.

Bannon thrived on the chaos he created and did everything he could to make it spread. When he finally made his way through the crowd to the back of the town house, he put on a headset to join the broadcast of the *Breitbart* radio show already in progress. It was his way of bringing tens of thousands of listeners into the inner sanctum of the "Breitbart Embassy," as the town house was ironically known, and thereby conscripting them into a larger project. Bannon was inordinately proud of the movement he saw growing around him, boasting constantly of its egalitarian nature. What to an outsider could look like a cast of extras from the Island of Misfit Toys was, in Bannon's eyes, a proudly populist and "unclubbable" plebiscite rising up in defiant protest against the "globalists" and "gatekeepers" who had taken control of both parties.

Just how Phil Robertson of *Duck Dynasty* figured into a plan to overthrow the global power structure wasn't clear, even to many of Bannon's friends. But, then, Bannon derived a visceral thrill anytime he could deliver a fuck-you to the establishment. The thousands of frustrated listeners calling in to his radio show, and the millions more who flocked to *Breitbart News*, had left him no doubt that an army of the angry and dispossessed was eager to join him in lobbing a bomb at the country's leaders. As guests left the party, a doorman handed out a gift that Bannon had chosen for the occasion: a silver hip flask with "Breitbart" imprinted above an image of a honey badger, the *Breitbart* mascot.

Bannon's cult-leader magnetism was a powerful draw for oddballs and freaks, and the attraction ran both ways. As he moved further from the cosmopolitan orbits of Goldman Sachs and Hollywood, there was no longer any need for him to suppress his right-wing impulses. Giving full vent to his views on subjects like immigration and Islam isolated him among a radical fringe that most of political Washington regarded as teeming with racist conspiracy theorists. But far from being bothered, Bannon welcomed their disdain, taking it as proof of his authentic conviction. It fed his grandiose sense of purpose to imagine that he was amassing an army of ragged, pitchfork-wielding outsiders to storm the barricades and, in Andrew Breitbart's favorite formulation, "take back the country." If Bannon was bothered by the incendiary views held by some of those lining up with him, he didn't show it. His habit always was to welcome all comers.

To all outward appearances, Bannon, wild-eyed and scruffy, a Falstaff in flip-flops, was someone whom the political world could safely ignore. But his appearance, and the company he kept, masked an analytic capability that was undiminished and as applicable to politics as it had been to the finances of corrupt Hollywood movie studios. Somehow, Bannon, who would happily fall into league with the most agitated conservative zealot, was able to see clearly that conservatives had failed to stop Bill Clinton in the 1990s because they had indulged this very zealotry to a point where their credibility with the media and mainstream voters was shot. Trapped in their own bubble, speaking only to one another, they had believed that they were winning, when in reality they had already lost.

To stop Hillary, Bannon believed, conservatives needed to exert influence beyond their own movement, which would require them to abstain from indulging every outlandish Clinton conspiracy theory, as they had fallen prey to doing in the 1990s, when important Republican politicians such as Dan Burton were running around shooting watermelons with a pistol. In order to gain the necessary influence, Bannon thought, conservatives needed to build a political case based on documented facts that would discredit Clinton in the eyes of the people whose support she would need to win the election—not just voters, but the media as well.

While *Breitbart News* could rally conservatives against Clinton, Bannon knew that such an openly partisan organ would never be seen as a credible messenger by Democratic voters or the guardians of mainstream news. "One of the things Goldman teaches you is, don't be the first guy through the door, because you're going to get all the arrows," said Bannon. "If it's junk bonds, let Michael Milken lead the way. Goldman would never lead in any product. Find a business partner." That's where the Government Accountability Institute came into play. Although it was funded by Mercer family money, GAI was, under the letter of the law, a nonpartisan 501(c)(3) research organization whose work, if it had merit, could safely be taken up by reporters and producers at nonpartisan media outlets without exposing them to charges of political bias. Leading GAI required Bannon to assume an entirely different profile from the one he cultivated at *Breitbart*. But having been so many things already in his career, he had no trouble adding a new role.

As befitted someone with his peripatetic background, Bannon

became a kind of Jekyll-and-Hyde figure in the complicated ecosystem of the right—he was two things at once. Through *Breitbart*, he could influence the right, and through GAI, he could exert a subtler influence over the left. This allowed him to marry the old-style attack journalism of *Breitbart News* with a more sophisticated approach, conducted through GAI, that built rigorous, fact-based indictments against major politicians and then partnered with mainstream media outlets to disseminate those findings to the broadest possible audience. The key was to pique the interest of a group of people every bit as obsessive and driven as hard-core partisans like Bannon: investigative reporters at major newspapers and TV networks.

"What Peter and I noticed is that it's facts, not rumors, that resonate with the best investigative reporters," Bannon said, referring to GAI's president. If they could amass enough unflattering facts about Clinton—ideally ones that hinted at larger stories—then reporters would eagerly chase after them. This would produce an elegant symbiosis. As negative stories sprouted up in the mainstream press, they would dampen enthusiasm among potential Clinton supporters, while serving as fodder for *Breitbart News* to stoke anti-Clinton outrage on the right.

The biggest product of this system was the project Bannon was so excited about at *Breitbart*'s CPAC party: Schweizer's investigative book, *Clinton Cash*. Its publication was the culmination of everything Bannon had learned during his time in Goldman Sachs, Internet Gaming Entertainment, Hollywood, and *Breitbart News*. It was, he thought, the key to orchestrating Hillary Clinton's downfall.

Most days, Bannon could be found in his Mr. Hyde persona, in the Washington offices of *Breitbart News*. That's where he was one day in late May 2015, a few days after *Clinton Cash* had rocketed to number two on *the New York Times* bestseller list. The book was creating a media frenzy that was pleasantly familiar to many *Breitbart* staffers.

Bannon's elevation to executive chairman of what was officially the Breitbart News Network had been sudden, but his new role was eased by the fact that the site was deeply imprinted with its founder's DNA. Breitbart had developed a visceral feel for what kinds of stories would resonate and keep readers coming back for more. "To me, that was Andrew's greatest skill set: knowing what stories would move the masses," said Alex Marlow, who began as Breitbart's assistant and later became the site's editor in chief. "He learned that from Matt Drudge, who is the greatest conversation starter in American history."

Breitbart's genius was that he grasped better than anyone else what the early twentieth-century press barons understood—that most readers don't approach the news as a clinical exercise in absorbing facts, but experience it viscerally as an ongoing drama, with distinct story lines, heroes, and villains. Breitbart excelled at creating these narratives, an editorial approach that lived on after his death. "When we do an editorial call, I don't even bring anything I feel like is only a one-off story, even if it'd be the best story on the site," said Marlow. "Our whole mind-set is looking for these rolling narratives." He rattled off the most popular ones, which *Breitbart* covers intensively from a posture of aggrieved persecution. "The big ones won't surprise you," he said. "Immigration, ISIS, race riots, and what we call 'the collapse of traditional values.' But I'd say Hillary Clinton is tops." Often, the site managed to inject these narratives into the broader discourse.

Although most famous for his outré media stunts, Breitbart

could spot stories that others couldn't (or wouldn't) see—stories downplayed or buried on the back pages of newspapers—and billboard them with screaming, transgressive headlines. A scathing press critic, he claimed that the greatest manifestation of liberal media bias was the stories that news outlets chose *not* to tell. "Andrew always said, 'If you look at the mainstream media, they're all fishing for stories in one pond,'" recalled *Breitbart* president Larry Solov. "'But there's a second pond, and nobody's fishing there.'" Only by wresting control of the news narrative away from mainstream outlets, Breitbart believed, could this imbalance be rectified. That was what *Breitbart News* aimed to do. "Our vision—Andrew's vision—was always to build a global center-right, populist, anti-establishment news site," said Bannon.

Yet Breitbart's definition of "news" differed markedly from that of the wire services in that it also encompassed political activism: it was news with a purpose. Much of the site's energy was devoted to skewering liberal hypocrisy and highlighting ostensibly outrageous instances of political correctness. Unlike reputable news outlets, *Breitbart* was willing to publish dubious investigative "sting" videos shot by conservative activists, such as the 2009 ACORN tape or the Shirley Sherrod tape that was misleadingly edited to portray the Obama Agriculture official as an anti-white racist. And there was no parallel anywhere to Breitbart's orchestration of Anthony Weiner's downfall, not in his decision to publish an unverified photo of the married congressman's crotch supposedly tweeted at a young paramour, and certainly not in the Barnum-like scene he created by hijacking Weiner's press conference after the story turned out to be true. Episodes such as these sent a galvanizing charge into readers that no other conservative site could match.

When Bannon took over, he wanted to ensure that Breitbart lost none of its combative zest. The main discernible difference under his leadership was an amplification of the nativist populism already evident in the site's coverage and an emboldened desire to attack "globalist" Republicans along with Democrats. Operating from the basement of the Breitbart Embassy, *Breitbart*'s pirate crew became tribunes of the rising Tea Party movement and champions of Sarah Palin, with whom Bannon was close, bedeviling GOP leaders and helping to drive the 2013 government shutdown.

Bannon made another decision that wasn't immediately obvious but that would have a significant effect on the size and nature of Breitbart's audience—and eventually on the 2016 presidential campaign. He wanted to attract the online legions of mostly young men he'd run up against several years earlier, believing that the Internet masses could be harnessed to stoke a political revolution. Back in 2007, when he'd taken over Internet Gaming Entertainment, the Hong Kong company that systemized gold farming in *World of Warcraft* and other massively multiplayer online games, Bannon had become fascinated by the size and agency of the audiences congregating on MMO message boards such as Wowhead, Allakhazam, and (his favorite) Thottbot. "In 2006, 2007, they were doing 1.5 billion page views a month," he recalled. "Just insane traffic. I thought we could monetize it, but it turned out I couldn't give the advertising away." Instead, the gamers ended up wrecking IGE's business model by organizing themselves on the message boards and forcing the companies behind *World of Warcraft* and other MMO games to curb the disruptive practice of gold farming.

IGE's investors lost millions of dollars. But Bannon gained a perverse appreciation for the gamers who'd done him in. "These guys, these rootless white males, had monster power," he said. "It was the pre-reddit. It's the same guys on Thottbot who were [later] on reddit" and 4chan—the message boards that became the birth-place of the alt-right.

When Bannon took over *Breitbart*, he wanted to capture this au-dience. Andrew Breitbart had drawn a portion of it enchanted by his aggressive provocations on issues such as race and political correct-ness. Bannon took it further. He envisioned a great fusion between the masses of alienated gamers, so powerful in the online world, and the right-wing outsiders drawn to *Breitbart* by its radical politics and fuck-you attitude. "The reality is, Fox News' audience was geriatric and no one was connecting with this younger group," Bannon said. But he needed a way to connect. He found it in Milo Yiannopoulos, a gay British tech blogger and Internet troll nonpareil.

Hoping to appeal to the gamer audience, Bannon found Yian-nopoulos through a friend while scouting for someone to launch a *Breitbart* tech vertical. "He sent me a résumé and the title of the book he was working on: *The Pathological Narcissism of the Silicon Valley Elite*," Bannon recalled. "I said, 'Whoa.' Then I met him. When I saw Milo, it was the first time I saw a guy who could connect culturally like an Andrew Breitbart. He had the fearlessness, the brains, the charisma—it's something special about those guys. They just had that 'it' factor. The difference was, Andrew had a very strong moral universe, and Milo is an amoral nihilist. I knew right away, he's gonna be a fucking meteor."

At its essence, the alt-right is a rolling tumbleweed of wounded male id and aggression.* Yiannopoulos showed a flair for manipu-

---

*While a handful of speakers and writers (such as Richard Spencer, the white supremacist head of the National Policy Institute) have tried to give "alt-right" an intellectual gloss, the bulk of the energy and activism attributed to the alt-right is driven by nihilistic, meme-obsessed gamer types whose use of racist and anti-Semitic language and iconography seems driven mainly by a warped sense of irony and a desire to upset their targets—and draw media attention. Bannon rejects any association with Spencer, whom he calls a self-promoting "freak" and a "goober."

lating it. In contrast to the gadget reviews and company news that compose tech coverage on other sites, *Breitbart* focused on incendiary cultural issues such as Gamergate, the controversy over sexism in the video-game industry that involved a loosely organized campaign of harassment against female programmers. Yiannopoulos's specialty became the intentionally offensive opinion piece that invariably provoked a high-traffic response, an editorial style adopted across *Breitbart*. Many of the site's most offensive headlines were his. He was also fluent in alt-right obsessions and iconography, such as the alt-right's mascot, Pepe the Frog.

Yiannopoulos didn't hide behind a keyboard; he also brought performative skills to his job. Like Breitbart himself, he delighted in taking the fight over "political correctness" to enemy turf, often liberal college campuses, where his visits would reliably incite an angry counterreaction that pointed out the hypocrisy of a censorious left supposedly committed to ideals of free speech and open debate.

The purpose of all this incitement, at least in Bannon's mind, was to entice the online legions into the *Breitbart* fold. "I realized Milo could connect with these kids right away," he said. "You can activate that army. They come in through Gamergate or whatever and then get turned onto politics and Trump." In this way, *Breitbart* became an incubator of alt-right political energy. Although Yiannopoulos was most interested in cultivating his own celebrity— Bannon thought he looked like "a gay hooker"—he was more than willing to do his part and make the political connection explicit. "How Donald Trump Can Win: With Guns, Cars, Tech Visas, Ethanol . . . And 4Chan" read the headline of an October 2015 article he wrote.

Trump himself would help cement this alt-right alliance by retweeting images of Pepe the Frog and occasional missives—always inadvertently, his staff insisted—from white nationalist Twitter accounts. Before long, denizens of sites such as 4chan and reddit were coordinating support for Trump's campaign. One aspect of this "support" was flooding the Twitter feeds of prominent journalists, particularly Jewish journalists, with vile anti-Semitic imagery. A study conducted by the Anti-Defamation League found that 2.6 million anti-Semitic tweets, many of them directed at journalists, were sent in the year leading up to the election and that the "aggressors are disproportionately likely to self-identify as Donald Trump supporters, conservatives, or part of the 'alt-right.'"

Sometimes, Bannon's impulse to attack led to egregious errors. The site republished as news a satirical story stating that Paul Krugman, the Nobel laureate and liberal *New York Times* columnist, had filed for bankruptcy (he hadn't). When Obama nominated Loretta Lynch for attorney general, a *Breitbart* reporter assailed her for having worked on Bill Clinton's defense team (it was a different Loretta Lynch). "Truth and veracity weren't his top priority," said Ben Shapiro, a writer for the site who quit in 2016 over frustrations with Bannon. "Narrative truth was his priority rather than factual truth." Bannon basically agreed. When the embarrassed Lynch reporter asked for time off, he refused to allow it, allergic to any hint of concession. "I told him, 'No. In fact, you're going to write a story every day this week.'" Bannon shrugged. "We're honey badgers," he explained. "We don't give a shit."

With backing from the Mercer family, Bannon plotted a global expansion, opening *Breitbart* bureaus in London and Texas. "We look at London and Texas as two fronts in our current cultural and political war," Bannon announced in 2014. "There is a growing global anti-establishment revolt against the permanent political class at home, and the global elites that influence them, which impacts everyone from Lubbock to London."

The type of reporters Bannon liked to hire were hyper-aggressive activist-journalists, whom he thought of as foot soldiers in the war he was waging. To lead his Texas bureau, he chose a former anarchist turned FBI informant. He described a pair of London hires as "real hell fighters in the *Breitbart* tradition." His Washington political editor, Matthew Boyle, was notorious for threatening Capitol Hill press secretaries in both parties with damning headlines about their bosses if they didn't immediately produce whatever information he was seeking.

Perhaps Bannon's most unusual *Breitbart News* reporting team—and one that shaped his thinking about how to go after Hillary Clinton, both before and after he joined the Trump campaign—was a group of beautiful young women whom he proudly referred to as "the Valkyries," after the war goddesses of Norse mythology who decided soldiers' fates in battle. They included Michelle Fields, an ambitious television and print journalist who, before joining *Breitbart*, had won early fame as a conservative YouTube celebrity and later became a Fox News contributor. There was also Alex Swoyer, a blond attorney and former beauty queen who had won the Miss Southwest Florida crown while attending the Ave Maria School of Law in Naples, Florida.

But Bannon's favorite Valkyrie, and his protégé, was Julia Hahn, a whip-smart twenty-five-year-old who was raised in Beverly Hills and studied philosophy at the University of Chicago, where she'd written a thesis examining "the intersection of psychoanalysis and post-Foucauldian philosophical inquiry." Hahn's cherubic visage and impeccably sweet manners belied an intense commitment to

Bannon's brand of populist nationalism and a ferocious pen. Her favorite target was Republican House Speaker Paul Ryan, whose devotion to global free trade and open borders drew her scorching disapproval. Hahn charged Ryan with being a "third-world migration enthusiast" and "double agent" secretly pulling for Clinton. Once, while visiting his Wisconsin district to profile a challenger, someone pointed out Ryan's home, which Hahn immediately noticed was surrounded by a sturdy fence. She leaped out of the car to snap pictures, which later accompanied her classic *Breitbart* article "Paul Ryan Builds Border Fence Around His Mansion, Doesn't Fund Border Fence in Omnibus." Bannon loved it. "When she comes into your life," he bragged, "shit gets fucked up."

As he schemed about how to impugn the Clintons, Bannon kept returning to the former president's sex scandals—a humiliating subject for Hillary Clinton but a dangerous one for Republicans, whose monomaniacal pursuit and impeachment of Bill Clinton was a leading example of the overreach Bannon was keen to avoid. The sudden downfall of Bill Cosby, whose serial predations had come roaring back into the news after the comedian Hannibal Buress brought them up in a show, led Bannon to wonder if the Clintons might not be newly vulnerable as well. Quizzing the Valkyries convinced him that they were. Bannon often used the young women as a kind of in-house focus group of millennial voter sentiment. The Clinton scandals might be old news to his generation, he admitted, "but these girls have never heard most of this stuff." Furthermore, millennials had just eclipsed baby boomers as the largest voting-eligible demographic in America.

By the time Trump joined the presidential race in June 2015, Bannon was fully convinced. "I'm a big believer in generational theory," he said one day, sitting in the dining room of the Breitbart Embassy. "There's a whole generation of people who love the news but were seven or eight years old when this happened and have no earthly idea about the Clinton sex stuff." While it was still too soon to make hay of this issue, a time would come when it would be ripe to be deployed. "I think that has to be concentrated and brought up," he said.

In the meantime, he had other avenues to pursue. While his Mr. Hyde persona ran *Breitbart News*, Bannon's Dr. Jekyll side was already posing a much greater problem for Hillary Clinton.

Tallahassee is about as far as you can get in the United States, geographically and psychically, from the circus of the presidential campaign trail. That's why Bannon chose to locate the Government Accountability Institute there—that, and the fact that Peter Schweizer, its president, had moved down from Washington. "There's nothing to do in Tallahassee, so I get a lot more work done," Schweizer joked to a visitor in the autumn of 2015. GAI is housed in a sleepy cul-de-sac of two-story brick buildings that looks like what you'd get if Scarlett O'Hara designed an office park. The unmarked entrance is framed by palmetto trees and sits beneath a large, second-story veranda with sweeping overhead fans, where the (mostly male) staff gathers in the afternoons to smoke cigars and brainstorm.

Established in 2012 to study crony capitalism and governmental malfeasance, GAI is staffed with lawyers, data scientists, and forensic investigators and has collaborated with such mainstream news outlets as *Newsweek*, *ABC News*, and CBS's *60 Minutes* on stories ranging from insider trading in Congress to credit-card fraud among presidential campaigns. It's a mining operation for political scoops that, for two years, had trained its investigative firepower on the Clintons.

What made *Clinton Cash* so unexpectedly influential is that mainstream news reporters picked up and often advanced Schweizer's many examples of the Clintons' apparent conflicts of interest in accepting money from large donors and foreign governments. ("Practically grotesque," wrote Harvard Law School professor Lawrence Lessig, who briefly sought the Democratic presidential nomination. "On any fair reading, the pattern of behavior that Schweizer has charged is corruption.") Just before the book's release, *The New York Times* ran a front-page story about a Canadian mining magnate, Frank Giustra, who gave tens of millions of dollars to the Clinton Foundation and then flew Bill Clinton to Kazakhstan aboard his private jet to dine with the country's autocratic president, Nursultan Nazarbayev. Giustra subsequently won lucrative uranium-mining rights in the country. The *Times* piece cited Schweizer's still-unpublished book as a source of its reporting, puzzling many readers and prompting a reaction from the paper's ombudswoman, Margaret Sullivan, who grudgingly concluded, while acknowledging that no ethical standards were breached, "I still don't like the way it looked."

The effect on Clinton's popularity was profound: the percentage of Americans who thought she was "untrustworthy" shot up into the 60s. Worse for Clinton was that the Democratic primary offered an attractive alternative. Bernie Sanders was an anti–Wall Street, good-government populist whose liberal purity put Clinton's ethical shortcomings into sharp relief.

For Bannon, the *Clinton Cash* uproar validated his personal theory about how conservatives had overreached the last time a Clinton was in the White House and what they should do differently. "Back then," he says, "they couldn't take down Bill because they didn't do that much real reporting, they couldn't get the mainstream guys interested, and they were always gunning for impeachment no matter what. People got anesthetized to outrage." What news conservatives did produce about the Clintons in the 1990s, such as David Brock's Troopergate investigation on Paula Jones in *The American Spectator*, was often tainted in the eyes of mainstream editors by its explicit partisan association. Now Bannon had found a "business partner" in the same media outlets conservatives had long despised. His intuition about the reporters on the investigative desks of major newspapers was also correct: they weren't the liberal ideologues of conservative fever dreams but kindred souls who could be recruited into his larger enterprise.

David Brock himself, who renounced conservatism and became a key liberal strategist, fund-raiser, and Clinton ally, was one of the few Democrats in 2015 who saw clearly the threat that the emerging *Clinton Cash* narrative posed to Hillary Clinton. What conservatives learned in the nineties, Brock said, was that "your operation isn't going to succeed if you don't cross the barrier into the mainstream." Back then, conservative reporting had to undergo an elaborate laundering process to influence U.S. politics. Reporters such as Brock would publish in small magazines and websites, then try to plant their story in the British tabloids and hope that a right-leaning U.S. outlet like the *New York Post* or the *Drudge Report* picked it up. If it generated enough heat, only then would it break through to a mainstream paper.

"It seems to me," Brock warned of Bannon and Schweizer, "what they were able to do in this deal with the *Times* is the same strategy, but more sophisticated and potentially more effective and damaging because of the reputation of the *Times*. If you were trying to create doubt and qualms about Hillary Clinton among progressives, the *Times* is the place to do it." He paused. "Looking at it from their point of view, the *Times* is the perfect host body for the virus."

Schweizer had begun his career as a researcher at the conservative Hoover Institution, digging through Soviet archives to learn how the Russians viewed Ronald Reagan during the Cold War. In 2004 he coauthored a well-regarded history of the Bush family, *The Bushes: Portrait of a Dynasty*, that drew on interviews with many of its members, including Jeb Bush. But Schweizer grew disillusioned with Washington and became radicalized against what he perceived to be a bipartisan culture of corruption. "To me, Washington, D.C., is a little bit like professional wrestling," he said. "When I was growing up in Seattle, I'd turn on Channel 13, the public-access station, and watch wrestling. At first I thought, *Man, these guys hate each other because they're beating the crap out of each other.* But I eventually realized they're actually business partners. Half the people watching know that, the other people don't know that. But what matters is that they create the spectacle. There's a lot in D.C. that's like professional wrestling. It's done for show, but ultimately there's a business partnership between the combatants."

Schweizer, fifty, is friendly, sandy-haired, and a little pudgy, a neighborly sort you'd meet at a barbecue and take an instant liking to. (Bannon nurtured this regular-Joe appeal by forbidding him from wearing a necktie when he's on television.) Bannon and Schweizer followed two principles when conceiving *Clinton Cash*. First, it would avoid nutty conspiracy theories. "We have a mantra," said Bannon. "'Facts get shares; opinions get shrugs.'" Second, they would heed the lesson Bannon learned at Goldman: specialize. Hillary Clinton's story, they decided, was too sprawling and familiar to tackle in its entirety. So they focused only on the past decade, her least familiar period, and especially on the hundreds of millions of dollars flowing into the Clinton Foundation. Bannon called this approach "periodicity."

As with so many of the Clintons' troubles, the couple's own behavior provided copious material for GAI's investigators. When Clinton became secretary of state, the foundation signed an agreement with the Obama White House to disclose all of its contributors. It didn't follow through. So GAI researchers combed tax filings, flight logs, and foreign-government documents to turn up what the Clinton Foundation had withheld. Their most effective method was mining the so-called Deep Web, the 97 percent or so of information on the Internet that isn't indexed for search engines such as Google and therefore is difficult to find.

"Welcome to the Matrix," said Tony,* GAI's head data scientist, as he mapped out the Deep Web on a whiteboard for a visitor. A presentation on the hidden recesses of the Web followed. "The Deep Web," he explained, "consists of a lot of useless or depreciated information, stuff in foreign languages, and so on. But a whole bunch of it is very useful, if you can find it." Tony specialized in finding the good stuff, which he did by writing software protocols that spider through the Deep Web. Because this requires heavy computing power, GAI struck a deal to use the services of a large European provider during off-peak hours. "We've got $1.3 billion of equipment I'm using at almost full capacity," he said. This effort yielded a slew of unreported foundation donors who appear to have

---

*We agreed I wouldn't publish his last name.

benefited financially from their relationship with the Clintons, including the uranium mining executives cited by *The New York Times* (who showed up on an unindexed Canadian government website). These donations illustrated a pattern of commingling private money and government policy that disturbed even many Democrats.

Clinton Cash caused a stir not only because of these revelations but also because of how they arrived. GAI is set up more like a Hollywood movie studio than a think tank. The creative mind through which all its research flows and is disseminated belongs to a beaming young Floridian named Wynton Hall, a celebrity ghostwriter who's penned eighteen books, six of them *New York Times* bestsellers, including Trump's 2011 book, *Time to Get Tough: Making America #1 Again.* Hall's job is to transform dry think-tank research into vivid, viral-ready political dramas that can be unleashed on a set schedule, like summer blockbusters. "We work very long and hard to build a narrative, storyboarding it out months in advance," Hall said. "We're not going public until we have something so tantalizing that any editor at a serious publication would be an idiot to pass it up and give a competitor the scoop."

To this end, Hall peppered his colleagues with slogans so familiar around the office that they became known by their acronyms. "ABBN—Always be breaking news" was one. Another slogan was "Depth beats speed." Time-strapped reporters squeezed for copy would gratefully accept original, fact-based research because most of what they're inundated with from PR flacks is garbage. "The modern economics of the newsroom don't support big investigative reporting staffs," said Bannon. "You wouldn't get a Watergate, a Pentagon Papers today, because nobody can afford to let a reporter spend seven months on a story. We can. We're working as a support function."

GAI does this because Bannon decided it's the secret to how

conservatives can hack the mainstream media. Hall has distilled this, too, into a slogan: "Anchor left, pivot right." It means that "weaponizing" a story onto the front page of *The New York Times* ("the left") is infinitely more valuable than publishing it on *Breitbart* ("the right") because the *Times* reaches millions of readers inclined to vote Democratic. This approach prompted a wholesale change in how Bannon and his confederates think about elite media. "We don't look at the mainstream media as enemies, because we don't want our work to be trapped in the conservative ecosystem," said Hall. "We live and die by the media. Every time we're launching a book, I'll build a battle map that literally breaks down by category every headline we're going to place, every op-ed Peter's going to publish. . . . Getting our message embedded in mainstream outlets is what gets us the biggest blast radius."

Once that work has permeated the mainstream—once it's found "a host body," in David Brock's phrase—then comes the "pivot." Heroes and villains emerge and become grist for a juicy *Breitbart News* narrative. The story takes on a life of its own. Hillary Clinton became the biggest narrative of all, even though none of the GAI reporting went directly to *Breitbart*. It didn't have to. "With *Clinton Cash*, we never really broke a story," said Bannon, "but you go to *Breitbart*, and we've got twenty things, we're linking to everybody else's stuff, we're aggregating, we'll pull stuff from the left. It's a rolling phenomenon. Huge traffic. Everybody's invested."

As devious as this plot was, it could never have succeeded to the degree that it did had Clinton not abetted it with such vigor. That summer, she failed to emerge as the overwhelming front-runner everyone had expected, weighed down by stories on Clinton

Foundation "buckraking" and the revelation that she had kept a private e-mail server as secretary of state and destroyed much of her correspondence. She also refused to release transcripts of highly paid speeches she'd delivered to Goldman Sachs and other Wall Street firms. In August, e-mails surfaced showing that Bill Clinton, through the foundation, had sought State Department permission to accept speaking fees in repressive countries such as North Korea and the Republic of the Congo. A poll the same day found that the word voters associated most with his wife was "liar."

Clinton's tone-deaf response to the steady drip of revelations only deepened their impact because it conveyed a sense of entitlement that was off-putting even to many Democrats. Confronted over her failure to disclose foreign donors, Clinton and her aides stonewalled, or scolded reporters for not focusing instead on the foundation's good works, or claimed it didn't matter. When *The Boston Globe* discovered that a local branch of the Clinton Foundation had "uniformly bypassed" Clinton's agreement with the White House to disclose foreign donors, a spokeswoman told the paper that they "deemed it unnecessary" to reveal those names, and refused.

Rehearsed in the rigors of right-wing attacks, Clinton's aides went after the source of so many of them: Peter Schweizer's book. They tried to discredit *Clinton Cash* as they had successfully done to numerous anti-Clinton polemics in the 1990s. But their efforts mostly failed because Schweizer's book was not filled with outlandish rumors and blind quotes, as the earlier books had been; it contained documentable facts that reporters could check out for themselves. To Bannon's delight, many did—and decided to pursue them further. "We've got the fifteen best investigative reporters at the fifteen best newspapers in the country all chasing after Hillary Clinton," he exulted that summer.

To the staff of GAI, Clinton looked like someone trapped in quicksand, whose flailing only worsened her plight. "Here we are, sitting here in flip-flops in Tallahassee," said Hall, "and this massive Clinton operation is coming at our little tiny nonprofit like we're some huge entity." He laughed. "We're up on the balcony smoking cigars and writing press releases, and their heads are exploding. It's kind of surreal."

Even amid Clinton's struggles, however, Democrats were confident she would ultimately prevail. Some were even willing to concede that Bannon and his ilk were more effective than the conservatives who targeted Bill Clinton twenty-five years earlier. "They've adapted into a higher species," said Chris Lehane, a Clinton White House staffer and hardened veteran of the partisan wars of the nineties. "But these guys always blow themselves up in the end."

Bannon disagreed, and, as always, had a historical analogy to explain why. What he was really pursuing was something like the old Marxist dialectical concept of "heightening the contradictions," only rather than foment revolution among the proletariat, he was trying to disillusion Clinton's natural base of support. Bernie Sanders's unexpected strength suggested to him that it was working. He was sure that Sanders's rise was destined to end in crashing disappointment. Having thrilled to his populist purity, his supporters would never reconcile themselves to Clinton, because the donors featured in *Clinton Cash* violated just about every ideal liberals hold dear. "You look at what they've done in the Colombian rain forest, look at the arms merchants, the war lords, the human trafficking— if you take anything that the left professes to be a cornerstone value, the Clintons have basically played them for fools," Bannon said. "They've enriched themselves while playing up the worst cast of characters in the world. Bill Clinton is not going around the world with Bill Gates, or the head of GE. By and large it's guys who need something and can't get access to the inner sanctums of world power on their own. It's Third World reputation laundering."

In the meantime, a new narrative was emerging—Bannon could see it in the *Breitbart* traffic numbers. Donald Trump had a bigger megaphone than anyone in politics, even Clinton, and he was showing an unparalleled ability to dictate media coverage that Bannon could only marvel at. What he wanted the media to cover, constantly and at length, was only one thing: Donald Trump.

EIGHT

"THE TRAFFIC IS
ABSOLUTELY FILTHY!"

Trump is a beast!" Bannon was cackling, practically giddy over what he had just witnessed. He still couldn't believe it. It was June 16, 2015. Trump had just glided down the Trump Tower escalator with Melania in tow, announced his entry into the presidential race—and then proceeded to unload a mind-bending, mostly improvised, forty-five-minute rant during which he casually referred to Mexican immigrants as "rapists" and criminals.

"When Mexico sends its people, they're not sending their best," Trump said, standing at a lectern and pointing to members of the audience. "They're not sending you. They're not sending you. They're sending people that have lots of problems, and they're bringing those problems with us. They're bringing drugs. They're bringing crime. They're rapists. And some, I assume, are good people."

To Republican Party leaders, Trump's performance was a horror show, the very antithesis of the message they yearned to project of a more welcoming, inclusive GOP than the one Mitt Romney had

led to defeat in 2012. After that loss, RNC chairman Reince Priebus had commissioned a rigorous postmortem of all that had gone
wrong and what the party could do to fix it. The report, which became known as the "Republican autopsy," concluded that the GOP
was committing demographic suicide by insulting and antagonizing
the fast-growing population of Hispanic voters, who didn't take
kindly to Romney's suggestion that illegal immigrants would resort
to "self-deportation" if only their lives were made unpleasant enough.
The autopsy's urgent recommendation was to reverse this approach—
and fast: "If Hispanic Americans perceive that a GOP nominee
or candidate does not want them in the United States (i.e., self-
deportation), they will not pay attention to our next sentence." It
continued: "We must embrace and champion comprehensive immigration reform. If we do not, our Party's appeal will continue to
shrink to its core constituencies only."

News of Trump's announcement speech instantly went viral,
rocketing across cable television and Twitter. But while party leaders winced, Trump's small coterie of advisers (with the exception of
his daughter, Ivanka) wasn't panicking over the "rapists" charge, as
any normal campaign would have, but was in fact relieved and excited that his presidential announcement had broken through. A
few days earlier, Trump and some aides had offered the exclusive
story of his upcoming entrance into the race to Maggie Haberman,
a star reporter at *The New York Times*—and had been rebuffed.
Trump's long history of self-promotional flirtations with running
had left most insiders skeptical that he would ever follow through.
Fearing that Trump might be ignored, his aides had pushed back his
announcement date. "We were originally trying to do it on June
fourteenth, which happens to be Flag Day and Mr. Trump's birthday," said Corey Lewandowski, his first campaign manager. "But it

fell on a Sunday, and we knew that we wanted to announce on a Tuesday or a Wednesday to get as much attention as we could," ideally enough to carry through into the Sunday shows.

Trump's attacks on Mexican immigrants and his vow to "build a great wall" at the U.S.–Mexico border ensured that a lack of attention was one problem Trump would not have to confront—not then, not ever. Leaving nothing to chance, he invited *Breitbart News'* Matthew Boyle up to his twenty-sixth-floor office immediately following his announcement for an exclusive interview and some extra anti-immigrant, anti-establishment jawboning, just to ensure that the Republican base heard his message loud and clear. They heard it, and they loved it. Bannon, who was ecstatic that Trump had not softened his message now that he was truly in the race, splashed the news across *Breitbart*. Then he got busy arranging a surreal visit Trump would make to the U.S.–Mexico border a few weeks hence, one that would further affix his anti-immigrant identity at the center of his presidential campaign.

Although it wasn't included in the sound bites broadcast on the evening news, Trump, just after he delivered his notorious "rapists" line, had given a citation for the charge. "I speak to border guards," he said, "and they tell us what we're getting." Trump really did do this, and it was an early example of the Trump-Bannon-*Breitbart* nexus that operated continually throughout the campaign, in varying degrees of public acknowledgment. While Trump was unquestionably his own chief strategist (and often a shrewd one), he had a constant thirst for input, whether it came in the form of cable-news punditry, phone calls with friends, or visits with politically sympathetic groups like the border guards.

One reason Bannon decided to establish a Texas bureau was to help *Breitbart* develop sources among the Immigration and Customs Enforcement agents and border patrol officers stationed at the U.S.–Mexico border. Many of them held fiercely restrictionist views on immigration that mirrored those of *Breitbart*'s editors and left the agents increasingly at odds with the pro-reform sentiment building among the leaders in both parties. By letting it be known that *Breitbart* was, as Bannon put it, "a safe pair of hands," the site became the go-to destination for border agents seeking a sympathetic media outlet in which to express their views or vent about immigration matters that they believed the mainstream media was purposely suppressing. This is how *Breitbart* became one of the first outlets to publicize the child migrant crisis at the U.S.–Mexico border in the summer of 2014: border agents took snapshots of overcrowded detention facilities and provided them to *Breitbart*, whose alarmist stories ("Border Open for Criminals as Agents Forced to Babysit Illegals") were amplified by the *Drudge Report* and spread to dozens of mainstream outlets.

In the weeks following Trump's announcement, Bannon arranged to have Local 2455, the Border Patrol Union in Laredo, Texas, invite Trump to the border for a visit on July 23. (The union's Laredo spokesman was a regular guest on Bannon's radio show.) Under pressure from the national union, Local 2455 was forced at the last minute to rescind the invitation. But Trump came anyway, trailing a massive press contingent—and was clearly welcomed by the local border agents.*

---

*The National Border Patrol Council, which represents 16,500 of the roughly 21,000 agents who work for the agency, later endorsed Trump—the first time the union had taken sides in a presidential race. The National Immigration and Customs Enforcement Council, which represents 7,600 ICE agents and employees, also endorsed Trump. This, too, was its first presidential endorsement.

From the moment the "Trump"-emblazoned Boeing 757-200 airliner touched down in Laredo, Trump's visit was sheer pandemonium. He had spent the days leading up to the trip bizarrely insisting that he was putting himself in grave danger—even though FBI statistics showed that Laredo was the nineteenth-safest city in the country. Trump didn't exactly dress for combat. He arrived at the Laredo airport in a gold-buttoned navy blazer, khakis, and white golf shoes, with a matching white "Make American Great Again" cap, and was besieged by more than a hundred reporters and dozens of camera crews. Still, he kept up the ruse. "People are saying, 'Oh, it's so dangerous what you're doing, Mr. Trump, it's so dangerous!'" a straight-faced Trump told the assembled press. "I have to do it. We're showing something."

Reporters piled into two charter buses furnished by Trump and followed his police-escorted motorcade to the World Trade Bridge, where eighteen-wheelers were lined up waiting to cross the border. In a brief press conference, Trump, always the ringmaster, attacked the anti-immigration bona fides of Texas governor Rick Perry, boasted about his own poll numbers, insisted that anti-Trump protesters along the highway "were all in favor of Trump," and reiterated his vow to build a wall and "stop the illegals." "I'll bring the jobs back," he declared. "And, you know, the Hispanics are going to get those jobs, and they're going to love Trump." He corrected himself: "They already do." And with that, Trump zipped back to the airport and went home to New York, having spent all of three hours on the ground.

The trip's purpose was pure theater. It was intended to show that Trump meant what he'd said and was willing to go to the border and say it there, too, without equivocation. It was also Trump's way of thumbing his nose at critics of his "rapists" comment, such as

Jeb Bush (who called it "extraordinarily ugly"), even as he denied Bush political oxygen by dominating presidential campaign coverage. In fact, Bush's support was already crumbling under the weight of Trump's steady, emasculating ("low energy") assaults. Three days before the Laredo visit, Trump had surged past Bush to take a commanding lead in the *Washington Post*–ABC News poll of Republican voters. He would never relinquish it.

It took a certain moxie to dream up stunts like the border visit. Trump loved moxie. And he liked the ideas he was getting from Bannon, especially the dropped-jaw reaction they produced on cable news. Although Trump didn't dwell on policy details, Bannon pitched in there, too. Trump was coming under fire because his campaign hadn't produced a single policy paper. So Bannon arranged for Nunberg and Ann Coulter, the conservative pundit, to quickly produce a white paper on Trump's immigration policies. (When the campaign released it, Coulter, without disclosing her role, tweeted that it was "the greatest political document since the Magna Carta.")

"Throughout the campaign—long before Steve actually joined the campaign—he was active through *Breitbart*, but also by providing very important and unsolicited advice," said Lewandowski. "He would call Mr. Trump, or he would call me, and say, 'Hey, here's a recommendation.' We talked to Steve a lot. I think for Mr. Trump, authenticity is the most important thing. Steve's authentic. His success financially gave him the freedom to not have to do things he doesn't want to do—not shave, not wear a tie. That's unheard-of in the world of Trump. But he's achieved a remarkable amount of personal success, and that matters a lot to Trump."

It helped, too, that Bannon's success included Hollywood and a background in entertainment. On *The Apprentice*, Trump rarely followed a script, instead taking a concept and improvising to fill the role. In politics, as in television, Trump could instantly spot a good idea, and then, through some combination of intuition and bravado, improvise with consistently successful results. As the world was learning, television and politics were not so different.

By August, Trump sat comfortably atop every major Republican presidential poll. The Laredo trip and, more broadly, his refusal to apologize for any transgression, no matter how crass or offensive, lit up a segment of the Republican base that had been dormant or uncommitted. Trump's celebrity and name ID had always gotten him a respectable percentage in the polls, usually somewhere in the low teens. Now he shot up into the mid to high twenties, which, in a crowded field of seventeen candidates, was enough to put him solidly in the lead. Even so, the party establishment took solace in the belief that Trump was heading for an inevitable fall. The first GOP debate, sponsored by Fox News, loomed on August 6 in Cleveland.

Within Fox, Trump was fast emerging as a polarizing figure. He had long been a friend of the network and cherished his weekly Monday call-in segment on *Fox & Friends*, but his entrance into the race and surprising strength in the Republican field were causing tension. Fox anchors, like other media figures, initially treated his candidacy with arched-eyebrow amusement. But as Trump pulled ahead of the field, that began to change. Murdoch and Ailes, both champions of immigration reform, had had a soft spot for Marco Rubio ever since the dynamic young Florida senator had pitched them on the merits of his Gang of Eight reform bill over a private dinner in 2013 in the executive dining room of News Corporation's Manhattan headquarters. In response, the network curbed its criticism of the reform plan.

But others at Fox News, Sean Hannity foremost among them, were ardent Trump backers with a direct line to Bannon (whose influence some Fox hosts knew about and didn't like. "Bannon is human garbage," one of them fumed). Lurking beneath it all was a worry that Trump's antics might tarnish the Republican brand and thereby ease Hillary Clinton's path to the White House.

Amid this uneasiness and suspicion, Megyn Kelly, who was set to co-moderate the Cleveland debate, was something of a wild card. A former defense attorney and political independent, Kelly was a rising star at Fox News, with pretensions to being a serious journalist. In May, Trump had appeared on her prime-time show, *The Kelly File*, without incident. But a week before the debate, Trump's network grew alarmed at Kelly's eagerness to tout a story published in *The Daily Beast* recounting accusations Trump's ex-wife Ivana made in a divorce deposition that he had raped her in 1989. Over two nights, Kelly did multiple segments on the story that included her sharp criticism of Trump's personal attorney, Michael Cohen, who had wrongly claimed, "You cannot rape your spouse. And there's very clear case law," and then made vague but ominous threats to *The Daily Beast* reporter.

Trump was scheduled to appear on *The Kelly File* three days before the debate, but lost his nerve and canceled at the last minute. Kelly had been hammering him all week, he complained to a friend, and he was certain she was out to get him.

It turned out he was right: Trump's toughest opponents in Cleveland were not his fellow candidates but the Fox News moderators, who went right after him—none with more gusto than Kelly.

As soon as the lights went up, she went straight for the jugular. "You've called women you don't like 'fat pigs,' 'dogs,' 'slobs,' and 'disgusting animals,'" she admonished him. "Does that sound to you like the temperament of a man we should elect as president?"

Trump saw the attack coming and cut her off. "Only Rosie O'Donnell," he barked.

"No, it wasn't," Kelly replied. "Your Twitter account—"

The audience interrupted with applause for Trump.

"Thank you," he replied.

"For the record, it was well beyond Rosie O'Donnell—"

"Yes, I'm sure it was."

"Your Twitter account has several disparaging comments about women's looks," Kelly continued. "You once told a contestant on *Celebrity Apprentice* it would be a pretty picture to see her on her knees. Does that sound to you like the temperament of a man we should elect as president? And how will you answer the charge from Hillary Clinton, who is likely to be the Democratic nominee, that you are part of the war on women?"

"The big problem this country has is being *politically correct*," Trump practically shouted, invoking conservatives' favorite term of disdain. "I've been challenged by so many people, and I don't frankly have time for total political correctness—and to be honest with you this country doesn't have time either."

The crowd roared again.

Trump continued hurling insults, going after O'Donnell, political reporters, Bowe Bergdahl, China, Mexico, Japan, money lenders, and just about everyone in Washington. "Our leaders are stupid," he declared. "Our politicians are stupid." He soon worked around to his greatest applause line. "We need to build a wall, and it has to be built quickly," he said. "We need to keep illegals out."

Although Kelly was correct in every citation, the audience in the hall was plainly with Trump, cheering and oohing at each thrilling provocation, as if they were ringside at a prizefight. The evening proved to be pivotal for Trump. Going in, he'd never had to debate his opponents, nor submit to steady, hostile questioning by seasoned journalists. Because Trump didn't even feign interest in the policy details that are the ammunition of most candidate debates, the broad expectation was that he was walking into a turkey shoot.

Yet not only was Trump unrattled, but his bravado and aggression set the tone for the debate. Every candidate strained to match his energy. Emulating Trump's swagger, New Jersey governor Chris Christie tore into Kentucky senator Rand Paul. But no one except Paul mustered the courage to directly attack Trump, and Paul may have regretted it, as Trump dispatched him with a devastating put-down ("You're having a hard time tonight") that was deadly because it was true. Consciously or otherwise, several candidates echoed Trump's points and some even genuflected before the unlikely front-runner. "Donald Trump is hitting a nerve in this country," Ohio governor John Kasich said at one point. "Mr. Trump is touching a nerve because people want to see a wall being built."

Going into the debate, the big battle was supposed to be between Trump and Jeb Bush. But Trump sensed that his real opponent was Fox News, and throughout the evening, he and his inquisitors battled back and forth like gladiators. Kelly did manage to inflict some wounds. Rattling off the liberal positions Trump had once held, she stopped him cold by asking: "When did you actually become a Republican?" Trump's bluster momentarily escaped him. "I've evolved on many issues over the years, and do you know who else has? Ronald Reagan," he answered feebly. "Very much evolved."

But Trump wasn't finished—not even when the moderators were

done. After the debate, he inaugurated what was soon to become a tradition of walking off the stage and directly to the television cameras to critique the event he'd just participated in. He didn't let up. The next evening, Trump lit into the Fox News moderators and complained about Kelly in particular. To CNN's Don Lemon, he said, "You could see there was blood coming out of her eyes, blood coming out of her wherever."

A media storm quickly ensued over whether Trump was suggesting that Kelly had gone after him unfairly because she was menstruating. But Trump's anger at Fox News and Kelly also set off another storm that didn't fully register until the next day—yet it opened up an enduring divide in the Republican Party that would carry through the election. The divide was between mainstream Republicans and those primarily loyal to Trump, and centered on whether Fox was subjecting Trump to ordinary journalistic inquiry or attacking him with the intention of destroying him to make way for a more acceptable candidate. Among other things, this divide split Fox News and *Breitbart*.

Within minutes of the debate's end, even as Trump was still nursing his grievances on live television, reporters began to realize that the revelations of his past behavior, so bluntly excavated by Kelly, had indeed caused an intense reaction among Republican voters—not against Trump, but against Fox News. One method reporters use to gauge voter sentiment is to arrange ahead of time to speak with supporters of a candidate as soon as a debate concludes. Among Trump supporters, the sense of betrayal was acute. "I had more emotion about Fox News tonight than I did about Donald Trump," said Janet Roberts, sixty-nine, a nurse in Bellville, Ohio, who was backing Trump. "Those questions were not professional questions. They were bullying. They were set up to purposely make them all look bad. Our country is a mess, and I feel like the debate was an example of that. I'm still with Trump."

Bannon and the *Breitbart* editors had the same reaction and immediately turned on Megyn Kelly, with a fusillade of negative articles. She became the newest *Breitbart* narrative: the back-stabbing, self-promoting betrayer-of-the-cause. And *Breitbart* became the locus of pro-Trump, anti-Fox conservative anger. Between Thursday night, when the debate took place, and Sunday evening, *Breitbart* published twenty-five stories on Kelly, and the site's editor in chief, Alex Marlow, went on CNN to accuse Fox News of "trying to take out Donald Trump" and staging "a gotcha debate."

The intensity of Republican anger stunned Fox News executives. The debate had drawn a record 24 million viewers. Now many of them were apoplectic at the network's top talent. "In the beginning, virtually 100 percent of the emails were against Megyn Kelly," a Fox source told *New York*'s Gabriel Sherman. "Roger was not happy. Most of the Fox viewers were taking Trump's side." Word spread through the building that Kelly was furious and had personally complained to Ailes. By Sunday, the attacks against her showed no sign of letting up, as other conservative opinion makers, such as radio host Mark Levin, agreed that her questions to Trump had been "unfair."

In a panic, Ailes called Bannon and begged him to call off the attacks.

"Steve, this isn't fair, and it's killing us," Ailes said. "You have to stop it."

"Fuck that, that was outrageous what she did!" Bannon retorted. "She pulled every trick out of the leftist playbook."

"You've gotta knock this crap off, Steve."

"Not until she backs off Trump—she's still going after him on her show."

"She's the star of this network! Cut it out!"

The call ended without resolution. Bannon and Ailes would not speak again for almost a year.

Kelly indeed refused to back down, and mocked Trump during a weekend Fox News appearance by posing a rhetorical question: "If you can't get past me, how are you going to handle Vladimir Putin?" On Monday's *Kelly File*, she addressed the controversy in a direct-to-camera statement. "Mr. Trump is an interesting man who has captured the attention of the electorate—that's why he's leading in the polls," she said. "Trump, who is the front-runner, will not apologize. And I certainly will not apologize for doing good journalism."

But what irritated Bannon even more was the sudden outpouring of support Kelly was receiving from people whom he considered sworn enemies of the conservative cause: Joe Scarborough and Mika Brzezinski of MSNBC's *Morning Joe*, the "whole fucking cast" of CNN, and—most gallingly—Hillary Clinton, who he felt never met a gender controversy she wouldn't exploit for political gain.

The next day, in a fit of pique, Bannon and Marlow composed a point-by-point indictment of Kelly's alleged transgressions and published it on *Breitbart*: "The Arrogance of Power: Megyn Kelly's 'Good Journalism.'" While it was an unvarnished depiction of *Breitbart* editorial sentiment, the piece served a double purpose: it kept the fight going. As Bannon confessed to an associate, "The [Web] traffic is absolutely filthy!"

The blowback against Kelly and Fox News kept mounting.

Trump was livid. Over the weekend, he had called Hannity and told him he was boycotting Fox. Fearful of the damage Trump could do to the Fox brand, Ailes relented and called him to apologize—a concession Trump tweeted out: "Roger Ailes just called. He is a great guy & assures me that 'Trump' will be treated fairly on @FoxNews. His word is always good!"

Bannon, however, remained a problem. *Breitbart* wasn't relenting. In fact, its attacks on Kelly were growing more personal. "Flashback: Megyn Kelly Discusses Her Husband's Penis and Her Breasts on Howard Stern," read a *Breitbart* headline on the one-week anniversary of the debate. Not knowing what else to do, Ailes dispatched his personal lawyer, Peter Johnson, Jr., to the Breitbart Embassy in Washington, D.C., to deliver a personal message to Bannon to end the war on Kelly.

Bannon loathed Johnson, whom he referred to privately as "that nebbishy, goofball lawyer on *Fox & Friends*"—Johnson had leveraged his proximity to Ailes to become a Fox News pundit. When he arrived at the Embassy, Johnson got straight to the point: if Bannon didn't stop immediately, he would never again appear on Fox News.

"You've got a very strong relationship with Roger," Johnson warned. "You've gotta stop these attacks on Megyn. She's the star. And if you don't stop, there are going to be consequences."

Bannon was incensed at the threat.

"She's pure evil," he told Johnson. "And she will turn on him one day. We're going full-bore. We're not going to stop. I'm gonna unchain the dogs."

The conversation was brief and unpleasant, and it ended with a cinematic flourish.

"I want you to go back to New York and quote me to Roger," Bannon said. "'Go fuck yourself.'"

Even as it captivated the public's attention, Trump's presidential campaign often seemed to exist as a thing apart from the real world of politics that only perpetuated itself through a willful collective suspension of disbelief. For all Trump's success in the polls and debates, the prevailing assumption in Washington was that voters would come to their senses before the first ballots were cast, and this strange moment in American politics would pass. Perhaps because Trump's insurgency had all the elements of a gripping reality-TV show, and he himself was *sui generis,* political analysts tended not to connect the Trump phenomenon to other developments occurring at the same time.

But signs were emerging everywhere that they should. In September, the rising populist tide that was about to wash away the GOP presidential field first swept another major Republican figure out of his job. For the better part of three years, House Speaker John Boehner had struggled to contain a growing mutiny among his hard-right flank. Twice before, its members had launched rebellions to topple Boehner and failed. But by the fall of 2015, driven by the same metastasizing energy fueling Trump's campaign, their influence had grown more substantial.

For House Republicans, building an anti-establishment identity was becoming so important that membership in the conservative Republican Study Committee, which denoted one's independence from party leadership, grew to encompass a majority of the caucus. This irked the most conservative members because it muddied the distinction they prized. So in early 2015, a few dozen broke off to form a new group, the House Freedom Caucus, that situated itself even further to the right. The group's chairman, Representative Jim

Jordan of Ohio, said the Freedom Caucus would be a "smaller, more cohesive, more agile, and more active" conservative group—"active" meaning "oppositional." Other Republicans resented the HFC's challenge. "They're not legislators, they're just assholes," complained one GOP aide. "The craziest of the crazy." Yet the HFC's strident refusal to accept anything less than total victory—even under a Democratic president—set a standard that was amplified across the conservative universe by *Breitbart News* and talk radio.

Over the summer, Mark Meadows, a North Carolina representative and founding member of the HFC, filed a motion that would trigger what amounted to a vote of no confidence in Boehner. It was a move that expressed the profound anger and frustration that had been building up in the party since at least the Tea Party wave of 2009. Republican leaders had repeatedly promised voters that if handed power they would unwind the major Obama achievements, from the Affordable Care Act to the Dodd-Frank financial reforms. And although they had gone so far as to shut down the government in 2013 in a failed bid to defund Obamacare, Republicans had controlled the House for almost five years and Obama's programs remained intact. Republican voters had cynically been promised fast, easy solutions—so when Boehner couldn't deliver, they were primed to chalk it up to betrayal.

As the Summer of Trump carried into the fall, and Republican fascination with the norm-smashing front-runner kept growing, taking down a major party leader came to seem like a measure of the new populist strength. On September 5, *Breitbart* took aim with a story titled "Behind the Scenes with John Boehner's Worst Nightmare: Mark Meadows Launches Mission to Fix Broken Congress." At the same time, Trump was telling the country how easy it would be to strike deals, if only voters would choose the right leaders. "We are led by very, very stupid people," Trump declared at a September 9 rally on Capitol Hill. But it didn't have to be that way. "We will have so much winning if I get elected," he vowed, "that you may get bored with the winning."

Caught between the pincers of *Breitbart* and Trump, Boehner had nowhere to go. On September 23, a Fox News poll showed that 60 percent of Republicans felt "betrayed" by their own party's leaders. Small wonder. The next day, Boehner announced his retirement.

The seismic news from Congress was enough to break through the wall-to-wall coverage of Trump and the presidential campaign. And the lesson it reinforced was the same one Trump was shouting from the campaign trail: if you don't like your party's leaders, you can get rid of them and install someone else.

NINE

"HONEST POPULISM"

Trump's fixation with Fox News was a powerful force throughout the campaign and the psychology of his relationship with Rupert Murdoch almost filial. He often told intimates of how Murdoch, whose approval he craved, had once humiliated him. As Trump was preparing to launch his campaign, recalled one person to whom Trump told the story, his daughter Ivanka arranged a lunch with Murdoch to share the news. "Rupert had never had any interest in me at all," Trump told this person. "He thinks real estate guys who made a bunch of money are a dime a dozen."

Soon after the three of them were seated and the waiter brought their soup, Ivanka spoke up: "My father has something big to tell you."

"What's that?" Murdoch said.

"He's going to run for president."

"He's not running for president," Murdoch replied, without looking up from his soup.

"No, he is!" she insisted.

Murdoch changed the subject.

Trump nursed the slight for months, seething at the indignity. "He didn't even look up from his soup!" he'd complain. The insult weighed heavily on him, and it made Fox News a perennially fraught subject.

Trump's willingness to flout any norm was a powerful source of his appeal. But sometimes it worked against him. Just before the Iowa caucuses, where Trump would at last subject himself to actual voters, he reared up and pulled a stunt that backfired.

Soon after the August détente between Trump and Ailes, Trump's feud with Fox News flared up again, driven by the issue he was most passionate about: his poll numbers. Throughout the fall, Trump took to Twitter to lambaste his nemesis, Megyn Kelly, for the alleged sin of highlighting polls that disfavored him while ignoring those in which he fared well. "Isn't it terrible that @megynkelly used a poll not used before (I.B.D.) when I was down, but refuses to use it now when I am up?" Trump tweeted in November. He kept after her, calling her "dopey @megynkelly" and "highly overrated and crazy" and twice retweeting others who called her a "bimbo."

Whether Trump's animus toward Kelly was emotional or strategic wasn't clear. Either way, she loomed as a problem. Fox News was hosting a debate in Des Moines, four days before the February 1 Iowa caucuses, and Kelly was set to reprise her role as moderator. Trump was determined to assert his primacy and force her off the stage. A week beforehand, he tweeted: "Based on @MegynKelly's conflict of interest and bias she should not be allowed to be a moderator of the next debate." But Ailes knew a showdown would be ratings gold and stood firm. Trump, unwilling to submit, announced he would boycott the debate and hold a competing event to raise money for veterans. "Let's see how much money Fox is going to make on the debate without me, okay?" he said.

Trump's confidence was aided by polls such as the Bloomberg Politics–*Des Moines Register* Iowa Poll, a legendary survey of support conducted by J. Ann Selzer, a longtime Iowa pollster widely regarded as the state's finest. By tradition, the political world awaited Selzer's final poll with bated breath, and when it arrived on January 30, it showed that Trump had overtaken Ted Cruz to seize a commanding 5-point lead, 28 percent to 23 percent. "Trump is leading with both the inner core of the caucus universe and the fringe—that's what any candidate would want," Selzer said.

Yet on caucus night, amid a record turnout, Cruz won in a huge upset. Powered by Iowa's large community of evangelical Christians, Cruz won 28 percent of the vote, Trump 24 percent, and Marco Rubio 23 percent. Trump, who had predicted "a tremendous victory," looked shattered. "I love you people," he told a crowd of supporters in West Des Moines that evening. "We will go on to get the Republican nomination, and we will go on to easily beat Hillary or Bernie or whoever the hell they throw out there."

No one believed him. What's more, the outcome seemed to ratify every doubt political experts held about him: he hadn't bothered to raise money or do the hard work of traditional campaigning, had little campaign infrastructure, no polling, a weak ground game, a volatile temperament, and what appeared to be a fatal inability to translate media attention into hard votes. It had taken quite a while, but in the end, just as those experts had predicted, voters had listened to Republican leaders and come to their senses. Even Trump admitted error: "I think some people were disappointed that

I didn't go into the debate." To all appearances, the voters had for-saken him.

But they hadn't. Eight days later, on February 9, Trump stormed to a blowout win in the New Hampshire primary, more than dou-bling the support of the second-place finisher, John Kasich. "Wow, wow, wow," a jubilant Trump declared afterward. "We are going to make America great again!" By any measure, Trump's victory was a historic event—had anyone proposed a year earlier that Donald J. Trump, tabloid fixture and star of *The Apprentice*, would overwhelm-ingly carry *any* GOP primary, they'd have been laughed out of the room.

All along, many of those closest to Trump believed that his true test would come in the Southern states that followed in the weeks after New Hampshire. During the fall, while other Republicans were blitzing states with early primaries such as Iowa, New Hampshire, and South Carolina, Trump was holding massive rallies in places like Alabama, which was bizarre according to conventional wisdom. Most reporters considered them an exercise in self-aggrandizement. In late August, Trump held a stadium event in Mobile, Alabama, which was so baffling to the local political cognoscenti that on the day he arrived, the front-page headline of the *Mobile Press-Register* read "Trump's stumping in Mobile, but why?"

There were two reasons for the perplexing strategy. The first was the Trump team's belief that it could quickly lock down the nomination by winning the "SEC primary"—a nickname derived from the Southeastern Conference, the college-athletics power-house whose member universities included many of the states hold-ing primaries immediately after New Hampshire's. They included South Carolina (February 20); Alabama, Arkansas, Georgia, Ten-nessee, Texas (March 1), Kentucky (March 5), and Mississippi

(March 8). Although there weren't many reliable public polls of these states during the fall, the few that were published showed Trump performing well. As a Trump adviser explained on the eve of the August stadium rally in Mobile, "With the lead he's got now in Texas, he feels that he can win the nomination on March 1 with a sweep of the populist, anti-establishment South." Trump was also relying on data beyond poll numbers. "His brand and sales are strongest in the South," the adviser added. "His TV ratings, his Trump resort guests—he thinks it'll pay off."

The other reason Trump was focused on the Deep South was that he was trying to win the support of the man who introduced him in Mobile (and, in fact, resided there): Alabama senator Jeff Sessions. Well into the primary season, Trump lacked any endorsements from elected Republicans. No politician was as closely aligned with his positions as was Sessions, whose views on immigration and the GOP leadership—he was mainly against both—had made him an outcast in the Senate. Sessions could see that he and Trump appealed to the same type of voters: "a lot of middle-class working people, who don't trust establishment messaging. I call it 'honest populism,'" Sessions said in October. But he had withheld his formal support.

Throughout the spring, Bannon was whipping the *Breitbart* staff like a jockey in the homestretch to champion Trump and scourge his opponents. Yet he rarely spoke directly with Trump, who didn't seem to need much help and was not even particularly aware of what Bannon was doing. Trump's singular media fixation was cable television—he didn't listen to talk radio or go online to read *Breitbart*. Instead, Bannon's major contribution during this period was brokering an alliance between Trump's world and Sessions's. In January, Bannon prevailed on Lewandowski to hire Sessions's top aide, Stephen Miller, who had been smitten with Trump since his

emergence as an immigration critic in 2014. Miller, too, shared
Trump's broader discontent. Just before joining the campaign as
Trump's senior speechwriter, Miller groused, "The Republican leadership is so out of touch with the conservative grass roots that I don't
have an adjective strong enough to describe it." (Luckily, Trump had
plenty.)

The urgency Bannon felt about Sessions and the South was alien
to most Republican strategists and thinkers. For the better part of
twenty years, the prevailing worry among the GOP's intellectual
class was that the party was *too* Southern—that its rootedness in
Southern folkways and values would inhibit its ability to appeal to a
rapidly diversifying national electorate, an idea whose clearest expression was Christopher Caldwell's 1998 essay "The Southern Cap-
tivity of the GOP" in *The Atlantic*. Bannon believed exactly the
opposite. He thought that the South—populist, patriotic, pro-
military, and skeptical of immigration—was in fact the party's sal-
vation. Having drifted too far toward secular globalism, it needed to
return to its roots.

The same week in 2013 that Marco Rubio pitched Ailes and
Murdoch on immigration reform over a secret dinner at News Corp.,
Bannon held a five-hour dinner of his own at the Breitbart Embassy
to try to talk Sessions into running for president. "You're not going
to be president, and you're not going to win the Republican nomination," Bannon told him, as Miller looked on. "However, we can bill
you as the agrarian populist and take trade and immigration and
pull them toward the top of the party's issue list."

In the end, Sessions wasn't convinced. "I can't do it," he said.
"But we'll find a candidate who will carry that message."

Three years later, that candidate had revealed himself, and

Sessions was sitting in a car at the Millington Regional Jetport in suburban Memphis waiting for him to arrive. But he was fretting over what he was about to do. It was February 27, 2016, and Trump had just upset Cruz to win the South Carolina primary. But Sessions was on the phone with Bannon—and had been for over an hour—anxious about the risk of becoming the first U.S. senator to endorse Trump. Fourteen months earlier, when Republicans took control of the Senate in the 2014 midterm elections, Sessions, the ranking member of the powerful Budget Committee, had been denied the chairmanship—punishment, he believed, for his aberrant ways. Now he wanted reassurance that giving his imprimatur to Trump wouldn't cost him his political career.

"Trump is a great advocate for our ideas," Sessions said. "But can he win?"

"One hundred percent," Bannon said, pacing back and forth in flip-flops in the front room of the Embassy. "If he can stick to your message and personify this stuff, there's not a doubt in my mind."

"They already took me off Budget," Sessions reminded him. "If I do this endorsement and it doesn't work, it's the end of my career in the Republican Party."

"It's do or die," Bannon replied. "This is it. This is the moment."

A day earlier, Chris Christie, a pillar of the GOP establishment, had stunned the political world by showing up unannounced to endorse Trump at a rally in Texas. Bannon reminded Sessions that a nod from him now, with the SEC primaries looming three days away, could be decisive. The South could rise and deliver the nomination to Trump.

Sessions agreed.

"Okay, I'm all-in," he said. "But if he doesn't win, it's over for me."

Just as the sun was beginning to set, Trump's jet rolled to a stop in front of an airport hangar where an eager crowd had packed in for the rally. Afterward, Sessions climbed aboard the jet to meet with Trump and formalize their arrangement. The next day, when Trump resumed campaigning, Sessions was with him at a rally in Madison, Alabama, to deliver his endorsement and signal that the Tea Party wing of the GOP was on board with Trump.

"I told Donald Trump this isn't a campaign, this is a *movement*," Sessions told the crowd. "Look at what's happening. The American people are not happy with their government."

He left no doubt about his motivation.

"You have asked for thirty years, and politicians have promised for thirty years, to fix illegal immigration," Sessions said. "Have they done it?"

"*No!*" the crowd roared.

"Well, Donald Trump will do it," Sessions said. "At this time, in my best judgment, at this time in America's history, we need to make America great again."

And with that, Sessions donned a red baseball cap with Trump's slogan emblazoned on the front.

Two days later, on March 1, Trump rolled up victories all across the South, winning the bulk of the remaining SEC primary states: Alabama, Arkansas, Georgia, Tennessee. One major prize—Texas—eluded him by going to a native son, Ted Cruz. But Cruz's victory was viewed as underwhelming because it fell far short of what he had once promised. "We are . . . very well positioned to do incredibly well on March 1," Cruz had told his supporters in mid-December. "You look at the states in that SEC primary— Georgia, Alabama, Tennessee, Arkansas, Oklahoma, and the great state of Texas—you couldn't color a better map in terms of strong conservative, Southern Baptist, evangelical, veteran, gun-owning, God-loving states." Over the next week, Trump racked up additional wins in Kentucky, Louisiana, and Mississippi, and then added Florida on March 15.

With Trump appearing all but unstoppable, the Republican establishment went into a full-blown panic and began exploring elaborate scenarios to deny him the nomination. Although most presidential hopefuls had by now dropped out of the race, Cruz, Rubio, and Kasich were still running and diluting the anti-Trump vote. One fleetingly popular scenario to stop Trump from becoming the nominee was for GOP delegates to coalesce around a white-knight alternative at the party convention in July. House Speaker Paul Ryan, who was Mitt Romney's vice presidential pick and had no shortage of political ambition, emerged as the chattering-class favorite. "Everyone thinks he's Republican Jesus," a Republican Senate staffer told *Politico*.

The possibility, however remote, that Ryan might steal the nomination from Trump sent Bannon into a panic of his own. He put *Breitbart*'s sharp-taloned Julia Hahn to the task of providing some less flattering comparisons. (An unnamed operative told her, "The Republican convention is the GOP establishment's prom, and Paul Ryan is their Prom Queen.") And he tried to rally his alt-right readers against the party's mandarins. "Pepe's gonna stomp their ass," he said, referring to the racist frog.

On April 11, as reporters filed in and out, Bannon sat in the Breitbart Embassy stabbing at a shrimp salad and plotting an all-out war to stop Ryan, of whom he was both fearful and dismissive— sometimes within the same sentence. Ryan, he fumed, was "a limp-dick motherfucker who was born in a petri dish at the Heritage Foundation," a conservative think tank too close to the "globalist donor class" for Bannon's tastes. He was also angry at the RNC, which had tried to get *Breitbart* to sponsor a primary debate and was now, he believed, conspiring with Ryan to box out Trump. "I wasn't going to pay them half a million dollars to associate *Breitbart* with a failed brand like the RNC," he said. "We drive the coverage."

The next day, the clamor over Ryan's entirely hypothetical presidential bid reached such a pitch that Ryan felt obligated to hold a press conference and respond. He didn't leave any wiggle room. "Count me out," he said. "I simply believe that if you want to be the nominee for our party, to be the president, you should actually run for it. I chose not to do this. Therefore, I should not be considered. Period. End of story."

Bannon didn't believe him. When a reporter who had interviewed him for a story about Ryan said he was dropping it in light of the news conference, Bannon was incredulous. "Just put the 'file' aside DON'T throw it away," he emailed.

His fears were overblown. On May 3, Trump won the Indiana primary in a rout, slamming the door shut on Cruz's slim hopes for a comeback. "I said I would continue on as long as there was a viable path to victory," a crestfallen Cruz said afterward. "Tonight, I'm sorry to say, it appears that path has been foreclosed." Thirty minutes later, a tweet from the account of RNC chairman Reince Priebus, ghostwritten by his deputy, Sean Spicer, a notoriously poor speller, made the news official: "@realDonaldTrump will be presumtive [sic]

@GOP nominee, we all need to unite and focus on defeating @HillaryClinton #NeverClinton."

The misfire seemed a portent of what was to come.

High up in his Trump Tower office, the nominee-in-waiting was greeting a steady procession of reporters, well-wishers, and shell-shocked Republican officials, sifting the elements of his upset victory. "It was a hard-fought battle," Trump said, sitting behind a hillock of newspapers and glossy magazines piled up on his desk. "It was a nasty battle. They say the nastiest ever in politics."

It was May 17. The world had had two weeks to process the news that it would be Trump facing off against Hillary Clinton in the fall. And yet the surreality persisted. Trump was attempting to explain how he'd seized control of the GOP and what his vision was for the party now that he was firmly in charge. But he kept returning to the subject of his victory.

"Let me just go here first," he said. "So when I first decided to—I always say—take the deep breath and go down the escalator with my wife, I had watched [Fox News contributor] Charles Krauthammer, shortly before that, saying these candidates are the finest group of political talent ever assembled in the history of the Republican Party. That was maybe a week before I decided to go. And I sort of said to myself, 'If that's true, what am I doing this for?' If they're really that good. But you know, many people have said that, governors, senators—the finest group of talent."

A copy of *Vanity Fair* with a buxom, corseted Amy Schumer on the cover slid from the top of his pile onto the floor. Trump took no notice.

Channeling a major theme on cable television, he wondered

aloud how all the experts had underestimated him. What had they missed? "Maybe me," he said, answering his own question. "Maybe they don't understand me. Plenty of people that know me said I was going to win. And I deal at a very high level."

The important thing now was that Trump, having won, intended to affix the Trump brand on the GOP, as he did on all his acquisitions—an imminence he believed the party should be grateful for. "If I didn't come along, the Republican Party had zero chance of winning the presidency," he said. So the Republican Party was going to change.

For all the drama he created, Trump alone had intuited that standard Republican dogma no longer appealed to large swaths of the party base. In fact, voters had grown frustrated, even disgusted, by the politicians who purveyed it. While overshadowed by his feuds and insults, Trump had conveyed and defended a clear set of ideas that drew record numbers of Republican primary voters, even though they frequently cut against right-wing orthodoxy: protect Social Security and Medicare benefits, defend Planned Parenthood, restrict free trade, avoid foreign entanglements, deport illegal immigrants, and build a wall. Trump had arrived at these heterodox views by doing exactly what politicians were supposed to do: listening to voters. "I'm not sure I got there through deep analysis," he admitted. "My views are what everybody else's views are. When I give speeches, sometimes I'll sign autographs and I'll get to talk to people and learn a lot about the party."

The problem, he'd concluded, was lousy marketing. Having absorbed the shortcomings of the Republican message, Trump had developed a better one: "America first." He waved off complaints that the slogan was redolent of the anti-Semitism of Charles Lindbergh's America First Committee during World War II. "I don't care," he said. "When you look at the voters, you see they want hope. There's no hope. No hope. We're taking care of everybody else. I'm for making America first." Under Trump, things would be different. "Five, ten years from now—different party," he said. "You're going to have a worker's party."

Trump thought the scale of his victory proved the strength of his proposals. "All these millions and millions of people," he said. "It's a movement." That movement, and his willingness to break with party orthodoxy, he believed, endowed him with the power to win states in the general election that ordinary Republicans hadn't carried in decades. "I think I'm going to do great in the state of Washington," Trump predicted. "Ted Cruz wouldn't even try. People say, 'You're wrong about this,' but I think Oregon . . . New Mexico . . . Florida, that's my second home, right? I think I'm going to do well in the three states they always talk about: Florida, Pennsylvania, Ohio."

He went on to make a series of preposterous-sounding claims—almost all of which would be borne out in the end: he would win a larger share of African Americans and Hispanics than Romney had (they loved him on *The Apprentice*!); he would open up new electoral college paths for the Republican Party; he would defeat Hillary Clinton; and he would do all this without raising the $1 billion to $2 billion that modern presidential campaigns were thought to require.

Trump didn't have the typical qualifications of a major-party presidential nominee, this he admitted. But he insisted it didn't matter. He had his movement, and his Twitter feed, and an instinct for devastating personal invective ("Lyin' Ted," "Little Marco") that would now be directed at Hillary. He understood the media and how to manipulate it. And he had something that he thought was even more important than presidential qualifications: "I have the loudspeaker."

Trump's ascension was all the more incredible because of the constant, churning chaos within his campaign. Early on, when he was still regarded as a political punch line, Trump got advice from the mercurial Roger Stone and his protégé, Sam Nunberg. When Corey Lewandowski was brought into the fold, he began feuding with Stone and Nunberg. In late July 2015, Nunberg was fired from the campaign after racist Facebook posts surfaced that he'd written years earlier. Nunberg blamed Lewandowski and vowed to exact revenge. Stone quit a week later, frustrated by Trump's attacks on Megyn Kelly at the GOP debate in Cleveland. (Trump claimed Stone was fired.)

Lewandowski, a tightly wound loyalist who guzzled Red Bull energy drinks all day, made enemies inside and outside the Trump campaign—and also, fatally, among the Trump family. Through Lewandowski, the campaign chaos spread like typhoid through the broader Trump universe, afflicting Bannon and *Breitbart*. On March 8, the night Trump won the Michigan and Mississippi primaries, Lewandowski forcefully grabbed Michelle Fields, the *Breitbart News* reporter, as she approached Trump to ask a question after a news conference in Jupiter, Florida. Fields claimed she'd been assaulted and tweeted a picture of her bruises. This set off an incendiary debate within *Breitbart*. Some staffers openly doubted Fields's account. Bannon, who was close to Lewandowski, did nothing to defend her. Aghast that *Breitbart* seemed to side with Trump and Lewandowski over its own employee, Fields and two other staffers quit in protest. Lewandowski, unrepentant, called Fields "delusional."

Jupiter police disagreed and charged him with battery; the charge was later dropped.

Although Lewandowski survived, he didn't last long. "Trump treats you like a son if he likes you," said Nunberg. "Corey's mistake was that he really thought he was one and that he could move against other members of the family." In June, amid growing Republican alarm over Trump's failure to prepare for the general election, Trump's adult children and his son-in-law, Jared Kushner, began to take a firmer hand. Sensing his authority threatened, Lewandowski quietly struck back. Nunberg found out from a reporter that his nemesis was trying to plant negative stories about Kushner in the press, and he shared this information with Trump's children. Ivanka Trump, Kushner's wife, was furious. Meanwhile, Stone worked to undermine Lewandowski by persuading Trump to hire Paul Manafort, Stone's ex–business partner, to oversee his delegate operation at the Republican convention.

On June 20, at a meeting with Trump and his two sons, Don Jr. and Eric, Lewandowski was fired. Stone and Nunberg had their revenge.* Manafort rose to replace Lewandowski and prepare Trump to run a viable general-election campaign. Once a powerful Republican operative, Manafort had helped Gerald Ford block Ronald Reagan's insurgency at the 1976 convention, and then worked for Reagan, George H. W. Bush, and Bob Dole. But he had long ago shifted his focus abroad to a roster of shady clients who included Viktor Yanukovych, the Ukrainian president and Vladimir Putin ally, who fled to Russia when violent protests drove him from

*According to a Trump associate, Lewandowski retaliated by persuading Trump to sue Nunberg for breaching a confidentiality agreement. In an affidavit responding to the lawsuit, Nunberg accused the married Lewandowski of having a "sordid and apparently illicit affair" with "a female Trump Campaign staffer." The parties later agreed to drop the suit.

the country; the Angolan UNITA guerrilla leader Jonas Savimbi; and Lynden Pindling, a former Bahamian prime minister accused of having ties to drug traffickers. But Manafort also owned a condominium in Trump Tower and would work for free—both qualifications that insinuated him into Trump's favor.

Where Lewandowski had encouraged Trump to follow his every impulse, Manafort tried, mostly in vain, to smooth the candidate's rough edges, curb his attacks, and prod him to do something he loathed: ask rich Republicans for money. But Trump bridled at the attempts to control him. On the eve of the Republican convention, Clinton had raised $264 million to Trump's $89 million. "It is like an epic disaster that is going to get worse," said Rob Jesmer, a former head of the National Republican Senatorial Committee. Trump was still banking on his ability to dominate news coverage, which was free. But here, too, a problem had emerged.

Fox News, which had dutifully fallen in line after Trump's win, was engulfed in scandal after Gretchen Carlson, a longtime anchor, filed a lawsuit on July 6 charging Roger Ailes with sexual harassment. Three days later, *New York* published the accounts of six more women who claimed Ailes harassed them. The TV legend, once thought invincible, suddenly looked less so. Rupert Murdoch had always protected him. But Murdoch was eighty-five years old, and his sons James and Lachlan, both top executives at Fox's parent company, 21st Century Fox, took a dim view of Ailes.

Desperate for allies who would aggressively defend him, Ailes reached out to Bannon through an intermediary. The two hadn't spoken since their fight over Megyn Kelly the year before. But Bannon was sympathetic, believing that the timing of the lawsuit against Ailes was no accident—and was meant to overshadow Trump's convention, set to begin on July 18.

He called Ailes at his home and reached his wife, Beth. "Steve, I'm so glad you called," she said, passing the phone to her husband.

Ailes was blunt: "I need air cover."

Bannon was surprised at his desperation. "He was babbling," he later told an associate. "He was in the fucking mumble tank."

The two men talked for an hour. In the end, Bannon agreed to put a reporter on the story and told Ailes he would "put up as spirited a defense as possible—typical *Breitbart* stuff."

But when 21st Century Fox hired the New York law firm Paul, Weiss, Rifkind, Wharton & Garrison to conduct an investigation of the charges, Bannon decided that Ailes was finished and called to tell him so.

"You know, it's over now," he said.

"What do you mean?" Ailes asked.

"They hired an outside firm," Bannon said. "They're moving it out of the building—and you watch, Megyn Kelly will turn on you."

Ailes scoffed. "Rupert's got my back," he said. "The boys want to kill me, but Rupert won't let me go."

The next day, Ailes called back, less sure of himself. He had tried calling the elder Murdoch, who was vacationing with his wife in the South of France and didn't take the call.

"It's too hard to get through; he's on a boat," Ailes ventured.

Bannon told him to get as much money as he could in a settlement and face up to the truth. "If somebody called him about a merger, he'd take the fucking call," Bannon told Ailes. "You're done."

On July 19, the news broke that Kelly had indeed told the Paul, Weiss investigators that Ailes had sexually harassed her. *Breitbart* dutifully published Ailes's last-ditch defense, a claim that Fox News' entire prime-time lineup would quit if Ailes was forced out. That evening, *New York* reported, Ailes was banned from the Fox building, and his company e-mail and phone were shut down. On July 21, just hours before Trump was to formally accept the Republican nomination in Cleveland, Ailes agreed to a $40 million exit package. He was finished.

Although Manafort averted a delegate revolt, the GOP Convention was not much sunnier. Instead of the patriotic pageantry Republicans typically produce, the four-day event was a strange, dark, almost dystopian affair whose attempt to unify the party was marred by Ted Cruz's public refusal to endorse Trump, prompting the crowd to boo him off the stage during prime time.

On Thursday night, in his acceptance speech, Trump declared that it was "a moment of crisis in our nation." He laid out a portrait of carnage, citing homicide rates and describing individual murders. "The attacks on our police, and the terrorism in our cities, threaten our very way of life," he warned. "Any politician who does not grasp this danger is not fit to lead our country."

Trump's speech was widely panned and seemed to foredoom his campaign. In the weeks that followed, his poll numbers slid further after he engaged in extended attacks on the parents of a slain Muslim American war hero, Khizr and Ghazala Khan, who had spoken at the Democratic convention. Trump also suggested that Cruz's father might have been involved in the assassination of John F. Kennedy. And he invited Russia to interfere in the U.S. election, stating at a news conference: "Russia, if you're listening, I hope you're able to find the thirty thousand e-mails [from Hillary Clinton's private server] that are missing. I think you will probably be rewarded mightily by our press."

By mid-August, Clinton's lead over Trump was nearing double

digits in many national polls, as pressure built in the Republican ranks for the RNC to cut off money to Trump's campaign to try to save its House and Senate majorities. Many of Trump's largest donors were desperate for him to shake up his campaign. One of them, Rebekah Mercer, boarded a helicopter and flew to meet Trump at the East Hampton estate of New York Jets owner Woody Johnson. She had insisted on a face-to-face meeting to deliver a message to Trump: it was time to make a change and let someone more aggressive run his campaign. She knew just the man.

TEN

BURN EVERYTHING DOWN

Rebekah Mercer was never one to hold back her thoughts. "This thing is over," she told Trump, "if you don't make a change fast." She'd spent hours fielding calls from anguished donors. Her own family was into Trump for $3.4 million, more if you counted ancillary support such as *Breitbart*. The RNC, she told him, was days away from cutting him loose and turning its focus to saving the Republican majorities in the House and Senate.

"It's bad," Trump admitted.

"No, it's not bad—it's over," she shot back. "Unless you make a change."

Earlier that day, *The New York Times* had published an unsparing account of the campaign's dysfunction ("Inside the Failing Mission to Tame Donald Trump's Tongue") that described how aides were so desperate to contain Trump's outbursts that they were sending old friends like Rudy Giuliani and Mike Huckabee to babysit him on the campaign trail. Mercer told Trump that he needed to get rid of Paul Manafort, whose ill-conceived attempt to moderate him into someone acceptable to swing voters had plainly failed. Furthermore, growing attention to Manafort's ties to pro-Kremlin autocrats was hurting Trump's campaign.

"Bring in Steve Bannon and Kellyanne Conway," Mercer told him. "I've talked to them; they'll do it."

Trump agreed.

It didn't hurt that Bannon, Conway, and David Bossie were already involved in a Super PAC that was aiding Trump. Informally called the "Defeat Crooked Hillary PAC," the Mercer-backed effort had been set up three months earlier, with a novel twist: it would only attack Clinton, not boost Trump. That way conservatives reluctant to support Trump could still donate in good conscience. (The give-to-stop-Clinton gambit didn't work. According to data compiled by the Center for Responsive Politics, the only substantial donations after the Super PAC shifted its focus to defeating "Crooked Hillary" came from Robert Mercer [$2 million] and Peter Thiel [$1 million].) After Cruz dropped out in May, Ivanka Trump and Jared Kushner had approached Mercer to ask if she would organize an effort to support Trump. She agreed. But the awkward truth was that most wealthy conservatives *didn't* support Trump. The Clinton angle was a move born of desperation, and one that risked skirting federal election law. "Some donors don't want to associate with something overtly pro-Trump," Bossie admitted. "Technically, the name of the Super PAC is going to be 'Make America Number 1.' If we call it 'Defeat Crooked Hillary,' it's an FEC violation."

That night, August 13, Trump and Bannon spoke by phone and agreed to a deal: Bannon would take over the campaign (forgoing a salary, as Manafort had) and Conway would be named campaign manager. Bossie would later join as her deputy. Trump told Bannon to meet him the next morning at his golf club in Bedminster, New Jersey.

The next day, a Sunday, Trump's top advisers gathered at Trump National Golf Club in Bedminster, unaware of the leadership change that had been instituted the night before—or of their boss's foul mood. At the table were Chris Christie, Giuliani, Ailes, who was now advising Trump, Manafort, and his deputy, Rick Gates. (Jared and Ivanka were yachting in Croatia with David Geffen and not present.)

Trump, who had been stewing over the *Times* article, exploded at Manafort.

"How can anybody allow an article that says your campaign is all fucked up?" Trump demanded to know, furious at his portrayal and at reports his aides were going on television in an effort to reach him.

"You think you've gotta go on TV to talk to me?" he shouted. "You treat me like a baby! Am I like a baby to you? I sit there like a little baby and watch TV and you talk to me? Am I a fucking baby, Paul?"

The room fell silent.

Manafort took the hazing in stride. It was hardly the first time Trump had lost his temper. And while he'd been demoted, he hadn't been fired. Besides, he had a bigger problem to worry about. After the meeting, Manafort headed home to his Trump Tower condominium. On his desk was a printout of an article, set to run in the next morning's *New York Times*. It explained how a Ukrainian government anticorruption team had discovered a secret handwritten ledger listing Manafort as the designated recipient of $12.7

million in previously undisclosed cash payments from a pro-Russian political party aligned with former president Viktor F. Yanukovych, Manafort's client.

Although *Times* reporters had been pressing him for weeks to comment, Manafort's attorney had advised him against it. Now Manafort was having doubts. He'd kept the news of the impending story from the Trump campaign. He'd even hidden it from his wife, who leaped up from the couch in fury when she found out that night.

On Monday morning, the Manafort story was splashed across the front page of *The New York Times* ("Secret Ledger in Ukraine Lists Cash for Donald Trump's Campaign Chief") and dominated the day's news, overshadowing a high-profile national-security speech Trump was delivering in Ohio that afternoon. (Twisting the knife in his old rival, Lewandowski tweeted out the *Times* story.) Manafort fed the story, and ensured it would continue for at least another day, by finally issuing an on-the-record denial. "The suggestion that I accepted cash payments is unfounded, silly, and nonsensical," he said, claiming that any payments were for staff, polling, and political research.

Manafort's story was, a top Trump adviser later conceded, "a kill shot" that infuriated everyone in the campaign, no one more than the candidate himself. Having held back the news of Bannon and Conway's takeover, the campaign announced it on Wednesday morning, hoping to snuff out the Manafort distraction. Initially, Trump's team billed the move as an "expansion" rather than what it obviously was: a demotion. But by late Thursday, Trump had had enough and demanded Manafort's scalp. "It's like the French Revolution," said Roger Stone. "The guys who are cutting people's heads off at the beginning wind up getting their own heads cut off at the end."

Kushner, now back from vacationing in Croatia, delivered the news at a Friday morning breakfast as diplomatically as he could. "We've really got a problem here, Paul," Kushner told him. "You're going to have to step down."

But Manafort objected. "Well, I don't want to do that, because it'll look like I'm guilty," he said.

Kushner pressed harder. "It would be helpful if you stepped down."

"Yes," Manafort replied, "but I can't do that."

At this, Kushner's demeanor hardened and he glanced at his watch. "We're putting out a press release at nine a.m. that says you've resigned," he said. "That's in thirty seconds."

Manafort's ouster extinguished the last vestige of hope for Republicans praying that Trump would at last pivot to a more statesmanlike approach. No one believed he had any chance of winning in November; their desperation, at this point, was driven purely by the desire to limit the scope of the expected GOP losses down the ticket. Bannon's elevation was simply unimaginable, the Republican establishment's worst nightmare come to life.

"This is the bunker scene in *Downfall*, only the Trump crowd won't tell Hitler the truth. It's utter madness," said Stuart Stevens, who ran Mitt Romney's 2012 presidential campaign. "Trump is a nut, and he likes to surround himself with nuts. It's a disaster for the Republican Party."

Although few Republicans knew Bannon personally, many were acquainted with *Breitbart*'s aggressive, hard-edged populism, often because they had been on the receiving end of one of its journalistic assaults. Bannon, they understood, would pay no heed at all to the sensitivities of down-ballot Republicans, and indeed would gladly indulge Trump's impulse to burn everything down.

"If you were looking for a tone or pivot, Bannon will pivot you in a dark, racist, and divisive direction," said the GOP consultant Rick Wilson. "It'll be a nationalist, hateful campaign. Republicans should run away."

By now, Bannon's term for his politics, and Trump's—"nationalism"—was already in wide circulation in the political press. But the term's meaning was (and remains) confusing and has never been fully explicated. While Trump's embrace of "America first" nationalism was chiefly due to its resonance as a campaign slogan, Bannon's attraction to it had a far deeper and more complicated lineage.

From an early age, Bannon was influenced by his family's distinctly traditionalist Catholicism and tended to view current events against the broad sweep of history. Though hardly a moralizing social conservative, he objected bitterly to the secular liberalism encroaching upon the culture. "We shouldn't be running a victory lap every time some sort of traditional value gets undercut," he said in 2015. While he was still in the Navy, Bannon, a voracious autodidact, embarked upon what he described as "a systematic study of the world's religions" that he carried on for more than a decade. Taking up the Roman Catholic history first instilled in him at Benedictine, his Catholic military high school, he moved on to Christian mysticism and from there to Eastern metaphysics. (In the Navy, he briefly practiced Zen Buddhism before wending his way back to Tridentine Catholicism).

Bannon's reading eventually led him to the work of René Guénon, an early-twentieth-century French occultist and metaphysician who was raised a Roman Catholic, practiced Freemasonry, and later became a Sufi Muslim. There are many forms of traditionalism in religion and philosophy. Guénon developed a philosophy often referred to as "Traditionalism" (capital "T"), a form of antimodernism with precise connotations. Guénon was a "primordial" Traditionalist, a believer in the idea that certain ancient religions, including the Hindu Vedanta, Sufism, and medieval Catholicism, were repositories of common spiritual truths, revealed in the earliest age of the world, that were being wiped out by the rise of secular modernity in the West. What Guénon hoped for, he wrote in 1924, was to "restore to the West an appropriate traditional civilization."

Guénon, like Bannon, was drawn to a sweeping, apocalyptic view of history that identified two events as marking the beginning of the spiritual decline of the West: the destruction of the Order of the Knights Templar in 1314 and the Peace of Westphalia in 1648. Also like Bannon, Guénon was fascinated by the Hindu concept of cyclical time and believed that the West was passing through the fourth and final era, known as the Kali Yuga, a six-thousand-year "dark age" when tradition is wholly forgotten.

The antimodernist tenor of Guénon's philosophy drew several notable followers who made attempts during the twentieth century to re-enchant the world by bringing about this restoration. The most notorious of these was Julius Evola, an Italian intellectual and the black sheep of the Traditionalist family. A monarchist and racial theorist who traced the descent of the Kali Yuga to interwar European politics, Evola, unlike Guénon (a pious Muslim chiefly interested in spiritual transformation), took concrete steps to incite societal transformation. By 1938, he had struck an alliance with Benito Mussolini, and his ideas became the basis of Fascist racial theory; later, after he soured on Mussolini, Evola's ideas gained currency in Nazi Germany.

The common themes of the collapse of Western civilization and
the loss of the transcendent in books such as Guénon's *The Crisis of
the Modern World* (1927) and Evola's *Revolt Against the Modern
World* (1934) are what drew Bannon's interest to Traditionalism (although he was also very much taken with its spiritual aspects, citing
Guénon's 1925 book, *Man and His Becoming According to the Vedanta*,
as "a life-changing discovery").*

Bannon, more synthesist than adherent, brought to Guénon's
Traditionalism a strong dose of Catholic social thought, in particular the concept of "subsidiarity": the principle expressed in Pope Pius
XI's 1931 encyclical, *Quadragesimo anno*, that political matters
should devolve to the lowest, least centralized authority that can
responsibly handle them—a concept that, in a U.S. political context,
mirrors small-government conservatism.

Everywhere Bannon looked in the modern world, he saw signs
of collapse and an encroaching globalist order stamping out the last
vestiges of the traditional. He saw it in governmental organizations
such as the European Union and political leaders such as German
chancellor Angela Merkel, who insisted that countries forfeit their
sovereignty, and thus their ability to maintain their national character, to distant secular bureaucrats bent on erasing national borders.
He saw it in the Roman Catholic Church, whose elevation of Pope
Francis, "a liberal-theology Jesuit" and "pro-immigration globalist,"
to replace Pope Benedict XVI so alarmed him that, in 2013, he established *Breitbart Rome* and took a Vatican meeting with Cardi-
nal Raymond Burke in an effort to prop up Catholic traditionalists
marginalized by the new Pope.

---

*The best modern primer on Guénon, Evola, and the Traditionalists is *Against the Modern
World: Traditionalism and the Secret Intellectual History of the Twentieth Century*, by Mark Sedgwick, a scholar at Aarhus University in Denmark.

More than anywhere else, Bannon saw evidence of Western collapse in the influx of Muslim refugees and migrants across Europe and the United States—what he pungently termed "civilizational jihad personified by this migrant crisis." Expounding on this view at a 2014 conference at the Vatican, Bannon knit together Guénon, Evola, and his own racial-religious panic to cast his beliefs in historical context. Citing the tens of millions of people killed in twentieth-century wars, he called mankind "children of that barbarity" whose present condition would one day be judged "a new Dark Age." He added, "We are in an outright war against jihadist Islamic fascism. And this war is, I think, metastasizing far quicker than governments can handle it."

Bannon's response to the rise of modernity was to set populist, right-wing nationalism against it. Wherever he could, he aligned himself with politicians and causes committed to tearing down its globalist edifice: archconservative Catholics such as Burke, Nigel Farage and UKIP, Marine Le Pen's National Front, Geert Wilders and the Party for Freedom, and Sarah Palin and the Tea Party. (When he got to the White House, he would also leverage U.S. trade policy to strengthen opponents of the EU.) This had a meaningful effect, even before Trump. "Bannon's a political entrepreneur and a remarkable bloke," Farage said. "Without the supportive voice of *Breitbart London*, I'm not sure we would have had a Brexit."

For all his paranoid alarm, Bannon believes that the rise of nationalist movements across the world, from Europe to Japan to the United States, heralds a return to tradition. "You have to control three things," he explained, "borders, currency, and military and national identity. People are finally coming to realize that, and politicians will have to follow." The clearest example of Traditionalist political influence today is in Russia. Vladimir Putin's chief ideologist, Alexander Dugin—whom Bannon has cited—translated Evola's work into Russian and later developed a Russian-nationalist variant of Traditionalism known as Eurasianism.

Bannon initially thought restoration lay in a rising political generation still some years off: figures such as Frauke Petry, of Germany's right-wing Alternative für Deutschland, and Marion Maréchal-Le Pen, niece of Marine, whose politics he approvingly described as "practically French medieval," adding: "She's the future of France." It took some time for him to realize that in Trump (whose familiarity with French metaphysics, we can be certain, is no more than glancing) he had found a leader who could rapidly advance the nationalist cause.

In the summer of 2016, Bannon described Trump as a "blunt instrument for us." But by the following April, Trump was in the White House and Bannon had raised his estimation of him to pathbreaking leader. "He's taken this nationalist movement and moved it up twenty years," Bannon said. "If France, Germany, England, or any of these places had the equivalent of a Donald Trump, they would be in power. They don't."

When he took over Trump's campaign in August, Bannon did indeed run a nationalist, divisive campaign in which issues of race, immigration, culture, and identity were put front and center. This wasn't by accident or lacking in purpose, even if the candidate himself didn't care to understand its broader historical context. By exhuming the nationalist thinkers of an earlier age, Bannon was trying to build an intellectual basis for Trumpism, or what might more accurately be described as an American nationalist-Traditionalism. Whatever the label, Trump proved to be an able messenger.

Bannon's ties to *Breitbart*'s inflammatory journalism, and the anguish he caused Republicans, became the dominant focus of the

political world in the wake of his elevation to run Trump's floundering campaign. This overshadowed a different, more salient point
about the shake-up: by installing Bannon, Conway, and later Bossie,
Trump was handing the reins of a half-billion-dollar political enterprise to a seasoned team of professional anti-Clinton operatives.
These three figures from the Republican fringe, and the menagerie
of characters they brought with them, were suddenly in charge of
running a major-party presidential campaign—against an opponent, Hillary Clinton, whom they'd been plotting to tear apart for
the better part of twenty-five years.

One weakness of Trump's campaign was that it was guided almost entirely by the candidate's impulses. Trump's focus, especially
when things were going badly, thrashed around like a loose firehose.
He would attack Megyn Kelly one day, then go after the parents of
a slain Muslim soldier the next. Another weakness was the lack of
opposition research that a campaign would typically draw upon to
frame its opponent—Trump's only input appeared to be cable news.

Bannon's arrival neatly solved both these problems. He kept
Trump focused on a clear target at which to direct his ample talent
for attacking and belittling people: "Crooked Hillary." And he
brought an encyclopedic knowledge of damaging material with
which to attack her, gleaned from having masterminded Peter Schweizer's book *Clinton Cash* while he was at GAI. The book also gave
Trump an overarching theme in which to fit his attacks, one that the
media, thanks partly to Schweizer's and Bannon's own efforts, was
already predisposed to accept: that Clinton was thoroughly corrupt.

And because Bannon's convulsive extremism was now going to
set the tone, there would be no holding back. "The campaign has
been too lethargic, too reactive," he said, shortly after his hiring.
"It's not going to be a traditional campaign."

On the first business day after Manafort's firing, Trump put out a statement intended to reframe the race: "Hillary Clinton is the defender of the corrupt and rigged status quo. The Clintons have spent decades as insiders lining their own pockets and taking care of donors instead of the American people. It is now clear that the Clinton Foundation is the most corrupt enterprise in political history. What they were doing during Crooked Hillary's time as Secretary of State was wrong then, and it is wrong now. It must be shut down immediately."

In the days that followed, the campaign flooded reporters and followers with dozens of press releases focused on the Clinton Foundation and the charge that Hillary was corrupt:

"Clinton's Corruption Exposed—Again" . . . "Hillary Clinton Short Circuits Trying to Defend the Clinton Foundation" . . . "ABC News Reports on New Clinton Foundation Corruption" . . . "Florida's Largest Newspaper Calls on Clinton to Make 'Clean Break' from Corrupt Foundation" . . .Clinton Campaign: If You Don't Like the Clinton Foundation, Don't Vote for Clinton" . . . "More Editorial Boards Attack 'Shady' Clinton Corruption" . . . "Clinton 'Used a Special Tool to Delete Emails so That 'Even God Can't Read Them'"

Out on the stump, Trump wholeheartedly embraced the theme, ratcheting up and extending his extravagant denunciations of Clinton's countless alleged perfidies. The crowd chant that had erupted during the Republican National Convention—"Lock her up! Lock her up!"—now became a mainstay of Trump's rallies, as popular

with audiences as his greatest hit, "Build the Wall!" Trump's supporters, many wearing "Hillary for Prison" T-shirts, came to antic-
ipate it, shaking their fists and shouting the refrain at the top of
their lungs.

None of this seemed to matter a whit, at least not in August or
September. Trump still trailed in nearly every national poll, as well
as in those of most critical swing states. What it seemed like instead was the parochial obsession of a bunch of right-wing cranks
who, having found themselves in charge of a presidential campaign,
were feeling their oats in a way they never imagined could be possible. And yet the consistent theme of Clinton's corruption, ham-
mered on day in and day out, was seeping into the consciousness of
millions of Americans who, despite what the polls were saying, had
not yet made up their minds.

Many Democrats privately exulted over Trump's choice of Bannon, believing that the pair would blow up the GOP. Clinton and
her staff sensed an opportunity. After Trump's string of early August setbacks, Clinton had granted herself license to take two weeks
off from the campaign trail, disappearing from the public eye as she
swept through wealthy enclaves such as the Hamptons, Nantucket,
and Beverly Hills, vacationing and fund-raising with the likes of
Justin Timberlake, Cher, and Jimmy Buffett. But the chance to
damage Trump by highlighting Bannon's extremism was enough to
lure her away, briefly, from the billionaires and celebrities.

The idea was hatched by two of her senior aides, Jennifer Pal-
mieri and Jake Sullivan: Clinton would deliver a major speech in
Reno, Nevada, highlighting Bannon's ties to the alt-right. The term
"alt-right" itself had no fixed meaning. In its broadest sense, it encompassed the spectrum of groups left over if you took everyone
to the right of center and subtracted mainstream Republicans and

neoconservative foreign-policy hawks: populists, libertarians, immigration restrictionists, reactionaries, paleoconservatives, white supremacists, and full-on neo-Nazis. This catchall definition is what Bannon had had in mind when, in July, he told a journalist at *Mother Jones* that he considered *Breitbart* a "platform for the alt-right."

But Clinton, in her August 25 speech, cleverly defined "alt-right" to mean *only* white supremacists and Nazis, taking the sins of the racist fringe and stretching them to cover the whole group. Clinton's staff debated whether to put "alt-right" in the headline of the press release, and finally decided that they should. "The term was just beginning to enter the political lexicon," a Clinton adviser explained, "and we thought it would be catnip that would fuel people's curiosity [about the alt-right] and what Bannon's place was in that world. Trump's campaign was built on stoking xenophobic impulses, so you could take a process story on Bannon's hire and turn it into a bigger critique of how Trump was uniquely unacceptable."

Clinton rose to the task. "Trump," she declared, to a multicultural audience at a community college, "is reinforcing harmful stereotypes and offering a dog whistle to his most hateful supporters. It's a disturbing preview of what kind of president he'd be. And that's what I want to make clear today: a man with a long history of racial discrimination, who traffics in dark conspiracy theories drawn from the pages of supermarket tabloids and the far, dark reaches of the Internet, should never run our government or command our military."

Having established her premise, Clinton turned her attention to Bannon and *Breitbart*: "The latest shake-up was designed to 'Let Trump be Trump.' To do that, he hired Stephen Bannon, the head of a right-wing website called Breitbart.com, as campaign CEO. To give you a flavor of his work, here are a few headlines they've published:

Birth Control Makes Women Unattractive and Crazy.
Would You Rather Your Child Had Feminism or Cancer?
Gabby Giffords: The Gun Control Movement's Human Shield.
Hoist It High and Proud: The Confederate Flag
Proclaims a Glorious Heritage.

She continued: "According to the Southern Poverty Law Center, which tracks hate groups, *Breitbart* embraces 'ideas on the ex-
tremist fringe of the conservative right.' This is not conservatism as
we have known it. This is not Republicanism as we have known
it. These are race-baiting ideas, anti-Muslim and anti-immigrant
ideas, anti-woman—all key tenets making up an emerging racist
ideology known as the 'alt-right.' . . . The de facto merger between
Breitbart and the Trump campaign represents a landmark achieve-
ment for the alt-right. A fringe element has effectively taken over
the Republican Party."

Most voters (and many journalists) were unfamiliar with the
term and accepted Clinton's definition of it, which set off a clamor
to explain and explore the murky underworld she had described. In
fact, Clinton's speech wasn't far off the mark—certainly not her line
about "the far, dark reaches of the Internet," nor her contention that
a fringe element was taking over the GOP.

And if Bannon didn't embrace anti-Semitism and white
supremacy—as he repeatedly insisted he did not, noting that both
Andrew Breitbart and Larry Solov were Jewish—neither did he appear to be especially troubled by it. Asked at the 2014 Vatican conference about the racist element found in many far-right parties, Bannon
replied that "over time it all gets kind of washed out." He seemed to
regard it as an unavoidable evil, a kind of way station on the path to
populist triumph. "When you look at any kind of revolution—and

this is a revolution—you always have some groups that are dispa-
rate," he'd said. "I think that will all burn away over time and you'll
see more of a mainstream center-right populist movement."

Clinton's speech struck a chord with many members of the media because it helped to explain the torrent of abuse they were expe-
riencing, especially on social-media platforms such as Twitter. The
story line that Clinton's staff hoped her speech would produce did
indeed emerge, and the negative coverage of Bannon and Trump
and their relationship to the alt-right carried on for weeks.

It was a subject any ordinary campaign would be toxically afraid
of. But it didn't produce the political dynamic Clinton expected:
her lead actually narrowed in the month after her speech, from six
points to two points in the RealClearPolitics average of polls. Bannon thought he knew why. "We polled the race stuff and it doesn't
matter," he said in late September. "It doesn't move anyone who isn't
already in her camp."

What became much more worrisome for the Trump campaign was
sex—and sexual assault. On October 7, David Fahrenthold, a
reporter at *The Washington Post*, was leaked outtake footage from a
2005 Trump appearance on the NBC show *Access Hollywood*. In the
tape, the recently married Trump is heard bragging in lewd and
graphic detail to the show's host, Billy Bush, about kissing, groping,
and trying to bed women. "When you're a star, they let you do it,"
Trump says. "You can do anything. Grab them by the pussy."

From the moment it posted at four p.m. on Friday, Fahrenthold's
story drew such heavy traffic that it briefly crashed the *Post*'s internal servers. Republican politicians seized up in panic. Many believed
it was the death knell of Trump's campaign (a prospect they secretly

welcomed, given the reliably orthodox conservatism and resolute dullness of Trump's running mate, Mike Pence). South Dakota senator John Thune, the third-ranking member of the GOP leadership, echoed many of his colleagues by calling on Trump to quit the race: "Donald Trump should withdraw and Mike Pence should be our nominee effective immediately." House Speaker Paul Ryan announced he would no longer support or defend Trump's campaign, though he didn't withdraw his endorsement. "I am not going to defend Donald Trump—not now, not in the future," Ryan told his House colleagues in a private conference call. RNC chairman Reince Priebus, scheduled to appear on the Sunday morning shows, promptly withdrew, and *New York* later reported that he went to see Trump at his penthouse and advised him to quit or "go down with a worse election loss than Barry Goldwater's."

Trump, who made it a point never to apologize for any offense, took the unprecedented step of expressing remorse in a hastily produced ninety-second Web video. "I said it, I was wrong, and I apologize," Trump said to the camera. But his apology quickly morphed into an attack on the Clintons that made clear he would not be dropping out. "I've said some foolish things," he said, but "Bill Clinton has actually abused women, and Hillary has bullied, attacked, shamed, and intimidated his victims. We will discuss this more in the coming days. See you at the debate on Sunday."

Inside Trump's campaign there was a frantic rush to stanch the damage. Trump was stung by the string of Republican defections, and he raged against Ryan and took note of who loyally stood by him: a small circle of family members, Bannon, Bossie, and Giuliani—but not Priebus, Ryan, or Christie. Kushner, too, was bitterly disposed toward Ryan, a dynamic Bannon worried about, despite his own history of antagonism, because he feared it would divide the GOP. "It takes coalitions to win wars," he said, drawing a characteristically dramatic analogy. "It's just like Americans working with the Russians in World War II. Defeat the Fascists, then we'll fight amongst ourselves. We can have the long, cold war after that." He tried, and mostly failed, to stop Trump from criticizing Ryan.

The loyal circle also included the Mercers. The next morning, Robert and Rebekah Mercer issued a rare public statement reaffirming their support for Trump (while signaling to Republicans who wanted their money that they should tread carefully): "Donald Trump's uncensored comments, both old and new, have been echoed and dissected in the media repeatedly in an effort to kindle among his supporters a conflagration of outrage commensurate with the media's own faux outrage. Can anyone really be surprised that Mr. Trump could have said to Mr. Bush such things as he has already admitted saying? No. We are completely indifferent to Mr. Trump's locker room braggadocio. . . . We have a country to save and there is only one person who can save it. We, and Americans across the country and around the world, stand steadfastly behind Donald J. Trump."

Still, by Saturday afternoon, Bannon could feel the crisis spiraling out of control. When a reporter reached him to ask what the campaign was planning for the next evening's debate against Clinton, and whether a show of contrition might be warranted, Bannon didn't miss a beat: "Attack, attack, attack, attack, attack."

Trump didn't wait for Sunday night's debate to deliver. Bannon had long been convinced from his conversations with the Valkyries, his young female *Breitbart* reporters, that Bill Clinton's womanizing and Hillary's complicity in covering it up had more political salience than conventional wisdom allowed and was something that "has to be concentrated and brought up" (as he'd put it a year earlier). His original thought was that re-litigating the scandals would demoralize a younger generation of feminist women, unfamiliar with the details, whom Clinton was counting on for support. But with the *Access Hollywood* tape, Bannon saw that injecting Clinton's accusers into the heat of the presidential race would muddy the waters and force the media to devote attention to more than just Trump's damaging tape. The trick was to do it in a way that couldn't be ignored.

On Sunday afternoon, ninety minutes before the start of the debate at Washington University in St. Louis, word spread among the press corps that Trump was about to hold an event. As reporters squeezed into a conference room, Trump was seated at the center of a makeshift dais draped with black cloth and flanked by four elderly women well known to veteran political reporters: Kathleen Willey, Juanita Broaddrick, Kathy Shelton, and Paula Jones. Willey, Broaddrick, and Jones had all accused Bill Clinton of sexual assault; in 1975, a judge had appointed Hillary Clinton, then a young lawyer, to defend a man accused of raping Shelton, who was then twelve years old.

After brief prefatory remarks from Trump, the women took turns defending him and attacking the Clintons. "Mr. Trump may have said some bad words, but Bill Clinton raped me," Broaddrick alleged. "And Hillary Clinton threatened me. I don't think there's any comparison." The shock of what was unfolding prompted frenzied live coverage on cable news, while the Trump campaign streamed the event on Facebook. As cameras panned the room, they captured Bannon standing in the back, grinning wickedly.

Even though reporters shouted questions at Trump about the *Access Hollywood* tape, the brazen theatrics of Bannon's gambit, and

the visual of Trump seated among Clinton's accusers, guaranteed
that the primary imagery on television would cease to be the *Access
Hollywood* footage, which had run in a nonstop loop for two days,
and would be replaced by Trump's latest outrageous stunt. Watching
Bill Cosby succumb to his accusers the year before, Bannon had
noticed that their on-camera testimony was especially powerful because most of the victims had been attacked decades earlier and
were now elderly women and thus inherently sympathetic. Bannon
thought a similar dynamic would apply to the Clinton accusers, and
he worked to get them as much camera time as he could.

One method he planned to use was to put the women at the
front of the debate audience in seats reserved for Trump's family, to
unnerve Hillary Clinton and assure them a steady presence in the
camera shot. He and Kushner had hit upon the plan after seeing
Mark Cuban, the billionaire owner of the Dallas Mavericks and an
outspoken Clinton partisan, seated in the front row during the first
debate on September 26. Trump personally approved the idea, understanding that it would create an indelible moment of TV drama:
the candidates' family members were to enter the debate hall at
the same time and shake hands, which would put Bill Clinton
face-to-face with his accusers.

"We were going to put the four women in the VIP box," Giuliani explained. "We had it all set. We wanted to have them shake
hands with Bill, to see if Bill would shake hands with them." But
minutes before the proceedings were to begin, Frank Fahrenkopf,
cochairman of the debate commission, learned of the plan and for-
bade Trump's staff from following through. Bannon urged them to
go ahead anyway, to no avail. "Fahrenkopf said no—verbally said
'no,' that security would throw them out," Giuliani said. "We pulled
it because we were going to have a big incident on national TV."

When Clinton was introduced, she refused the traditional pre-debate handshake with Trump.

In the end, defusing the Bannon-Kushner plan made little difference, because Trump quickly took matters into his own hands. As 67 million people watched, Trump waited for the inevitable *Access Hollywood* question and sprung his counterattack. "If you look at Bill Clinton, far worse," he said. "Mine are words, and his was action. His was—what he's done to women, there's never been anybody in the history of politics in this nation that's been so abusive to women. . . . Hillary Clinton attacked those same women and attacked them viciously. Four of them are here tonight."

Afterward, Bannon marveled at Trump's fearlessness. "It's awe inspiring," he said. "You have to have a certain psychological construct to do that—he's got that. Classic honey badger. He crushed her."

Two days later, Trump's internal tracking polls gave some credence to Bannon's enthusiasm. By now, Trump's campaign was following a familiar pattern: whenever he made news for some negative event (attacking the Khans, a poor first debate performance) his support would erode . . . but then recover, like a balloon pushed underwater. In the first debate, on September 26, Trump had looked badly overmatched and he lost support. Within a week, his numbers were climbing. Then the *Access Hollywood* tape landed on October 7 and they dropped again. But four days later, they once again began to recover.

Outside the campaign, Trump's tape fiasco was regarded as a mortal blow and the Clinton-accuser gambit a transparently cynical ploy to change the subject. But on the inside, Trump's brain trust was seeing numbers that said attacking Clinton was the way to go—besides, they couldn't have stopped Trump if they'd wanted to. A smattering of public polls indicated the same thing, including one from October 12 taken by NBC News/SurveyMonkey, which showed more respondents improved their opinion of Trump than they did Clinton after watching the second debate.

But that same day, a Wednesday, multiple women came forward to accuse Trump of having groped or kissed them without their consent. Two went public in a front-page *New York Times* story; a third told *The Palm Beach Post* that Trump had "grabbed my ass" ten years earlier; the fourth, a former *People* magazine reporter, published an essay recounting how Trump had forcibly kissed her at his Mar-a-Lago resort in Florida before an interview she was going to conduct with him and his pregnant wife, Melania. Twisting the knife, Michelle Obama went after Trump directly in a speech the next day. "This wasn't just 'locker-room banter,'" she told a crowd in Manchester, New Hampshire. "This was a powerful individual speaking freely and openly about sexually predatory behavior."

Trump was incensed at the ambush and delivered an angry rebuttal at a rally in West Palm Beach, charging his accusers with being part of a "global conspiracy" and attacking them individually. "The Clinton machine is at the center of this power structure," Trump said, delivering prepared remarks that bore the mark of Bannon. "Anyone who challenges their control is deemed a sexist, a racist, a xenophobe, and morally deformed. They will attack you; they will slander you; they will seek to destroy your career and your family. . . . They will lie, lie, lie."

Democrats were giddy, believing that they were finally witnessing the self-destruction of a candidate who seemed impervious to so much. Paul Begala, an adviser to the Clinton-aligned Super PAC Priorities USA, watched Trump's rally and pronounced him finished. "To quote the late, great Nelson Mandela, it's like drinking poison and thinking it's going to hurt your enemy," Begala said. "He's a billionaire tycoon in a total meltdown, and he's going to try to take as many people down with him. It's not a political strategy, but it will be an unlovely twenty-six days until we dispatch him to the ash heap of history."

The wave of new accusers put Trump's campaign on a war footing. With Trump himself appearing increasingly unhinged, Bannon's instinctive hyper-aggressiveness met no internal resistance. The distinction they needed to draw, he told staffers, was between Trump's "locker room" behavior and what he alleged was Hillary Clinton's history of enabling sexual violence. "This has nothing to do with consensual sexual affairs and infidelities," Bannon said in a strategy meeting that week. "This is Bill. We're going to turn him into Bill Cosby. He's a violent sexual predator who physically abuses women who he assaults. And she takes the lead on the intimidation of the victims."

Bossie reached out to reporters to explain how the campaign intended to drive this narrative. Clinton had tweeted in November: "Every survivor of sexual assault deserves to be heard, believed and supported." The juxtaposition of that claim and the aggressiveness with which she and her allies had attacked her husband's accusers over the years was, Bossie claimed, a glaring hypocrisy. "It's untenable and it's farcical," he said. "With rape culture being what it is, these facts are going to shock millennial women. There will not be a millennial woman who will want to vote for her when these facts come out." Summing up the strategy for the final stretch of the race, a Trump adviser said, "We're gonna go buck wild."

Trump was certainly game. At a fund-raiser that week, he declared himself "unshackled" and seemed to relish the prospect of ramping up his attacks on Clinton, who he and Bannon both believed was orchestrating the parade of accusers. "A vote for Hillary is a vote to surrender our government to public corruption, graft, and cronyism that threatens the survival of our constitutional system itself," he told an Arizona crowd soon after. "What makes us exceptional is that we are a nation of laws and that we are all equal under those laws. Hillary's corruption shreds the principle on which our nation was founded."

On television and on the front pages of the major newspapers, Trump clearly seemed to be losing the election. Each new woman who came forward with charges of misbehavior became a focal point of coverage, coupled with Trump's furious reaction, his ever darkening speeches, and the accompanying suggestion that they were dog whistles aimed at racists and anti-Semites. "Trump's remarks," one *Washington Post* story explained, summing up the media's outlook, "were laced with the kind of global conspiracies and invective common in the writings of the alternative-right, white-nationalist activists who see him as their champion. Some critics also heard echoes of historical anti-Semitic slurs in Trump's allegations that Clinton 'meets in secret with international banks to plot the destruction of U.S. sovereignty' and that media and financial elites were part of a soulless cabal."

This outlook, which Clinton's campaign shared, gave little consideration to the possibility that voters might be angry at large banks, international organizations, and media and financial elites for reasons other than their basest prejudices. This was the axis on which Bannon's nationalist politics hinged: the belief that, as Marine Le Pen put it, "the dividing line is [no longer] between left and right but globalists and patriots." Even as he lashed out at his accusers and threatened to jail Clinton, Trump's late-campaign speeches put his own stamp on this idea. As he told one rally: "There is no global anthem, no global currency, no certificate of global citizenship. From now on, it's going to be 'America first.'"

Anyone steeped in Guénon's Traditionalism would recognize the terrifying specter Trump conjured of marauding immigrants, Muslim terrorists, and the collapse of national sovereignty and identity as the descent of a Dark Age—the Kali Yuga. For the millions who were not familiar with it, Trump's apocalyptic speeches came across as a particularly forceful expression of his conviction that he understood their deep dissatisfaction with the political status quo and could bring about a rapid renewal.

Whether it was a result of Trump's apocalyptic turn, disgust at the Clintons, or simply accuser fatigue—it was likely a combination of all three—the pattern of slippage in the wake of negative news was less pronounced in Trump's internal surveys in mid-October. Overall, he still trailed. But the data were noisy. In some states (Indiana, New Hampshire, Arizona) his support eroded, but in others (Florida, Ohio, Michigan) it actually improved. When Trump held his own at the third and final debate on October 19, the numbers inched up further.

The movement was clear enough that Nate Silver and other statistical mavens began to take note of it. "Is the Presidential Race Tightening?" he asked in the title of an October 26 article. Citing Trump's rising favorability numbers among Republicans and red-state trend lines, he cautiously concluded that probably it was. By November 1, he had no doubt. "Yes, Donald Trump Has a Path to Victory" read the headline for his column that day, in which he noted that Clinton's lead in national polls had shrunk from seven points in mid-October down to three or four points. "Trump remains an underdog," Silver wrote, "but no longer really a long shot."

By that point, Trump's data scientists had already arrived at the same conclusion. And then, peering into their models, they'd gone a step further and convinced themselves that the electorate was going to look different from what almost anyone else was anticipating. If they were right, there was a much clearer path to 270 electoral votes than most experts were allowing, one that stretched across the industrial upper Midwest.

To Bannon, this made intuitive sense, but one thing gave him pause: the Clinton campaign showed no sign at all that the midwestern states Trump's scientists now considered winnable were even in play. As he had done periodically throughout the fall, he posed a question to a reporter he knew that had nagged at him for weeks. "What is Clinton doing? What's their strategy? It's a week from Election Day and she's in Arizona."

ELEVEN

"THE FBI HAS LEARNED OF
THE EXISTENCE . . ."

Throughout everything, Hillary Clinton was seeing a different race. From the earliest days of her campaign, when private polls suggested that some 10 million people who'd voted Democratic in 2012 now said they were supporting Trump, she and her advisers had refused to believe it. Those voters may be frustrated and disillusioned, they may be "sending a message," but in the end they were Democrats—they would come home to Clinton. She need not waste time and resources to persuade them.

So certain of this was Clinton's campaign that in the final weeks of the race, confident of victory and hoping for a landslide, she traveled to red states such as Arizona that she imagined were within her grasp, and ignored the upper Midwest until it was too late. "We're already seeing the effects of climate change, and I have a plan to increase renewable energy that will create millions of clean-energy jobs that can't be exported—they've gotta be done right here in

Arizona!" Clinton belted out to ten thousand rally goers in Tempe, a week before the election.

This bid to broaden the map was no head fake. "Arizona ain't an indulgence," tweeted her communications director, Brian Fallon. "It's a true battleground. Perhaps even more favorable-looking right now than some other places we've been on TV." Clinton's plan all along was to reactivate the same coalition of Democratic-leaning groups that had twice delivered Barack Obama to the White House: young people, minorities, and suburban women. That's why she embraced the Black Lives Matter movement and vowed to protect from deportation a larger segment of the illegal immigrant community than Obama had. And if she could also carry states like Arizona that Obama hadn't won, then her electoral mandate would be that much bigger.

The reason Clinton's moves so puzzled the Trump campaign is that just before she traveled to Arizona, Trump's data analysts had become convinced, based on absentee ballots and early voting, that the people who were going to show up on Election Day would be older, whiter, more rural, and more populist than almost anyone else believed—so they re-weighted their predictive models to reflect a different electorate. As much as anything, this was a leap of faith. It's what gnawed at Bannon and other Trump advisers in the closing days of the race. But, in the end, what other choice did they have?

"If he was going to win this election, it was going to be because of a Brexit-style mentality and a different demographic trend than other people were seeing," said Matt Oczkowski, a senior official at Cambridge Analytica working in Trump's campaign.

Imagining a more Trump-friendly turnout changed the composition of the electoral map—and with it, Trump's strategy for the closing weeks of the race. On October 18, before the numbers had been re-weighted, the campaign's internal election simulator, dubbed the "Battleground Optimizer Path to Victory," gave Trump a 7.8 percent chance of winning the 270 electoral votes he needed. His long odds were mainly due to the fact that he trailed (albeit narrowly) in most of the states that looked like they would decide the election, including the all-important state of Florida.

Re-weighting the model to reflect an older, whiter electorate changed the polls by only a couple of percentage points in most of the major battleground states. But it shifted the odds of victory substantially in Trump's direction because it either put him ahead or made him newly competitive in states such as Florida, Michigan, Pennsylvania, and Wisconsin, where he'd previously trailed or hadn't looked to have a real chance. (Arizona wasn't competitive for Clinton in either of Trump's models.) Trump's path to victory was now illuminated.

Something else was happening, too. On October 25, Trump's internal polls showed his support ticking up in nearly every battleground state, a trend that continued over the next three days. Out on the trail, Trump was stepping up his angry screeds, traducing Clinton, whom he accused of plotting "the destruction of U.S. sovereignty in order to enrich these global financial powers, her special interest friends, and her donors.'"

At first, this seemed like an expression of primal rage from a man of towering ego who understood, even if only subconsciously, that he was headed for a historic comeuppance. But then Republican voters started to respond in a way that established politicians couldn't have imagined just two weeks earlier, when the *Access Hollywood* tape upended the race. Against all odds, Trump's support steadily consolidated—and forced Republican lawmakers who had piously abandoned him to make a humiliating volte-face.

The most satisfying for several Trump advisers was that of Utah representative Jason Chaffetz, a media-hungry weathervane of popular sentiment who had been among the first to withdraw his endorsement of Trump in the wake of the tape scandal. "I'm out. I can no longer in good conscience endorse this person for president," Chaffetz told Utah's Fox 13 News on October 8. "My wife, Julie, and I, we have a fifteen-year-old daughter," he said to CNN's Don Lemon later that night. "Do you think I can look her in the eye and tell her that I endorsed Donald Trump for president when he acts like this?"

Not three weeks later, on October 26, under pressure from angry constituents, Chaffetz flip-flopped and announced on Twitter that he would indeed be voting for Trump.

And then the bombshell landed. Early in the afternoon of Friday, October 28, James Comey, the director of the FBI, sent a letter to Congress announcing that new evidence had emerged in the case relating to Hillary Clinton's e-mails. "In connection with an unrelated case, the F.B.I. has learned of the existence of emails that appear to be pertinent to the investigation," he wrote. The "unrelated case" involved sexually explicit text messages sent by former representative Anthony Weiner to a fifteen-year-old girl in North Carolina. Weiner was married to Huma Abedin, one of Clinton's close aides, who had saved some of Clinton's e-mails on Weiner's laptop. Having declared the Clinton e-mail case closed in July, when he delivered an unprecedented public rebuke of her "extremely careless" conduct, Comey now told Congress that he was reopening the Clinton investigation.

Ever since *The New York Times* broke the news on March 2, 2015, that Clinton used a personal e-mail account and private server as secretary of state, risking exposure of classified documents to hostile foreign powers, the subject of her e-mails had stalked her campaign, fusing with the damaging *Clinton Cash* narrative to undermine the public's trust in her. Clinton had persevered through a criminal referral from the Justice Department, through countless congressional hearings, and through a nonstop barrage of attacks from hostile Republicans. Now a controversy she thought was behind her came roaring back into the white-hot crucible of the presidential race.

Clinton and her staff were incredulous. "We are eleven days out from perhaps the most important national election of our lifetimes," she said at a hastily arranged evening news conference. "Voting is already under way in our country. So the American people deserve to get the full and complete facts immediately. The director himself has said he doesn't know whether the e-mails referenced in his letter are significant or not. . . . Therefore it's imperative that the bureau explain this issue in question, whatever it is, without any delay."

Inside Trump's campaign, the mood was ecstatic. Bannon's phone lit up with frantic text messages from reporters racing to get a comment on the shocking revelations. Bannon demurred. "Don't want to step on Comey's lines," he texted back. As the cable news networks hit DEFCON 1, he understood that the worst thing the Trump campaign could do was to distract in any way from this damaging story.

When the news broke, Trump was just about to take the stage at a rally in Manchester, New Hampshire. As soon as he reached the lectern, he delivered the clip he knew the networks were waiting for. "I need to open with a very critical breaking news announcement," Trump said. "The FBI"—he paused as the crowd cheered—"has just sent a letter to Congress informing them that they have discovered new e-mails pertaining to the former secretary of state Hillary Clinton's investigation." He paused once more, as chants of *Lock her up!* swept through the hall. "They are reopening the case into her criminal and illegal conduct that threatens the security of the United States of America. Hillary Clinton's corruption is on a scale we have never seen before. We must not let her take her criminal scheme into the Oval Office."

By the time Trump arrived at his next event, in Lisbon, Maine, he had hit upon an even better sound bite to capture Clinton's travails. "This," he told the audience, "is the biggest political scandal since Watergate."

O ver the next eleven days, Trump did something that he hadn't managed to do in months: he kept focused. Somehow, at this decisive final moment, he stuck to a script that extolled Bannon-style, "America first" nationalism while issuing elaborate condemnations of Clinton's character and moral corruption. He had reason to be encouraged. His internal polls, which showed him already ascending before the Comey letter, now had him turning sharply upward in every state and continuing to climb.

On November 3, a report was circulated among Trump's top advisers that took note of the Comey effect. "The last few days have proven to be pivotal in the minds of voters with the recent revelations in reopening the investigation of Secretary Clinton," it read. "Early polling numbers show declining support for Clinton, shifting in favor of Mr. Trump, suggesting this may have a fundamental impact on the race."

Five days out, Trump still trailed Clinton in nearly every public poll, and his forecasting model, although it showed improved odds of victory, still implied that a loss was the likelier outcome. And the Comey letter was not a panacea. The report noted that the jolt it gave Trump was already leveling off in all but a few places. "As of today, we have started to realize what the 'ceiling' is in many states, though four states continue to rise: PA, IN, MO, and NH," the report said. "We will continue tracking these states to hopefully understand where the continued movement takes us."

Throughout the general election, both campaigns battled for a group of voters who would ultimately decide the race. While media outlets fixated on distinct character types considered representative of the election—the dispossessed factory worker registering to vote for Trump, the elderly woman longing to see a female president—the real competition between the campaigns was for voters of a less vivid hue.

Trump's data analysts gave them a nickname: "double haters." These were people who disliked both candidates but traditionally showed up at the polls to vote. They were a sizable bloc: 3 to 5 percent of the 15 million voters across seventeen battleground states that Trump's staff believed were persuadable. Early on, many indicated support for third-party candidate Gary Johnson. But after a series of televised flubs, including Johnson's admission that he didn't know what "Aleppo" was (it was a city caught in the middle of Syria's civil war), they largely abandoned him. What made the double haters so vexing to Trump's analysts was that their intentions were difficult to discern. Many refused to answer pollsters' questions or declared themselves undecided.

The Clinton campaign thought of these persuadable voters as being mainly "pocketbook Republicans"—people whose votes were driven by kitchen-table economic concerns but were made deeply uncomfortable by Trump's racist and sexist outbursts. These were the voters Clinton had hoped to shear off from Trump with her "alt-right" speech in August.

"What we found is that they were very fickle: they'd toggle between telling pollsters that they were leaning Clinton or leaning Trump, depending on where the news cycle was that week," said Fallon. "This is the largest piece of fallout we ascribe to the Comey letter. In ending the campaign on a note where people were reminded about the worst of our controversies, we saw those fickle, Republican-leaning voters that we'd been successfully attracting off and on throughout the general election revert back to Trump at the end."

For all their many differences, on this subject the campaigns generally agreed. Comey's letter had the effect of convincing the double haters to finally choose an affiliation—or, in the case of many who had been leaning toward Clinton, choose to stay home. "What we saw is that it gave them a reason to vote against her instead of voting for him," said Matt Oczkowski. "They were finally able to admit that to pollsters without feeling any guilt. All of those double haters and last-minute undecideds started to break heavily toward Trump in the polling and research when, deep down, they were probably going to vote for him anyway. Now they had a reason."

There was nothing Clinton could do to stop them.

As midnight approached on November 7, a restive Trump audience was packed into the DeVos Place Convention Center in Grand Rapids, Michigan. On this single day, the last before Election Day, Trump had barnstormed across many of the states his campaign was now certain were in play: Florida, North Carolina, Pennsylvania, New Hampshire, and then one final rally in Michigan. Too late, Clinton had awoken to the danger of the tightening race: she, too, had swept through Pennsylvania (twice) and North Carolina, and had also visited Grand Rapids earlier in the day.

Before Trump appeared, Ted Nugent hit the stage in a camouflage jacket and cap to play "The Star-Spangled Banner" on an electric guitar, shouting "This is real Michigan!" It was past midnight when Pence took the lectern to introduce "the next president of the United States, Donald Trump."

"So you know, we added this stop about twelve minutes ago, and look at this place—is this incredible?" Trump said. "We don't need Jay Z or Beyoncé, we don't need Jon Bon Jovi. We don't need Lady Gaga. All we need is great ideas to make America great again."

For the last time as a candidate, Trump worked through all his famous tropes, pausing wistfully at times and basking in the crowd's energy. "We're hours away from a once-in-a-lifetime change," he said. "Today is our Independence Day."

"Today the American working class is going to strike back," he said, marveling at the thought. "The election is now. Can you believe it? It's today."

Soon, Trump and his audience slid into the familiar call-and-response rhythms of his rallies.

"Hillary Clinton is the most corrupt person ever to seek the presidency of the United States."

Lock her up! Lock her up!

"Our jobs are being stolen like candy from a baby—not going to happen anymore, folks."

Booooo!

"It used to be, the cars were made in Flint and you couldn't drink the water in Mexico. Now the cars are made in Mexico and you can't drink the damned water in Flint. What the hell?"

Trump! Trump! Trump!

"We're going to fix our inner cities. Right now they're so unsafe, you walk to the store to pick up a loaf of bread, you get shot."

"A Trump administration will also secure and defend the borders of the United States. And yes, we will also build a great, great wall."

Build the Wall! Build the Wall!

At this, Trump stepped back from the lectern and opened his arms, smiling at the audience. "I just want to ask you one question, if you don't mind, at one in the morning," he said. "Who is going to pay for the wall?"

Mexico!

"One hundred percent," he said. "They don't know it yet, but they're going to pay."

In the end, he came back to his signature phrase, emblazoned on hats and placards throughout the hall: "To all Americans tonight in all of our cities and all of our towns, I pledge to you one more time, together, we will make America wealthy again. We will make America strong again. We will make America safe again. And we will make America great again."

And then Trump delivered one final importunement to the crowd.

"Go to bed!" he told them. "Go to bed right now! Get up and vote!"

On Election Day, Trump's forecasting model indicated that he probably wouldn't make it. Some of his advisers said his odds of victory were 30 percent; others went as high as 40 percent. At least one adviser said, "It will take a miracle for us to win."

And then the world turned upside down.

On the morning after the election, Bannon had barely slept. The sudden rush of victory, the drama of Clinton's concession call as Trump was about to take the stage, the glare of the spotlight in his eyes as he gazed out on the drunken, jubilant revelers in MAGA hats at the victory party—it left him in a fugue state.

But now, as the sun came up over Manhattan, he could see how everything had come together exactly according to script. "Hillary Clinton was the perfect foil for Trump's message," Bannon marveled to a reporter. "From her e-mail server, to her lavishly paid speeches to Wall Street bankers, to her FBI problems, she represented everything that middle-class Americans had had enough of."

The beauty of it was that no one had seen her downfall coming. "Their minds are totally blown," he said, laughing. Clinton's great mistake—the Democrats' great mistake—was one he recognized all too well, since he'd watched Republicans commit it during their anti-Clinton witch hunts of the nineties: they'd become so intoxicated with the righteousness of their cause, so thoroughly convinced that a message built on identity politics would carry the day and drown out the "deplorables," that they became trapped in their own bubble and blind to the millions who disagreed with them—"and that goes for you guys in the media, too," he added.

Now Trump had shattered that illusion, and the wave that had swept across Europe and Great Britain had come crashing down on America's shores. "Trump," Bannon proclaimed, "is the leader of a populist uprising. . . . What Trump represents is a restoration—a restoration of true American capitalism and a revolution against state-sponsored socialism. Elites have taken all the upside for themselves and pushed the downside to the working- and middle-class Americans." Bernie Sanders had tried to warn them, but the Democrats hadn't listened and didn't break free of crony capitalism. "Trump saw this," Bannon said. "The American people saw this. And they have risen up to smash it."

For all his early-morning bravado, Bannon sounded as if he still couldn't quite believe it all. And what an incredible story it was. Given the central role he had played in the greatest political upset in American history, the reporter suggested that it had all the makings of a Hollywood movie.

Without missing a beat, Bannon shot back a reply worthy of his favorite vintage star, Gregory Peck in *Twelve O'Clock High*.

"Brother," he said, "Hollywood doesn't make movies where the bad guys win."

AFTERWORD: KALI YUGA

In the shell-shocked aftermath of the election, President Obama, looking shaken, appeared in the White House Rose Garden to deliver public remarks intended to project a sense of calm—a sense, really, that the basic stability of the country remained intact. "The sun is up," Obama said. "I know everybody had a long night. I did as well. I had a chance to talk to President-elect Trump last night—about 3:30 in the morning, I think it was—to congratulate him on winning the election." The next day, when the two men appeared together in the Oval Office, it felt as if the world had slipped through the looking glass. Trump quickly named Bannon his chief White House strategist. Republicans controlled every branch of government. With Trump's ability to defy every political norm, anything seemed possible. Who could argue otherwise after what had just transpired?

And yet within days of his inauguration, Trump's White House was plunged into chaos and scandal from which it has not recovered—and may never. Bannon, the imaginative reconceiver of U.S. politics, hung streams of paper listing Trump's "promises" from the walls of his West Wing office. His strategy, as always, was to launch furious attacks, this time to "shock the system" and rapidly reorient the federal government in a more nationalist direction. He called this, with what I took to be intentional irony, a "shock and awe approach" to asserting Trump's power. But Trump's flurry of activity quickly ran into problems. There was his executive order, sprung a week after his inauguration, banning immigrants from seven majority-Muslim countries, which set off nationwide protests and was blocked by the courts; his firing two weeks later of national security director Michael Flynn for contacts with the Russians; the collapse of his first major legislative initiative, a bill to repeal Obamacare; his firing of FBI director James Comey; and the swift descent of the West Wing into a viper's nest of backstabbing and leaks.

This quick turn toward a crackup was hardly unforeseeable or even altogether surprising. But it contrasted sharply with the success of a candidate who had dominated his opponents, shaped news coverage, and shown himself to be all but impervious to forces that overwhelm other politicians.

Bannon, whose wild gambits in the campaign had invariably paid off, seemed to run out of magic tricks once Hillary Clinton was no longer a target. The government wasn't as malleable to Trump and Bannon's aggressions as the Republican Party and the cable news channels had been, and they found themselves consistently thwarted and undermined—by the courts, by right-wing hardliners in Congress, by their own inexperience and Trump's errant tweets, and by the bureaucracy they were now overseeing. The crises these failures precipitated in the White House cost Bannon much of his influence and soon threatened Trump's presidency.

While it's still early in his term, the possibilities that Trump's most ardent supporters once imagined for his presidency already seem to be mostly foreclosed. I think there are three main reasons why Trump's administration has so quickly fallen into disorder and confusion.

Trump thought being president was about asserting dominance. Just after he'd locked up the GOP nomination, Trump said something to me that crystallized his view of politics and explains, to my mind, much of his subsequent difficulties. "I deal with people that are very extraordinarily talented people," he told me. "I deal with Steve Wynn. I deal with Carl Icahn. I deal with killers that blow these [politicians] away. It's not even the same category. This"—he meant politics—"is a category that's like nineteen levels lower. You understand what I'm saying? Brilliant killers."

Trump was equating politics with business and the presidency with the job of being a big-shot CEO, a "killer." He filled the upper ranks of his administration with people of a similar mindset: Gary Cohn, Wilbur Ross, Steve Bannon—aggressive, domineering men accustomed to getting their way by dint of their position. None had government experience (nor did many others in the West Wing), so none anticipated the problems this approach to governing would cause. Trump's self-conception as the all-powerful *Apprentice* boss blinded him to a fundamental truth of the modern presidency: that the president needs Congress more than Congress needs the president. Trump's domineering instinct served him poorly, since most members of Congress are secure in their jobs and accountable mainly to their own constituents. And it backfired disastrously when Trump fired Comey after he refused to submit to a pledge of loyalty to the big boss.

Trump ran against the Republican Party, Wall Street, and Paul Ryan, but then took up their agenda. Populists often struggle to govern. But Trump scarcely attempted to lead the populist revolution he promised. In May, he'd told me he would transform the GOP into a "workers' party." But while he kept voicing populist shibboleths, the legislative agenda he took up was the standard conservative fare pushed by Paul Ryan. During the GOP primary, Trump had shrewdly sensed its weak point: Ryan's desire to finance tax cuts for the rich by cutting programs such as Social Security and Medicaid harmed the party's white, blue-collar base. Trump told me he'd made this point to Ryan directly: "I said, 'There's no way a Republican is going to beat a Democrat when the Republican is saying, "We're going to cut your Social Security" and the Democrat is saying, "We're going to keep it and give you more."'"

Yet Trump's first legislative push was for Ryan's bill repealing the Affordable Care Act, which would eliminate health insurance coverage for twenty-four million people, cutting Medicaid, which benefits Trump's working-class voters, to pay for high-end tax cuts. Not only was the bill deeply unpopular—a Quinnipiac poll in March found that only 17 percent of Americans supported it—but it galvanized grassroots Democratic opposition to Trump. Bannon went along because he thought Ryan had become a convert to nationalism, in the belief that it could give the GOP an electoral hammerlock on the upper Midwest. Bannon also thought Ryan's tax plan, funded by a tax on imports, was "the most nationalist feasible plan" and that his former enemy could deliver on it.

The great fear among Democratic leaders was that Trump would be true to his word and lead a populist rebellion that would cripple their party. "I know what you're doing, and I'm not going to let it happen," Senator Charles Schumer, the Democratic leader, told Bannon in the early days of the administration. Schumer feared that Trump would begin by pursuing a $1 trillion infrastructure bill—a massive project of roads and bridges that would neatly align with Trump's "builder" image, produce tangible benefits, win over union voters Democrats rely on, and stand as a testament to what "America first nationalism" could mean. As it turned out, Schumer needn't have worried.

Trump doesn't believe in nationalism or any other political philosophy—he's fundamentally a creature of his own ego. Over the years, Trump repeated certain populist themes: the United States is being ripped off in trade deals by foreign competitors; elites and politicians are stupid crooks. These were expressions of an attitude—a marketing campaign—rather than commitments to a set of policies. When Trump sensed nationalism was no longer generating a positive response for him, he abandoned it, announcing in April, "I'm a nationalist and a globalist," as if the two weren't opposed. At heart, Trump is an opportunist driven by a desire for public acclaim, rather than a politician with any fixed principles.

An early indicator was his decision to fill his administration with veterans of Goldman Sachs. Trump was gratified that they wanted to work for him, and he was willing to heed their counsel despite vilifying Goldman as a candidate. This opened up a rift that didn't exist in his campaign between "nationalists" like Bannon and "globalists" like Cohn, a top Goldman executive who became head of the National Economic Council.

Bannon's fall from his exalted status as Trump's top adviser wasn't the result of a policy dispute, but the product of Trump's annoyance that Bannon's profile had come to rival his own. Trump grew incensed at the popular notion that Bannon was the one really running the show—that he was, as an infamous *Time* cover put it, "The Great Manipulator." Soon afterward, Bannon was unceremoniously demoted, though he kept his job and clawed back to a position of influence. "I like Steve, but you have to remember, he was not involved in my campaign until very late," Trump told the *New York Post*. "I'm my own strategist."

For a certain segment of people around the world, the Trump brand holds powerful appeal. It was powerful enough to drive the greatest upset in American political history. Before that, it induced a succession of business partners in places as far flung as Miami and Moscow, Dubai and Azerbaijan, to team up with Donald Trump. The lure is always the same: that forming a partnership will be a mutually profitable arrangement. No one can sell that idea like Trump. More often than not, however, those partners seem to end up disappointed.

As Trump's presidency drifts and the scandals around him mount, the idea that he will follow through on the robust nationalist agenda he campaigned on seems less and less likely, and would be difficult to pull off even if he was inclined to try. Still, every president changes the contours of American politics, and Trump will, too. It may not be nearly as aggressively as Bannon envisioned when the two joined forces, or even necessarily in the direction he wanted, but it is also true that after Trump Republicans will have a harder time pursuing free trade and open immigration. Perhaps even more significant, the effects of Jeff Sessions's elevation to attorney general will reverberate for years in a way that populist-nationalists will approve of.

But in the end, it's hard to imagine that Bannon and the legions he spoke for will wind up as anything other than the latest partners disappointed when their deal with Trump turns sour.

—June 5, 2017

ACKNOWLEDGMENTS

On November 8, 2016, the world shifted for just about everybody, including me. As strange as Trump's victory was the realization that I'd had a front-row seat to many of the events that led to his presidency and had spent years getting to know many of the people responsible for it. At the outset of the election cycle, I'd approached the job of covering the Trump campaign as an interesting lark and a narrative bounty—a roller-coaster ride that, whatever its ups and downs, was certain to end on election day. It didn't, of course. But trapped as we all are on the roller coaster, it seemed worthwhile to try to tell the full story.

This book would never have come to be without Josh Tyrangiel, my editor at *Bloomberg Businessweek* in 2015, who allowed me to spend eight months researching what became an eight-thousand-word feature story on an ex-Goldman Sachs banker with grandiose plans to upset U.S. politics whom practically no one had heard of at the time: Steve Bannon. Few editors show that kind of faith in their writers, which is why few are as highly regarded as Josh. Ellen Pollock and Brad Wieners, who rate in the same category, put the story on *Businessweek*'s cover and gave it an unforgettable headline ("This Man Is the Most Dangerous Political Operative in America") that was far more apt than any of us realized at the time. I want to give special thanks to my beloved story editor, John Homans, who, in addition to greatly improving the original feature story with his deft editing, also read (and greatly improved) the chapters in this book. A special thanks as well to my *Bloomberg* bosses, Mike Bloomberg, John Micklethwait, Reto Gregori, and Wes Kosova, for allowing me time to work on this book, even amid the most news-intensive early presidency in memory.

I'm deeply indebted to several current and former *Bloomberg* colleagues who went far beyond the call of duty in sharing their reporting and expertise. Zachary Mider, in particular, who got to the story of Robert and Rebekah Mercer before almost anyone else did and is undoubtedly the most knowledgeable journalist on the subject, generously provided notes and on-the-ground reporting to help me re-create the scenes of the Mercers' 2015 Christmas party. His published work on the Mercers also informed this book in several places. Sasha Issenberg was an invaluable collaborator and traveling companion during the presidential campaign's stretch run and into the bleary early morning hours after election day, when we pieced together for *Businessweek* exactly how Trump had pulled it off. Sasha's unparalleled knowledge of data analytics, modeling, and cutting-edge campaign survey research (and his ability to explain it in plain English) made our pieces, and this book, much better than I ever could have managed on my own. Jennifer Epstein, a campaign road warrior who traveled with Hillary Clinton throughout, also generously shared her reporting notes and recollections.

My thanks also to Mark Lilla for his guidance on French intellectual history and antimodernist philosophy, and especially to Mark Sedgwick, both for his fascinating history of the Traditionalists and for generously critiquing a draft of my chapter on Bannon's fascination with them.

One of the most unexpected and interesting areas of reporting, for me, was unearthing the history of corporate America's fondness for *The Apprentice* and the multicultural audience Trump drew. I was first alerted to the liberal skew of Trump's viewers by Will Feltus back in 2011, during the "birther" craze. Since then, Will and the staff of National Media, Inc., have produced fascinating demographic research for me on several occasions, and for this I will always be grateful. I'd like to thank Eric Leininger of the Kellogg School of Management (and before that, McDonald's Corporation) for explaining how Fortune 500 corporations decide where to advertise and for connecting me with several sources involved in the ad-buying process during the early years of *The Apprentice*. I'd also like to thank Monique Nelson of UniWorld for her insights on minority representation in prime-time television. As a reporter for a business magazine, I have not encountered a sharper and more thoughtful CEO. Thanks as well to Henry Schafer of The Q Scores Company for several informative conversations.

This book drew on stories I wrote during the campaign that were often assigned, edited, and published by a talented group of journalists who include Mike Nizza, Elizabeth Titus, Kelly Bare, Allison Hoffman, Matthew Philips, and Howard Chua-Eoan. Several source relationships were deepened or made possible by my stints guest hosting the Bloomberg TV show *With All Due Respect*. I thank Mark Halperin and John Heilemann for that opportunity. Thanks also to Joe Scarborough and Mika Brzezinski of *Morning Joe*, and to Jesse Rodriguez. It's a cliché of Washington journalism that a lot of reporting is done in greenrooms—it also happens to be true. I'm grateful to Bloomberg's publicists Rachel Nagler and Julia Walker for putting me there so often.

Brad Stone, David Frum, and Jonathan Kelly provided helpful advice and encouragement at critical points. My editor at Penguin Press, Scott Moyers, was a joy to work with throughout the writing process, from our first conversation, when he outlined the book, through the final days of what sometimes felt to me like Trumpian chaos, but was in fact a finely choreographed display of publishing prowess. That process was aided by Christopher Richards, Kiara Barrow, Liz Calamari, Bill Peabody, Karen Mayer, Ann Godoff, Matt Boyd, Sarah Hutson, and Tricia Conley, as well as John Lawton and Christopher Dufault. Thanks also to Darren Haggar and Amanda Dewey.

Any campaign narrative is informed by the work of dozens of talented reporters. That was certainly the case here. There are too many to list individually, but I'm grateful to all those whose work has shaped and informed my understanding of American politics. They're a put-upon lot, and naming them wouldn't be professionally helpful, so I'd like to collectively thank the many current and former Trump staffers, officials, and advisers who served as sources for my reporting—one even hiding me in a Trump Tower pantry so we could speak undetected. I also had help from an assortment of people at *Breitbart News*, GAI, and Fox News.

My agent, Gail Ross, was instrumental in putting this project together quickly, but also paused to make sure that it wouldn't be suicidal from a psychic and family-balance perspective. It wasn't (quite) thanks to the support of friends and family. Diane Roberts gave me writing space high above the barking dogs and leaf blowers. My sister and brothers-in-law—Abby and Chris Forhan and Alec Woodard—have loved and bolstered my family through years of deadlines. My in-laws, Mark and Susie Woodard, took in my family so that I would have time alone to write. My parents, Gary and

Priscilla Green, modeled and encouraged the writing life, and reassured me during moments of despondency as only parents can.

More than anyone else, I want to thank my wife, Alicia, and my two young kids. After promising them throughout the campaign that the stress and time away would end in November, I made their lives more difficult by deciding to write this book. From the first mention of it, Alicia was unflagging in her support—through absences and meltdowns, missed family functions, and unexpected midnight phone calls from Trump officials. I missed my wife and kids tremendously, I love them deeply, and I'm happiest of all to be back in their presence.

NOTES

Preface

ix **My piece argued:** "The Tragedy of Sarah Palin," Joshua Green, *The Atlantic*, June 2011.

Chapter Two: "Where's My Steve?"

23 **"It's like poison":** The Trump-Winn story is drawn from George Anastasia, "Donald Trump Vs. Steve Wynn," *Philadelphia Inquirer,* March 12, 2000.

26 **"a relentless ferret":** Francis X. Clines, "'Pit Bull' Congressman Gets Chance to Be More Aggressive, *New York Times,* March 9, 1997, http://www.nytimes.com /1997/03/09/us/pit-bull-congressman-gets-a-chance-to-be-more-aggressive.html.

26 **A volunteer firefighter:** Lloyd Grove, "A Firefighter's Blazing Trail," *Washington Post,* November 13, 1997, www.washingtonpost.com/archive/lifestyle/1997/11 /13/a-firefighters-blazing-trail/b9beb874-fd7b-4dfe-b285-ffcd385501a2/.

27 **Waxman's team discovered:** George Lardner Jr. and John Mintz, "Burton Releases Hubbell Tapes," *Washington Post,* May 5, 1998, www.washingtonpost.com /wp-srv/politics/special/clinton/stories/hubbell050598.htm.

27 **The show's host, Tim Russert:** David Brock, "Sunday, Bloody Sunday," *New York,* May 18, 1998, nymag.com/nymetro/news/media/features/2732/.

28 **"The Burton investigation":** Paul Kane, "Rep. Dan Burton, Who Transformed House Panel into a Feared Committee, to Retire," *Washington Post,* January 31, 2012, www.washingtonpost.com/politics/rep-dan-burton-who-transformed-house -panel-into-a-feared-committee-to-retire/2012/01/31/gIQACFD2fQ_story. html.

32 **George Clooney, who once stormed:** Elizabeth Leonard, "George Clooney Unloads on Casino Owner Steve Wynn," *People,* May 2, 2014, people.com/celebrity /george-clooney-unloads-on-casino-owner-steve-wynn/.

32 **Trump had accepted both invitations:** PageSix.com staff, "Doubled Up," *New York Post,* March 25, 2011, pagesix.com/2011/03/25/doubled-up/.

33 **"I'm fine with this stuff":** Roxanne Roberts, "I Sat Next to Donald Trump at the Infamous 2011 White House Correspondents' Dinner," *Washington Post,* April 28, 2016, www.washingtonpost.com/lifestyle/style/i-sat-next-to-donald -trump-at-the-infamous-2011-white-house-correspondents-dinner/2016/04/27 /5cf46b74-0bea-11e6-8ab8-9ad050f76d7d_story.html.

36 **"incredibly gracious and engaged":** Maggie Haberman and Alexander Burns, "Donald Trump's Presidential Run Began in an Effort to Gain Stature," *New York Times,* March 12, 2016, www.nytimes.com/2016/03/13/us/politics/donald -trump-campaign.html?_r=0.

36 **Trump had indeed toyed:** "Before 2016, Donald Trump Had a History of Toying with a Presidential Run," *PBS NewsHour* transcript, PBS.org, July 20, 2106, www.pbs.org/newshour/bb/2016-donald-trump-history-toying -presidential-run/.

37 **One day that fall:** Michael Kruse, "The True Story of Donald Trump's First Campaign Speech—in 1987," *Politico,* February 5, 2016, www.politico.com /magazine/story/2016/02/donald-trump-first-campaign-speech-new -hampshire-1987-213595.

39 **"People have birth certificates":** "Trump on Obama's Birth Certificate: 'Maybe It Says He's a Muslim,'" FoxNews.com, nation.foxnews.com/donald-trump /2011/03/30/trump-obama-maybe-hes-muslim.

40 **National polls taken in mid-April:** "Poll: Donald Trump Leads 2012 GOP Field," USNews.com, April 15, 2011, www.usnews.com/news/articles/2011/04 /15/poll-donald-trump-leads-2012-gop-field.

40 **"Is the birther debate":** *Newsmakers,* "Newsmakers with Reince Priebus," C-SPAN, April 8, 2011, www.c-span.org/video/?298925-1/newsmakers-reince -priebus.

41 **"I realized," he said:** Haberman and Burns, "Donald Trump's Presidential Run Began in an Effort to Gain Stature," op. cit.

43 **George Conway earned:** Ryan Lizza, "Kellyanne Conway's Political Machinations," *New Yorker,* October 17, 2016, www.newyorker.com/magazine/2016/10 /17/kellyanne-conways-political-machinations.

45 **"I'm very honored":** "Donald Trump Offers Obama 5 Million Dollars," posted on October 24, 2012, www.youtube.com/watch?v=I-lWv0cpCnM.

46 **An analysis of his Twitter feed:** Charles Warzel and Lam Thuy Vo, "Here's Where Donald Trump Gets His News," BuzzFeed News, December 3, 2016, www.buzzfeed.com/charliewarzel/trumps-information-universe?utm_term= .alYW6Dqgx#.hhxxJnvK4.

Chapter Three: Bildungsroman

49 **moved to a leafy neighborhood:** Graham Moomaw, "Steve Bannon Talks Richmond Roots, Says Trump Will Condemn All Forms of Racism," *Richmond Times-Dispatch,* November 26, 2016, www.richmond.com/news/local /government-politics/article_0f87d838-4aaa-5e4f-b717-6a342a00b89c.html.

50 **"We were Kennedy freaks":** Matt Viser, "Harvard Classmates Barely Recognize the Bannon of Today," *Boston Globe,* November 26, 2016, www.bostonglobe .com/news/politics/2016/11/26/look-steven-bannon-and-his-years-harvard -business-school/B2m0j85jh5jRKzKbMastzK/story.html.

50 **"He would come home"**: Ibid.

53 **an insurgent campaign for president**: Matea Gold, Rosalind S. Helderman, Gregory S. Schneider, and Frances Stead Sellers, "For Trump Adviser Stephen Bannon, Fiery Populism Followed Life in Elite Circles," *Washington Post*, November 19, 2016, www.washingtonpost.com/politics/for-trump-adviser-stephen -bannon-fiery-populism-followed-life-in-elite-circles/2016/11/19/de91ef40 -ac57-11e6-977a-1030f822fc35_story.html.

60 **"We were all very involved"**: Michael Kranish and Craig Whitlock, "How Bannon's Navy Service During the Iran Hostage Crisis Shaped His Views," *Washington Post*, February 10, 2017, www.washingtonpost.com/politics/how-bannons -navy-service-during-the-iran-hostage-crisis-shaped-his-views/2017/02/09 /99f1e58a-e991-11e6-bf6f-301b6b443624_story.html?utm_term=.55daec272e01.

61 **"He was not a rebel"**: Matt Viser, "Harvard Classmates Barely Recognize Bannon of Today, *Boston Globe*, November 26, 2016, https://www.bostonglobe.com /news/politics/2016/11/26/look-steven-bannon-and-his-years-harvard-business -school/B2m0j85jh5jRKzKbMastzK/story.html.

Chapter Four: "A Dangerous Way to Look at the World"

74 **Bannon started a production company**: Daniel Miller, "Inside the Hollywood Past of Stephen K. Bannon, Donald Trump's Campaign Chief," *Los Angeles Times*, August 20, 2016, www.latimes.com/entertainment/envelope/cotown /la-et-ct-stephen-bannon-donald-trump-hollywood-20160830-snap-story.html.

75 **a shady, little-known Italian**: David McClintick and Anne Faircloth, "The Predator: How an Italian Thug Looted MGM, Brought Crédit Lyonnais to Its Knees, and Made the Pope Cry, *Fortune*, July 8, 1996, archive.fortune.com /magazines/fortune/fortune_archive/1996/07/08/214344/index.htm.

76 **Parretti was arrested**: "Rob Wells, Financial Settles Fraud Charges with SEC," *The Hour* (Norwalk, CT), January 5, 1996, news.google.com/newspapers?nid= 1916&dat=19960105&id=yxVJAAAAIBAJ&sjid=jwYNAAAAIBAJ&pg= 4634,444961, James Bates, "Ex-Studio Owner Parretti Arrested on Fraud Warrant," *Los Angeles Times*, October 19, 1995, articles.latimes.com/1995-10-19 /business/fi-58839_1_giancarlo-parretti.

77 **global media conglomerates**: Stephen Prince, *A New Pot of Gold: Hollywood Under the Electronic Rainbow, 1980–1989* (Oakland, CA: University of California Press, 2002), 158.

78 **Crédit Lyonnais sold MGM**: Lisa Bannon and Bruce Orwall, "Kerkorian Group to Acquire MGM for $1.3 Billion," *Wall Street Journal*, July 17, 1996, www.wsj.com/articles/SB837557246545964000.

79 **"We were wrong by a factor of five"**: "Bannon's claim to have a piece of the *Seinfeld* rights has drawn a good deal of attention since I first published it in *Bloomberg Businessweek* in 2015, with *Forbes* suggesting the rights could be worth as much as $32 million, and the *New Yorker*'s Connie Bruck raising the question of

whether they exist at all. According to a source familiar with the terms of the deal, Bannon's *Seinfeld* rights went to the French bank Société Générale when it acquired Bannon's firm so that Bannon and his partner could defer income rather than pay a lump-sum tax on the total assets. The *Seinfeld* money flows to Bannon through Société Générale, income that is reflected on Bannon's White House disclosure statement. According to the source, Bannon and his partner have each collected close to $2 million and counting.

80 **"great intellectual property":** Carl DiOrio and Josef Adalian, "Hypnotic Wins Big in Vegas," *Variety,* January 8, 2004, variety.com/2004/film/markets-festivals /hypnotic-wins-big-in-vegas-1117898069/.

80 **helped orchestrate its great coup:** Sharon Waxman, "Firm Believer," *Washington Post,* July 8, 2002, www.washingtonpost.com/archive/lifestyle/2002/07/08/firm -believer/c1a53bfe-f8f0-4888-a5b7-8315d85aa78e/.

81 **Amid charges of cocaine use:** Sharon Waxman, "Firm Believer," *Washington Post,* July 8, 2002.

81 **The business centered on:** The next three paragraphs draw on Julian Dibbell, "The Decline and Fall of an Ultra-Rich Gaming Empire," *Wired,* November 2008.

81 **Internet Gaming Entertainment:** Julian Dibbell, "The Decline and Fall of an Ultra Rich Online Gaming Empire," *Wired,* November 24, 2008, www.wired .com/2008/11/ff-ige/.

86 **"Politics is downstream from culture":** Steve Oney, "Citizen Breitbart," *Time,* March 25, 2010, content.time.com/time/magazine/article/0,9171,1975339,00 .html?iid=pw-ent.

90 **a "villain," a "prick":** Michael Calderone, "Not All Kennedy Critics Hold Fire," Politico.com, August 26, 2009, www.politico.com/story/2009/08/not-all -kennedy-critics-hold-fire-026475.

Chapter Five: Nobody Builds Walls Like Trump

94 **falling behind its major competitors:** Emily Yahr, Caitlin Moore, and Emily Chow, "How We Went from 'Survivor' to More Than 300 Reality Shows: A Complete Guide," *Washington Post,* May 29, 2015, www.washingtonpost.com /graphics/entertainment/reality-tv-shows/.

95 **Mark Burnett, the show's creator:** Michael Kranish and Marc Fisher, "The Inside Story of How 'The Apprentice' Rescued Donald Trump," *Fortune,* September 8, 2016, fortune.com/2016/09/08/donald-trump-the-apprentice-burnett/.

97 **Randal D. Pinkett, an African American:** Kathleen Fearn-Banks and Anne Burford-Johnson, *Historical Dictionary of African American Television* (Lanham, MD: Rowman & Littlefield, 2014).

98 **known as "visual diversity":** "Race Becomes More Central to TV Advertising," NBCNews.com, March 1, 2009, www.nbcnews.com/id/29453960/ns/business -us_business/t/race-becomes-more-central-tv-advertising/.

98 **"Going forward, all advertising"**: "Race Becomes More Central to TV Advertising," NBCNews.com.

99 **no Republican had won**: R. W. Apple, Jr., "G.O.P. Tries Hard to Win Black Votes, but Recent History Works Against It," *New York Times*, September 19, 1996, www.nytimes.com/1996/09/19/us/gop-tries-hard-to-win-black-votes-but -recent-history-works-against-it.html.

99 **John McCain had pulled**: "How Groups Voted in 2008," Roper Center for Public Opinion Research, Cornell University, n.d., ropercenter.cornell.edu/polls /us-elections/how-groups-voted/how-groups-voted-2008/.

100 **"Muggers and murderers"**: Sarah Burns, "Why Trump Doubled Down on the Central Park Five," *New York Times* Op-Ed, October 17, 2016, www.nytimes .com/2016/10/18/opinion/why-trump-doubled-down-on-the-central-park -five.html?_r=0.

101 **Nielsen ratings for *The Celebrity Apprentice:*** Joshua Green, "Trump's Birther Antics Are Driving Away His Liberal Audience," *Atlantic*, April 27, 2011, www .theatlantic.com/politics/archive/2011/04/trumps-birther-antics-are-driving -away-his-liberal-audience/237965/.

104 **"the Inspector Clouseau"**: Michael Isikoff, "The Strange Case of Christopher Ruddy, *Slate*, October 19, 1997, http://www.slate.com/articles/arts/books/1997 /10/the_strange_case_of_christopher_ruddy.html.

104 **There he befriended Trump**: Caitlin Huey-Burns, "Q&A with Chris Ruddy: Trump SpokesPal, Newsmax Chief," RealClearPolitics.com, March 2, 2017, www.realclearpolitics.com/articles/2017/03/12/qa_with_chris_ruddy_trump _spokespal_newsmax_chief.html.

105 **"Trump Declines Prime-Time"**: Jim Meyers, "Trump Declines Prime-Time GOP Convention Speech." *Newsmax*, August 9, 2012, www.newsmax.com /Newsfront/trump-convention-gop-romney/2012/08/09/id/448081/.

105 **Ruddy even arranged**: Jeremy W. Peters, "Trump to Moderate Republican Debate," *New York Times, The Caucus* (blog), December 2, 2011, thecaucus.blogs .nytimes.com/2011/12/02/trump-to-moderate-republican-debate/.

105 **The debate was canceled**: Alexander Burns, "Trump Debate Appearance Canceled," Politico.com, *Burns & Haberman Blog*, December 13, 2011, www.polit ico.com/blogs/burns-haberman/2011/12/trump-debate-appearance -canceled-107281.

105 **"He had a crazy policy"**: Ronald Kessler, "Donald Trump: Mean-Spirited GOP Won't Win Elections, *Newsmax*, November 26, 2012, http://www.newsmax .com/Newsfront/Donald-Trump-Ronald-Kessler/2012/11/26/id/465363/

107 **"I believe that if we're successful"**: Byron Tau, "Obama: Republican 'Fever' Will Break After the Election," Politico.com, June 1, 2012, www.politico.com/blogs /politico44/2012/06/obama-republican-fever-will-break-after-the -election-125059.

108 **Rupert Murdoch, the CEO of News Corp.:** Rupert Murdoch, "Immigration Reform Can't Wait," *Wall Street Journal*, June 18, 2014, www.wsj.com/articles /rupert-murdoch-immigration-reform-cant-wait-1403134311.

109 **"God bless Fox":** Ryan Lizza, "Getting to Maybe," *New Yorker*, June 24, 2013, www.newyorker.com/magazine/2013/06/24/getting-to-maybe.

109 **"We have to make America strong again":** Transcript of Donald Trump's Remarks (2013 Conservative Political Action Conference, March 15, 2013, Washington, DC), Democracy in Action, www.p2016.org/photos13/cpac13 /trump031513spt.html.

110 **Cantor's defeat was "a great signal":** Matthew Boyle, "Donald Trump: Cantor's Defeat Shows 'Everybody' in Congress Is Vulnerable if They Support Amnesty," Breitbart.com, June 12, 2014, www.breitbart.com/big-government/2014/06/12 /donald-trump-cantor-s-defeat-shows-everybody-in-congress-is-vulnerable -if-they-support-amnesty/.

113 **"He made it clear":** Susanne Craig and David W. Chen, "Donald Trump Considered Path to Presidency Starting at the Governor's Mansion in New York," *New York Times*, March 5, 2016, https://www.nytimes.com/2016/03/06/nyre gion/donald-trump-new-york-governor.html.

116 **"She thought that it was possible":** Ryan Lizza, "Kellyanne Conway's Political Machinations," *New Yorker*, October 17, 2016, http://www.newyorker.com /magazine/2016/10/17/kellyanne-conways-political-machinations.

Chapter Six: The Alt-Kochs

120 **Christmas party at Owl's Nest:** Owl's Nest Party research: Zachary Mider, "What Kind of Man Spends Millions to Elect Ted Cruz?" Bloomberg.com, January 20, 2016, www.bloomberg.com/politics/features/2016-01-20/what-kind -of-man-spends-millions-to-elect-ted-cruz-.

121 **"He's a very independent thinker":** Jane Mayer, "The Reclusive Hedge Fund Tycoon Behind the Trump Presidency," *New Yorker*, March 27, 2017.

122 **"We need samples of your urine":** Oregon Institute of Science and Medicine, mailer, n.d., www.oism.org/Sample_Bank_A_34_For_Internet_op.pdf.

122 **"I don't know him very well":** Dan Eggen, "Concerned Taxpayers of America Supported by Only Two Donors," *Washington Post*, October 16, 2010, www.wash ingtonpost.com/wp-dyn/content/article/2010/10/16/AR2010101602804.html.

124 **the Mercer family had given:** Elise Viebeck and Matea Gold, "Pro-Trump Megadonor Is Part Owner of Breitbart News Empire, CEO Reveals," *Washington Post*, February 24, 2017. According to *The Washington Post*, between 2009 and 2014, the family donated $35 million to conservative think tanks and at least $36.5 million to individual GOP races, www.washingtonpost.com/politics/pro -trump-megadonor-is-part-owner-of-breitbart-news-empire-ceo-reveals/2017 /02/24/9f16eea4-fad8-11e6-9845-576c69081518_story.html?utm _term=.86e1f0f5e7c4.

128 **modern speech-recognition:** Zachary Mider, "What Kind of Man Spends Millions to Elect Ted Cruz?," *Bloomberg Politics*, January 20, 2016, https://www.bloomberg.com/politics/features/2016-01-20/what-kind-of-man-spends-millions-to-elect-ted-cruz-.

132 **"Bob told me he believed":** Jane Mayer, "The Reclusive Hedge-Fund Tycoon Behind the Trump Presidency," *New Yorker,* March 27, 2017, www.newyorker.com/magazine/2017/03/27/the-reclusive-hedge-fund-tycoon-behind-the-trump-presidency.

134 **The film debuted:** Joshua Green, "'Clinton Cash' Has Been Made into a Movie," Bloomberg.com, April 28, 2016, www.bloomberg.com/politics/articles/2016-04-28/clinton-cash-has-been-made-into-a-movie.

134 **Robert Mercer became principal owner:** Jane Mayer, "The Reclusive Hedge-Fund Tycoon Behind the Trump Presidency."

135 **"One of the realities":** Davis Richardson, "Hillary Spokesman: We Didn't Account for the 'Breitbart Effect,'" Daily Caller, March 29, 2017, dailycaller.com/2017/03/29/hillary-spokesman-we-didnt-account-for-the-breitbart-effect/.

Chapter Seven: A Rolling Tumbleweed of Wounded Male Id and Aggression

137 **Trump had made his annual:** "Donald Trump Remarks at CPAC," C-SPAN, February 26, 2015, www.c-span.org/video/?324558-11/donald-trump-remarks-cpac.

148 **"Truth and veracity":** Matthew Garrahan, "Breitbart News: from Populist Fringe to the White House and Beyond," *Financial Times,* December 7, 2016, www.ft.com/content/a61e8e12-bb9c-11e6-8b45-b8b81dd5d080.

149 **To lead his Texas bureau:** Josh Harkinson, "How a Radical Leftist Became the FBI's BFF," *Mother Jones*, September/October 2011.

149 **They included Michelle Fields:** McKay Coppins, "Young, Pretty, and Political: The Highs and Lows of Conservative Media Stardom," BuzzFeed, March 10, 2014, www.buzzfeed.com/mckaycoppins/the-highs-and-lows-of-being-a-ris?utm_term=.pkDJX4vB0n#.xnYV9w4l3M.

149 **There was also Alex Swoyer:** Terri, "New Miss Southwest Florida Is Crowned," Cape Coral Internet Services, February 21, 2011, capecoralinternetservices.com/new-miss-southwest-florida-is-crowned/; "Alex Swoyer Joins Breitbart News as Newest Capitol Hill Reporter," Breitbart.com, March 29, 2015, www.breitbart.com/big-journalism/2015/03/29/alex-swoyer-joins-breitbart-news-as-newest-capitol-hill-reporter/.

149 **Julia Hahn, a whip-smart:** Andrew Marantz, "Becoming Steve Bannon's Bannon," *New Yorker,* February 13 and 20, 2017, www.newyorker.com/magazine/2017/02/13/becoming-steve-bannons-bannon.

150 **"Paul Ryan Builds Border Fence":** Julia Hahn, "Paul Ryan Builds Border Fence Around His Mansion, Doesn't Fund Border Fence in Omnibus," Breitbart.com, December 7, 2015, www.breitbart.com/big-government/2015/12/17/paul

-ryan-builds-border-fence-around-mansion-doesnt-fund-border-fence
-omnibus/.

150 **millennials had just eclipsed:** Richard Fry, "Millennials Overtake Baby Boomers as America's Largest Generation," Pew Research Center, Fact Tank, April 25, 2016, www.pewresearch.org/fact-tank/2016/04/25/millennials-overtake-baby-boomers/.

152 **"Practically grotesque," wrote Harvard:** Lawrence Lessig, "Democrats Embrace the Logic of 'Citizens United,'" *Washington Post,* May 8, 2015, https://www.washingtonpost.com/opinions/the-clintons-citizens-united-and-21st-century-corruption/2015/05/08/7f11a0d6-f57b-11e4-b2f3-af5479e6bbdd_story.html?utm_term=.c4341d792faa.

152 **"On any fair reading":** Lawrence Lessig, "Democrats Embrace the Logic of 'Citizens United,'" *Washington Post,* May 8, 2015, www.washingtonpost.com/opinions/the-clintons-citizens-united-and-21st-century-corruption/2015/05/08/7f11a0d6-f57b-11e4-b2f3-af5479e6bbdd_story.html?utm_term=.c4341d792faa.

152 **Giustra subsequently won lucrative:** Jo Becker and Mike McIntire, "Cash Flowed to Clinton Foundation Amid Russian Uranium Deal," *New York Times,* April 23, 2015.

152 **"I still don't like the way it looked.":** Margaret Sullivan, "An 'Exclusive' Arrangement on a Clinton Book, and Many Questions," *New York Times,* April 23, 2015, publiceditor.blogs.nytimes.com/2015/04/23/an-exclusive-arrangement-on-a-clinton-book-and-many-questions/?_r=0.

158 **"deemed it unnecessary":** Annie Linsky, "Clinton Charity Never Provided Foreign Donor Data," *Boston Globe,* April 30, 2015, www.bostonglobe.com/news/politics/2015/04/29/clinton-health-charity-failed-report-foreign-grant-increases-required-under-agreement-for-hillary-clinton-confirmation/yTYoUTi3wGhy3oDonxy6gI/story.html.

Chapter Eight: *"The Traffic Is Absolutely Filthy!"*

162 **with the exception:** Gabriel Sherman, "The Trump Campaign Has Descended into Civil War—Even Ivanka Has Gotten Involved," *New York,* August 6, 2015, nymag.com/daily/intelligencer/2015/08/trump-campaign-has-descended-into-civil-war.html.

162 **Trump and some aides:** Dylan Byers, "Maggie Haberman: The *New York Times* Reporter Trump Can't Quit," Money.CNN.com, April 7, 2017, money.cnn.com/2017/04/07/media/maggie-haberman-trump/.

164 **one of the first outlets:** Brandon Darby, "Leaked Images Reveal Children Warehoused in Crowded U.S. Cells, Border Patrol Overwhelmed," Breitbart.com, June 5, 2014, www.breitbart.com/texas/2014/06/05/leaked-images-reveal-children-warehoused-in-crowded-us-cells-border-patrol-overwhelmed/.

164 **"Border Open for Criminals":** Robert Wilde, "Border Patrol Union Spokesman: Border Open for Criminals as Agents Forced to Babysit Illegals," Breitbart.com, June 30, 2014, www.breitbart.com/big-government/2014/06/30/border-patrol-agent-interview-claims-70-of-manpower-not-patrolling-border/.

164 **Local 2455, the Border Patrol Union:** David Sherfinsky, "Local Union for Border Patrol Agents Pulls Out of Donald Trump Events," *Washington Times,* July 23, 2015, www.washingtontimes.com/news/2015/jul/23/local-union-border-patrol-agents-pull-trump-events/.

164 **The National Border Patrol Council:** Richard Marosi, "Union for Border Patrol Agents Under Fire for Endorsement of Trump," *Los Angeles Times,* May 12, 2016, www.latimes.com/nation/politics/la-na-border-patrol-trump-20160511-snap-story.html.

165 **Laredo was the nineteenth-safest:** Amelia Acosta and Annmargaret Warner, "The 20 Safest Cities in America," BusinessInsider.com, July 25, 2013, "http://www.businessinsider.com/safe-cities-in-america-2013-7.

166 **called it "extraordinarily ugly":** Patrick Healy, "Indignant Jeb Bush Says He Takes Donald Trump's Remarks Personally," *New York Times,* July 4, 2015, www.nytimes.com/politics/first-draft/2015/07/04/an-angry-jeb-bush-says-he-takes-donald-trumps-remarks-personally/.

166 **Trump had surged past Bush:** Dan Balz and Peyton M. Craighill, "Poll: Trump Surges to Big Lead in GOP Presidential Race," *Washington Post,* July 20, 2015, www.washingtonpost.com/politics/poll-trump-surges-to-big-lead-in-gop-presidential-race/2015/07/20/efd2e0d0-2ef8-11e5-8f36-18d1d501920d_story.html?tid=a_inl.

167 **over a private dinner in 2013:** Jason Horowitz, "Marco Rubio Pushed for Immigration Reform with Conservative Media," *New York Times,* February 27, 2016, www.nytimes.com/2016/02/28/us/politics/marco-rubio-pushed-for-immigration-reform-with-conservative-media.html?_r=0.

168 **a story published in:** Brandy Zadrozny and Tim Mak, "Ex-Wife: Donald Trump Made Me Feel 'Violated' During Sex," *Daily Beast,* July 27, 2015, www.thedailybeast.com/articles/2015/07/27/ex-wife-donald-trump-made-feel-violated-during-sex.html.

172 **"trying to take out Donald Trump":** Ian Hanchett, "Breitbart's Editor Alex Marlow: Fox News 'Trying to Take Out Trump' for GOP Establishment," Breitbart.com, August 7, 2015, www.breitbart.com/video/2015/08/07/breitbarts-editor-alex-marlow-fox-news-trying-to-take-out-trump-for-gop-establishment/.

172 **"In the beginning, virtually 100 percent":** Gabriel Sherman, "Donald Trump and Roger Ailes Make Up—for Now," *New York,* August 10, 2015, nymag.com/daily/intelligencer/2015/08/donald-trump-and-roger-ailes-make-up-for-now.html.

173 **"If you can't get past me":** Pam Key, "Megyn Kelly: 'If You Can't Get Past Me, How Are You Gonna Handle Vladimir Putin?,'" Breitbart.com, August 9, 2015,

www.breitbart.com/video/2015/08/09/megyn-kelly-if-you-cant
-get-past-me-how-are-you-gonna-handle-vladimir-putin/.

173 **"Mr. Trump is an interesting man"**: Megyn Kelly, "Megyn Kelly Addresses Donald Trump's Remarks," *The Kelly File*, August 10, 2015, video.foxnews.com /v/4412819805001/?#sp=show-clips.

173 **"The Arrogance of Power"**: Stephen K. Bannon and Alexander Marlow, "The Arrogance of Power: Megyn Kelly's 'Good Journalism,'" Breitbart.com, August 11, 2015, www.breitbart.com/big-journalism/2015/08/11/the-arrogance-of -power-megyn-kellys-good-journalism/.

174 **"Roger Ailes just called"**: Donald J. Trump, Twitter post, August 10, 2015, 8:35 A.M., twitter.com/realdonaldtrump/status/630764447716540417.

174 **"Flashback: Megyn Kelly"**: Katie McHugh, "Flashback: Megyn Kelly Discusses Her Husband's Penis and Her Breasts on Howard Stern," Breitbart.com, August 12, 2015, www.breitbart.com/big-journalism/2015/08/12/flashback -megyn-kelly-discusses-her-husbands-penis-and-her-breasts-on-howard -stern/.

176 **"smaller, more cohesive"**: Sabrina Eaton, "It's Official: Rep. Jim Jordan Now Chairs the House Freedom Caucus," Cleveland.com, February 11, 2015, www.cleveland.com/open/index.ssf/2015/02/its_official_rep_jim_jordan _no.html.

176 **"The craziest of the crazy"**: Matt Fuller, "House Freedom Caucus Looks to Be a Force—in Leadership and Lawmaking," *Roll Call*, February 4, 2015, www .rollcall.com/218/house-freedom-caucus-looks-to-be-force-in-leadership-and -lawmaking/.

176 **"Behind the Scenes"**: Matthew Boyle, "Behind the Scenes with John Boehner's Worst Nightmare: Mark Meadows Launches Mission to Fix Broken Congress," *Breitbart*, September 5, 2015, http://www.breitbart.com/big-government/2015 /09/05/exclusive-behind-the-scenes-with-john-boehners -worst-nightmare-mark-meadows-launches-mission-to-fix-broken-congress/.

177 **"We will have so much winning"**: Ian Schwartz, "Trump: 'We Will Have So Much Winning if I Get Elected That You May Get Bored with Winning,'" RealClearPolitics.com, www.realclearpolitics.com/video/2015/09/09/trump_we _will_have_so_much_winning_if_i_get_elected_that_you_may_get_bored _with_winning.html.

177 **60 percent of Republicans:** "Fox News Poll: 2016 Election, Pope Francis' Popularity," Fox News, September 23, 2015, www.foxnews.com/politics/interac tive/2015/09/23/fox-news-poll-2016-election-pope-francis-popularity.html.

Chapter Nine: "Honest Populism"

181 **"Let's see how much money"**: Brian Stelter, "Donald Trump Will Skip Fox News Debate on Thursday," Money.CNN.com, January 27, 2016, money.cnn .com/2016/01/26/media/donald-trump-poll-debate-fox/index.html.

181 **"I love you people"**: Jonathan Martin, "Ted Cruz Wins Republican Caucuses in Iowa," *New York Times,* February 1, 2016, www.nytimes.com/2016/02/02/us /ted-cruz-wins-republican-caucus.html?_r=0.

181 **"I think some people"**: Jeremy Diamond, "Trump Says Skipping Debate Might Have Cost Him in Iowa," CNN.com, February 3, 2016, www.cnn.com/2016 /02/02/politics/donald-trump-iowa-new-hampshire/.

182 **"Wow, wow, wow"**: Stephen Collinson, "Outsiders Sweep to Victory in New Hampshire," CNN.com, February 10, 2016, www.cnn.com/2016/02/09/poli tics/new-hampshire-primary-highlights/.

182 **"Trump's stumping in Mobile"**: Dave Weigel, Twitter post, August 21, 2015, 7:14 a.m., twitter.com/daveweigel/status/634730184508317696.

187 **"We are . . . very well positioned"**: Todd J. Gillman, "Ted Cruz's Southern Strategy Is No Longer the Sure Bet He Hoped For," Dallasnews.com, February 28, 2016, www.dallasnews.com/news/local-politics/2016/02/28/ted-cruz-s -southern-strategy-is-no-longer-the-sure-bet-he-hoped-for.

187 **Trump racked up additional wins:** Wilson Andrews, Kitty Bennett, and Alicia Parlapiano, "2016 Delegate Count and Primary Results," *New York Times,* July 5, 2016, nytimes.com/interactive/2016/us/elections/primary-calendar-and-results .html.

187 **"Everyone thinks he's Republican Jesus"**: Eli Stokols and Alex Isenstadt, "GOP Establishment on the Ropes," Politico.com, March 16, 2016, www.polit ico.com/story/2016/03/trump-contested-convention-establishment -plans-220848.

187 **"The Republican convention"**: Julia Hahn, "Concerns About Paul Ryan Emerging Out of Ted Cruz-Created Contested Convention as Nominee Domi- nate Wisconsin," Breitbart.com, April 2, 2016, www.breitbart.com/2016 -presidential-race/2016/04/02/concerns-paul-ryan-emerging-ted-cruz -created-contested-convention-nominee-dominate-wisconsin/.

188 **"Count me out"**: Katie Reilly, "Paul Ryan Says He Doesn't Want and Won't Accept the GOP Nomination," Time.com, April 12, 2016, time.com/4291293 /paul-ryan-republican-nomination/.

188 **"@realDonaldTrump"**: Reince Priebus, Twitter post, May 3, 2016, 8:58 p.m., twitter.com/jeneps/status/727664278908620800.

193 **persuading Trump to hire:** Gideon Resnick, "Roger Stone Convinced Trump to Hire Paul Manafort, Former Officials Say," *Daily Beast,* April 21, 2017, www .thedailybeast.com/articles/2017/04/21/roger-stone-convinced-trump-to-hire -paul-manafort-former-officials-say.html.

193 **But he had long ago shifted:** Steven Mufson and Tom Hamburger, "Inside Trump Adviser Manafort's World of Politics and Global Financial Dealmaking," *Washington Post,* April 26, 2016.

193 **"sordid and apparently illicit affair"**: "Read Ex-Aide Samuel Nunberg's Re- sponse to Donald Trump's Lawsuit," *Guardian,* July 13, 2016, www.theguardian

.com/us-news/ng-interactive/2016/jul/13/donald-trump-samuel-nunberg
-affidavit.

193 **The parties later agreed:** Chris Dolmetsch, "Former Trump Adviser Nunberg Agrees to Drop Campaign Suit," Bloomberg.com, August 11, 2016, www .bloomberg.com/politics/trackers/2016-08-11/former-trump-adviser-nunberg -agrees-to-drop-campaign-suit.

194 **Clinton had raised $264 million:** Bill Allison, Mira Rojanasakul, and Brittany Harris, "Tracking the 2016 Presidential Money Race," Bloomberg.com, July 21, 2016, www.bloomberg.com/politics/graphics/2016-presidential-campaign -fundraising/july/public/index.html.

194 **"It is like an epic disaster":** Lauren Fox and Tierney Sneed, "Why Trump's Fundraising Struggles Spell Disaster for the Entire GOP," *Talking Points* memo, June 22, 2016, talkingpointsmemo.com/dc/donald-trump-down-the -ballot-fundraising.

194 *New York* **published:** Gabriel Sherman, "6 More Women Allege That Roger Ailes Sexually Harassed Them," *New York*, July 9, 2016, nymag.com/daily/intelli gencer/2016/07/six-more-women-allege-ailes-sexual-harassment.html.

195 *Breitbart* **dutifully published:** Matthew Boyle, "Exclusive—Fox News Stars Stand with Roger Ailes Against Megyn Kelly, More Than 50 Fox Contributors, All Primetime, Willing to Walk," Breitbart.com, July 19, 2016, www.breitbart .com/big-government/2016/07/19/exclusive-fox-news-stands-roger -ailes-megyn-kelly-50-fox-contributors-primetime-willing-walk-ailes/.

196 **Ailes was banned:** Gabriel Sherman, "The Revenge of Roger's Angels," *New York*, September 2, 2016, nymag.com/daily/intelligencer/2016/09/how-fox-news -women-took-down-roger-ailes.html.

Chapter Ten: Burn Everything Down

199 **Her own family:** Matea Gold and Anu Narayanswamy, "Six Donors That Trump Appointed Gave Almost $12 Million with Their Families to Back His Campaign and the Party," *Washington Post,* December 9, 2016, www.washington post.com/news/post-politics/wp/2016/12/09/the-six-donors-trump-appointed -to-his-administration-gave-almost-12-million-with-their-families-to-his -campaign-and-the-party/?utm_term=.2ca68c2efbe8&tid=a_inl.

199 *The New York Times* **had published:** Alexander Burns and Maggie Haberman, "Inside the Failing Mission to Tame Donald Trump's Tongue," *New York Times,* August 13, 2016, www.nytimes.com/2016/08/14/us/politics/donald -trump-campaign-gop.html.

200 **"Defeat Crooked Hillary PAC":** Joshua Green and Zachary Mider, "New Super-PAC Launches for Donors Who Won't Back Trump but Loathe Clinton," Bloomberg.com, June 21, 2016, www.bloomberg.com/politics/articles/ 2016-06-22/new-super-pac-launches-for-donors-who-won-t-back-trump-but -loathe-clinton.

200 **Robert Mercer [$2 million]:** "Contributors, 2016 Cycle" Opensecrets.org, n.d., www.opensecrets.org/pacs/pacgave2.php?cmte=C00575373&cycle=2016.

201 **Jared and Ivanka were yachting:** Chris Spargo, "Yachting with the Enemy: Ivanka Trump and Jared Kushner Take the Jet Skis Out and Relax on Democratic Hollywood Billionaire David Geffen's $200m Mega-Yacht Off the Coast of Croatia," *Daily Mail* (UK), August 16, 2016, www.dailymail.co.uk/news /article-3743316/Yachting-enemy-Ivanka-Trump-Jared-Kushner-jet-ski -Croatia-Democratic-Hollywood-billionaire-David-Geffen-s-200m-boat.html.

202 **"Secret Ledger in Ukraine":** Andrew E. Kramer, Mike McIntire, and Barry Meier, "Secret Ledger in Ukraine Lists Cash for Donald Trump's Campaign Chief," *New York Times,* August 14, 2016, www.nytimes.com/2016/08/15/us /politics/paul-manafort-ukraine-donald-trump.html.

202 **"The suggestion that I accepted":** David E. Sanger and Maggie Haberman, "Donald Trump's Terrorism Plan Mixes Cold War Concepts and Limits on Immigrants," *New York Times,* August 15, 2016, www.nytimes.com/2016/08/16 /us/politics/donald -trump-terrorism.html.

203 **"This is the bunker scene":** Joshua Green, "Steve Bannon's Plan to Free Donald Trump and Save His Campaign," Bloomberg.com, August 18, 2016, www .bloomberg.com/politics/articles/2016-08-18/trump-resuscitate-campaign.

204 **"If you were looking for a tone":** Robert Costa, Jose A. DelReal, and Jenna Johnson, "Trump Shakes Up Campaign, Demotes Top Adviser," *Washington Post,* August 17, 2016, www.washingtonpost.com/news/post-politics/wp/2016 /08/17/trump-reshuffles-staff-in-his-own-image/.

205 **Evola's ideas gained currency:** Nicholas Goodrick-Clarke, *Black Sun: Aryan Cults, Esoteric Nazism, and the Politics of Identity* (New York: New York University Press, 2002).

210 **"Lock her up! Lock her up!":** Peter W. Stevenson, "A Brief History of the 'Lock Her Up!' Chant by Trump Supporters Against Clinton," *Washington Post,* November 22, 2016, www.washingtonpost.com/news/the-fix/wp/2016/11/22/ a-brief-history-of-the-lock-her-up-chant-as-it-looks-like-trump-might-not-even-try/.

213 **"over time it all gets kind of washed out":** J. Lester Feder, "This Is How Steve Bannon Sees the Entire World," BuzzFeed, November 15, 2016, updated November 16, 2016, www.buzzfeed.com/lesterfeder/this-is-how-steve-bannon -sees-the-entire-world?utm_term=.ulolXPzAad#.ck2Px3AGgn.

214 **David Fahrenthold, a reporter:** David Fahrenthold, "Trump Recorded Having Extremely Lewd Conversation About Women in 2005," *Washington Post,* October 8, 2016, www.washingtonpost.com/politics/trump-recorded-having-extremely -lewd-conversation-about-women-in-2005/2016/10/07/3b9ce776-8cb4-11e6 -bf8a-3d26847eeed4_story.html.

214 **it briefly crashed:** Paul Farhi, "A Caller Had a Lewd Tape of Donald Trump. Then the Race to Break the Story Was On," *Washington Post,* October 7, 2016,

www.washingtonpost.com/lifestyle/style/the-caller-had-a-lewd-tape-of-donald
-trump-then-the-race-was-on/2016/10/07/31d74714-8ce5-11e6-875e-2c1bfe
943b66_story.html.

215 **"Donald Trump should withdraw"**: Alex Pappas, "Here Are the Republicans
Calling on Donald Trump to Withdraw," Daily Caller, October 8, 2016, daily
caller.com/2016/10/08/here-are-the-republicans-calling-on-donald-trump
-to-withdraw-video/.

215 **"I am not going to defend"**: Paul Ryan conference call: Matthew Boyle,
"Exclusive—Audio Emerges of When Paul Ryan Abandoned Donald Trump: 'I
Am Not Going to Defend Donald Trump—Not Now, Not in the Future,'" Bre
itbart.com, March 13, 2017, www.breitbart.com/big-government/2017/03/13
/exclusive-audio-emerges-of-when-paul-ryan-abandoned-donald
-trump-i-am-not-going-to-defend-donald-trump-not-now-not-in-the-future/.

215 **"go down with a worse election"**: Gabriel Sherman, "Trump's Transition Team
'Is Like Game of Thrones,'" *New York*, December 8, 2016, nymag.com/daily
/intelligencer/2016/12/trumps-transition-team-is-like-game-of-thrones.html.

216 **"Donald Trump's uncensored comments"**: Matea Gold, "GOP Mega-Donors
Robert and Rebekah Mercer Stand by Trump, *Washington Post*, October 8, 2016,
www.washingtonpost.com/news/post-politics/wp/2016/10/08/gop-mega
-donors-robert-and-rebekah-mercer-stand-by-trump/.

217 **a judge had appointed:** Kim LaCapria, "Hillary Clinton Freed Child Rapist,"
Snopes.com Fact Check, May 2, 2016, updated August 13, 2016, www.snopes
.com/hillary-clinton-freed-child-rapist-laughed-about-it/.

218 **"We were going to put"**: Robert Costa, Dan Balz, and Philip Rucker, "Trump
Wanted to Put Bill Clinton's Accusers in His Family Box. Debate Officials Said
No," *Washington Post*, October 10, 2016, www.washingtonpost.com/news/post
-politics/wp/2016/10/10/trumps-debate-plan-to-seat-bill-clintons
-accusers-in-family-box-was-thwarted/?postshare=811476078962605&tid=
ss_tw.

220 **NBC News/SurveyMonkey:** Christine Wang, "Positive Opinions of Trump
Grow After Second Debate, NBC/Surveymonkey Poll Says," CNBC.com,
October 12, 2016, www.cnbc.com/2016/10/11/positive-opinions-of-trump-grow
-after-second-debate-nbcsuveymonkey-poll-says.html.

221 **"To quote the late, great Nelson Mandela"**: Philip Rucker and Sean Sullivan,
"Trump Says Groping Allegations Are Part of a Global Conspiracy to Help Clinton," *Washington Post*, October 13, 2016, www.washingtonpost.com/politics
/trump-says-groping-allegations-are-part-of-a-global-conspiracy-to-help
-clinton/2016/10/13/e377d7e4-915a-11e6-a6a3-d50061aa9fae_story.html.

221 **"We're gonna go buck wild"**: Joshua Green, "Trump to Intensify Attacks on
Clinton over Husband's Accusers," Bloomberg.com, October 12, 2016, www
.bloomberg.com/politics/articles/2016-10-12/trump-takes-a-back-to-the
-future-focus-on-bill-clinton-s-women.

223 **"Is the Presidential Race Tightening?":** Nate Silver, "Election Update: Is the Presidential Race Tightening?," *FiveThirtyEight, New York Times,* October 26, 2016, fivethirtyeight.com/features/election-update-is-the-presidential-race -tightening/.

223 **"Yes, Donald Trump Has a Path to Victory":** Nate Silver, "Election Update: Yes, Donald Trump Has a Path to Victory," *FiveThirtyEight, New York Times,* November 1, 2016, fivethirtyeight.com/features/election-update-yes-donald -trump-has-a-path-to-victory/.

Chapter Eleven: "The FBI Has Learned of the Existence . . ."

225 **"We're already seeing the effects":** "Hillary Clinton Speaks to Estimated Crowd of 10,000+," AZCentral.com, November 2, 2016, www.azcentral.com /story/news/politics/elections/2016/11/02/hillary-clinton-arizona-asu -presidential-campaign-rally/93143352/,

226 **"Arizona ain't an indulgence":** Brian Fallon, Twitter post, October 29, 2016, 9:41 a.m., twitter.com/brianefallon/status/792043601463283713.

228 **"I'm out. I can no longer":** Cristiano Limo, "'I'm Out': Rep. Chaffetz With- draws His Endorsement of Trump," Politico. com, October 8, 2016, www.polit ico.com/story/2016/10/rep-chaffetz-withdraws-his-endorsement-of -trump-229335.

228 **"My wife, Julie, and I":** Daniella Diaz, "Chaffetz Explains Why He's Pulling Support for Trump," CNN.com, October 8, 2016, www.cnn.com/2016/10/08 /politics/jason-chaffetz-donald-trump-republican-2016-election/.

Afterword: Kali Yuga

240 **a Quinnipiac poll in March:** http://www.businessinsider.com/quinnipiac-poll -shows-17-percent-of-american-support-trumpcare-ahca-2017-3.

242 **"I'm my own strategist":** http://nypost.com/2017/04/11/trump-wont-definitively -say-he-still-backs-bannon/.

INDEX